SONS OF FRANCE: PÉTAIN AND DE GAULLE

JEAN-RAYMOND TOURNOUX

SONS OF FRANCE
PÉTAIN AND DE GAULLE

TRANSLATED BY OLIVER COBURN

NEW YORK · THE VIKING PRESS

944,081
T729

To my wife

with homage
to all the fighters for freedom who
made the writing of this book possible

Author's Note

I began collecting material for this book in 1934 in the garrison town of Metz. I continued to collect before, during and after the war; and eventually finished the book at Paris in 1964. Much of the documentation comes from private records and oral testimony, in many cases previously unpublished. The main sources and references are given at the end of the book.

CONTENTS

ILLUSTRATIONS

(following page 182)

SONS OF FRANCE: PÉTAIN AND DE GAULLE

1

The World of Henri de Gaulle

The lecturer's voice suddenly lost its familiar rhythm. He took a deep breath, then went into the charge. 'Napoleon I, a usurper ... Napoleon III, a new Caesar. ... There is no example of a plebiscite where the instigator did not get the result he wanted, even the ratification of a *coup d'état*. A plebiscite is mob law, and mob law is folly.'*

Standing there on the rostrum, a crucifix on the white wall behind him, he drew himself up to his full height and continued with his lecture, discussing, summarizing, explaining, commentating. The words flowed on, full of light and shade, in the glitter of a rich vocabulary. Now they would open out into bold historical pictures, now illustrate a point in philosophy, now lead up to an aphorism. 'Honour for a man is like virtue for a woman. Once lost, it is never regained.'* Or: 'My friends, pride is the cardinal sin. It brought down Lucifer.'*

Carried away by his own eloquence, completely absorbed in what he was saying, he would often pace up and down in front of his class. There was no buzz, no noise or whispering, the boys were too much absorbed. No one thought of cutting the lecture; on the contrary, if the time-table allowed, the room often filled up with boys from other classes.

Such was M. Henri de Gaulle, father of Charles, a teacher at the College of the Immaculate Conception, founded by the Jesuits, in the rue de Vaugirard, Paris, and also at the Sainte-Geneviève School, rue des Postes, for boys preparing for university or other higher education. He was doctor of letters, science and law, and soon after 1900 became vice-principal of the College. Then he founded a teaching establishment in the rue du Bac which he called École Fontanes (after Louis de Fontanes, friend of Chateaubriand and Chancellor of the University under the Empire). He was headmaster of this school till just after the First World War.

* A star indicates a remark or phrase recalled by M. de Gaulle's former pupils (from the author's unpublished records).

1

One of the remarkable things about Henri de Gaulle was the universality of his knowledge: he had a prodigious memory, and taught with equal ease in different subjects, literature and history, Latin and Greek, besides deputizing very competently for the science master on occasions. Though his name was little known in the outside world, he enjoyed genuine popularity within all his schools. He was benevolent as well as erudite, kind as well as cultured, with a natural breeding and courtesy which were equally evident in his ordinary conversation.

Among his pupils at the Sainte-Geneviève School was the future writer Marcel Prévost, elected to the Académie Française in 1909, although at school young Prévost's style was not always appreciated by his masters – but at least M. de Gaulle gave him 18 out of 20 for French at the end of the year! At any rate Prévost later portrayed his teacher in a novel, *Le Scorpion*, putting into his mouth the words: 'It is France you love at this school. In speaking to you of France, I know I am repeating myself. You can all testify, all of you: in the ten years I have addressed you here, I have never done so without speaking of France.'

He was interrupted, says Prévost, by frantic applause. The hall was electrified. Officers' hands went 'instinctively to the hilts of their swords . . . a moment of grandeur in which all care for private interest disappeared: the hour when conspirators swear loyalty to their cause . . .'

The episode took place in 1880 at a school celebration which turned into a political meeting. It was a time of bitter conflict about religious education. Jules Grévy was President of the Republic, and at the ministry of education Jules Ferry – called by the Right such names as 'Nero', 'Diocletian', 'precursor of the Anti-Christ' – was defending his bill to deprive religious congregations of the freedom to teach, suppressing the toleration enjoyed by 20,000 monks and nuns. The main objects of attack were the Jesuits, against whom Jules Ferry inveighed in parliament in these terms: 'The Society of Jesus is not only not authorized, it is forbidden by our whole history. We must close these houses which are the breeding ground for counter-revolution, which teach children to hate and abuse the ideas that are the glory of modern France and the reason for its existence.'[1]

At the school where Henri de Gaulle taught, the debates in

[1] *Histoire de la IIIe République*, Jacques Chastenet.

2

parliament roused a high pitch of emotion. A Jesuit father called Chabrier cried: 'Surely we can find a good general to chuck out all this riff-raff, straight away too – and declare bankrupt the Chamber, the Senate and their vile Republic into the bargain!'

'*Vile république*': the expression was used by many teachers, including Henri de Gaulle. Père Chabrier, however, a fanatical Bonapartist, was really an exception. Almost all the teachers and their pupils were loyal to the monarchy. 'I am a legitimist,' declared Henri de Gaulle.

In 1890, ten years after these events, Charles, his second son, was born at Lille. Mme. de Gaulle (*née* Maillot, a family from Burgundy which had settled in Flanders) was a second cousin of her husband's, and she went to stay with her parents for the confinement.[1]

Charles was brought up in an exceptional family atmosphere, an 'island of resistance' to current ideas, which it is very difficult to imagine seventy-five years later: an inflexible moral code, an old-time sense of honour, principles allowing for no weakness, the cult of integrity taken to its furthest limits. France, Religion, Order. God and the King.

The Third Republic was only twenty years old in 1890. To many people in the aristocracy, the upper classes, the army and the church, Marianne still looked a young and dangerous adventuress. The officers, priests and judges came mostly from the old leading families, and few of these had rallied to the régime. Deep in their hearts they still believed in the monarchy, which had built up France's greatness and forged her unity. The two schools where Henri de Gaulle taught contained many pupils from such families; for them the cry '*Vive la France!*' was still hard to separate from the cry '*Vive le Roi!*'

These pupils would leave school on the smug side, even arrogant. They were nationalist and anti-Semitic, the latter tendency being encouraged by many of their masters. The anti-

[1] The original coat of arms of the de Gaulle family (written sometimes with one L, sometimes with two) consisted of three gall-nuts in a triangle in the centre of a shield. The family was ruined by the Revolution of 1789, at which date Henri's great-grandfather signed his name Degaulle. There seems to be no historical basis for the hypothesis that the particle 'de' is a deformation of the Flemish article: although there is a Belgian branch of the de Gaulles, the father's side of the family does not come from the *départements* near Belgium.

Semitism was tempered on occasions by Christian charity, and was not of the rabid kind: everyone in his place, the Jew's place being in a shop. They were ardent patriots, and the schools' war memorials had the names inscribed in gold letters of old boys who had fallen gallantly beneath Prussian bullets in the war of 1870. Above the names was the proud motto of the Maccabees: 'Better die in war than see the miseries of our nation – and of the saints.'

Such patriotism, of course, was not confined to a single class. Édouard Herriot, growing up at about the same time in a fairly humble environment, republican and radical, has portrayed his father, an army private who became an officer, as one of those soldiers who 'take the idea of duty to its furthest consequences, strict and noble, simple in morals and language, thinking only of family and country. He could be summed up in the motto on his sword-belt: Honour and Country.'

Henri de Gaulle, with his very different background, was certainly the most uncompromising guardian of the glories and traditions of the past He could develop happily in this sort of world. A burly figure, slightly bent, he was inclined to cross his hands behind the tails of his frock-coat. All through his classes he would constantly be pulling out a small white handkerchief to wipe his steel-rimmed pince-nez, which he then brandished between finger and thumb of his right hand – extended in support of the points he was making.

His teaching, of course, was anything but impartial. He could never forgive the men of the eighteenth century like Rousseau, Voltaire, Diderot and the rest. He was merciless in judgement on the revolutions of 1789 and 1848. He had little use for the Orléans dynasty, in fact detested it; but acknowledged a certain *bourgeois* merit in the reign of Louis-Philippe.

Napoleon III? He allowed Germany to become Prussianized. And the Liberal Empire had started a process which led to social disorder. 'You can see proof of it every day.' Gambetta? That 'Genoese',* that 'one-eyed savage'.* (Charles did not adopt all his father's doctrines. In *La France et son armée* he painted a very favourable portrait of Gambetta, 'personifying France's reawakening in the face of history'.)

In Henri de Gaulle's eyes universal suffrage was a bad thing, for it gave equal weight to the votes of 'charwomen'* and of the *élite*. He approved of the conquest of Algeria, an extension of

4

France beyond the Mediterranean. *'Ense et aratro'*,* by the sword and the plough. As to the value of history, he denied that history repeated itself: 'It is true that the same causes always produce the same effect, but History never passes again by the same path.'*

Educated, moulded, intellectually nurtured by the Jesuits, to whom he remained deeply grateful and gave his undisguised admiration, he was fond of quoting Ignatius Loyola as an ideal to follow: a priest and a soldier, the type of genius who in his own way successfully altered the course of history.

When he dealt with the war of 1870, Henri de Gaulle lost his normal calm and poise. He was a man obsessed, and the obsession was revenge. This was the reverse side of his *idée fixe*, the idea of France: France and her dignity, her security, her greatness. If the country seemed to be in decline, if petty factions seemed triumphant, one hope reassured him: the king will save France. As time went on, however, with the Third Republic growing stronger all the time, Henri de Gaulle became profoundly discouraged, realizing that the monarchy would probably never be restored.

The army, instrument of revenge, represented for him, according to a friend, 'the sanctuary of all that is noble, pure and disinterested amidst the tribulations and ignominies of politics'. Yet even the army was not above criticism, especially where honesty and respect for truth were in jeopardy. With the Dreyfus affair, for instance, he was naturally not one of the immediate supporters of Captain Dreyfus, but soon came to doubt the man's guilt, and was outspoken enough on the subject to make himself unpopular among many of his friends. At school he would forgive any pupil courageous enough to confess to a misdeed of his own accord, and when taking Latin or Greek he would often quote examples of mercy as 'Christian behaviour'.

He was very shocked by the South African War. Speaking in class on Queen Victoria's death, he said: 'I hope Her Majesty was able to make peace with her conscience before appearing in front of her Maker.' As to *'perfide Albion'*, 'I doubt if the epithet is strong enough.'

In the patriarchal family atmosphere all these ideas and attitudes must have left a deep impression on the growing boy Charles de Gaulle.

2

The Child Is Father of the Man

One of the well-known stories told about Charles's boyhood is
that the following dialogue frequently occurred:

'Charles, come here!'

No answer.

'Charles, come here!'

'Yes, Papa.'

'What have you been doing today? Not bullying your little
brother again, I hope.'

'No, Papa.'

'Good. Then here's two sous for you.' And Henri de Gaulle
would pull a coin out of his pocket.

Similar episodes are a commonplace of all families, of course,
but it illustrates at least that Charles was not an easy child. He
was neither open nor obedient, but unruly, impetuous, provok-
ing – often a thorough nuisance. He was mainly responsible for
the noise in the schoolroom with books and notebooks all over
the place. 'If Charles appears,' it was admitted in the family
circle, 'that's the end of peace and quiet.' He soon showed a
striking independence of character, and detested the constraints
of school. Not that he was lazy; far from it. He was studious, but
only where he liked the subject, and for instance had a strong
dislike of German lessons. His imagination strayed into realms
of fantastic adventure stories, so that his father, a man more
ready with kindly smile, sometimes felt obliged to administer
corporal punishment.

Self-willed and overbearing, Charles expected his brothers to
obey him. One of their war games was Crusaders and Saracens,
and there was an occasion when nine-year-old Pierre, bearing a
message from the Saracens, let himself be caught by the enemy,
then failed to carry out his instructions: at all costs to swallow
the paper with the message. The wretched messenger ran home
in tears. A stern commander-in-chief (Charles) had boxed him
hard on the ears for neglect of duty. Charles, however, was a
more complex character than his father. At school, for instance,

when he found boys who were the victims of bullying or teasing, he set himself up as their protector – and in this role was certainly a force to be reckoned with. But whether in generous or harsh vein, he rarely showed much warmth. His family, noting this characteristic, periodically made remarks to the effect that 'Charles must have fallen into the ice-box'.

The de Gaulle children owned a magnificent collection of lead soldiers. They shared out armies not as field-marshals but as sovereigns, the thrones being allotted by a sort of tradition: thus Xavier was usually King of England, Jacques the Emperor of All the Russias, and Charles invariably insisted on being ruler of France. There was a frequent difficulty about finding someone to be King of Prussia or the Kaiser, and on this point the war game sometimes degenerated into a family quarrel. Otherwise the troops took part in skilful manœuvres. Each brother, studying the campaigns of the Consulate and the Empire, reproduced heroic battles.

In any case, with their father directing their upbringing, the five children lived continuously with History. Anatole France once said: 'Towns may surely be picture books in which we can see our ancestors.' When the de Gaulles took a walk in Paris, they never went through a district or followed a road without Papa evoking national glories for them: the Louvre, Alésia, Bouvines, Fontenoy, Colbert, Louvois. . . .[1] At table there was often discussion on the comparative merits of Caesar and Pompey, on the plays of Racine, Molière and Corneille, on honour and passion. Racine, alas, gave undue importance to passion, while Molière was much too ready to sacrifice virtue; his comedies illustrated baser humanity. So all votes went to Corneille, whose heroes triumphed over the obstacles with which Destiny confronted them. 'Remember what Napoleon said,' Henri de Gaulle would tell his sons: "If Pierre Corneille were alive today, I would make him a prince."

The old French songs were sung in the de Gaulle home, of course, but with some of the erotic allusions censored: '*amant*' was replaced by '*Maman*', and the expurgated version of '*Auprès de ma blonde*' gave '*Auprès de ma mère, qu'il fait bon dormir.*'

On their mother's birthday the drawing-room was turned into

[1] Later on he was less pleased to point out the various rues Jean-Jaurès! Henri de Gaulle died in May 1932 at the age of eighty-three.

a theatre, and the boys would act scenes from the classics, especially Corneille, in whatever costumes were to hand. Here Charles could display a facility in which he took after his father – an amazing memory. He and his brothers were experts in made-up secret languages like *siacnarf* (*français* backwards), and he was always learning by heart whole pages of heroic couplets or Latin and Greek verse.

On occasions he composed poetry himself, though he was not one for the tender Muse. When he was fourteen, however – a tall boy already, with a romantic lock over his forehead and a long neck emerging from his stiff collar – he wrote a sketch in verse called *Une mauvaise Rencontre* (Unlucky Meeting), somewhat after the style of Rostand, which apart from its precocious brilliance throws an interesting light on the ideas of the growing boy. In one book (*Charles de Gaulle*) Georges Cattaui writes of a 'satire on cowards and a lesson in political philosophy which would have been very valuable for the future dupes of Hitler'. Alfred Fabre-Luce, on the other hand (in *Le plus illustre des Français*), concludes that 'Cunning and panache both attracted him already'.

The little play was first performed *en famille* during the summer of 1905 with Charles as the Brigand and his cousin Jean de Corbie as the Traveller. It won an award in a small literary competition, the author being offered the choice between a money prize and having it published. He chose the latter, and it appeared in print the following year.

During the German occupation, in July 1943, three performances of it were given in the grounds of a manor in Normandy owned by his brother Pierre. Next month another three performances were given in a neighbouring manor, in which Voltaire had lived, for the benefit of French prisoners of war. This manor was occupied by soldiers of the *Wehrmacht*, who paid their money and applauded the play – not suspecting the author's identity. (A few weeks before, General de Gaulle's sister, Mme. Cailliau, and her husband were arrested and deported, their last child, aged thirteen, being left on his own. Three weeks before that, Pierre de Gaulle had been arrested in Paris; his wife and five children just managed to get away from the manor and escape through the Pyrenees, then under snow, to reach Morocco.)

UNLUCKY MEETING

Characters: THE BRIGAND, THE TRAVELLER

The scene is a road crossing a wood in the background. A thicket on the other side of the road. It is night. When the curtain rises, the BRIGAND *is stretched out on a rostrum up right, lying across the road, rolled up in his big dark cloak.*

TRAV. (*entering* R., *with some caution*)
  Brrh! If I'd known it was as cold as this —
  An extra cloak would not have come amiss. (*Shivers*)
  How dark it is! Those trees there in the gloom
  Are like black spectres rising round their tomb.
  I'm rash to go home quite so late at night.
  Who's there?... Dead silence... Nobody in sight.
(*Challenges one of the trees. While talking, he reaches the* BRIGAND, *and knocks against his foot.*)
BRIG. Oh! (*Jumping to his feet.*) Dammit, sir!
TRAV. A highwayman – oh dear!
BRIG. You scared me, sir.
TRAV. He's laughing now. That's queer.
BRIG. As on this road so sound asleep I lay,
  Peacefully dreaming...
TRAV. (*aside*) Of his crimes, I'd say.
BRIG. ... Of some police whose skulls I split in two.
TRAV. (*in horror*) Oh! (*Advancing on him*)
BRIG. Please believe, sir, what I'm telling you.
TRAV. (*backing*) Of course! I do believe you (*aside*) My poor wife!
BRIG. (*familiarly*) You seem a pleasant chap – upon my life
  I like you!
TRAV. Really? Charmed. (*Aside*) Now mercy me!
BRIG. And want to save you!
TRAV. Save me? How?
BRIG. You'll see.
  This wood – but please forgive me, should I not
  First introduce myself? I quite forgot. (*Salutes*)
  César-Charles Rollet. Known in every place,
  Qualified highway robber, by God's grace.

9

Some are born kings or princes, potentates,
Provincial governors, generals, magistrates.
One's born a brewer, one is born a drayman,
Butcher or baker; I was born highwayman —
As doubtless from my costume you'd have said.

A feather used to wave upon my head,
While as for footwear, I was wont to use
What's generally called a pair of shoes.
But times are changed; of this my erstwhile dress,
You see, sir, on me, all that I possess.
I scarcely like to mention here my hat,
And yet how fine a garment once was that!

Ah, memories that linger in my breast,
Why must I still recall that noble crest,
By cruel cudgel shattered in its prime?
And why recall the patterns so sublime
Which that fair plume once sketched against the sky?
Oh, deadly day: alas, sir, all must die!

Ghastly and grim was that tremendous fight,
Fierce and horrific as the Stygian night,
The direst mêlée that I ever saw,
A brigand 'gainst an officer of law.
My plume fell when he tumbled off his horse,
His stomach gaping!
TRAV. (*terrified*) Oh!
BRIG. You're shocked, of course.
 All very well for you, but I don't know:
 Everyone hates and harries us, and so (*lovingly brandish-*
 ing his pistols)
 We take our vengeance quietly upon
 Our enemies. You're trembling?
TRAV. Please go on. It's nothing.
BRIG. Well, shorn of its feathers fine,
 My hat grew sad and went into decline.
 Proud and defiant still upon my head,
 For that lost plume what tears it would have shed,
 If it had had a heart – but anyhow,

A pauper, sir, you see before you now,
No money, shoes, no doublet, as you see,
But above all no hat – so pity me.
Who would not weep at such a tale as that?
(*Changing tone*)
    But still I've got two pistols, let me say.
    Look!
TRAV. (*in dismay*)
    Yes, I see them. Please put them away.
    You will, I hope, accept from me this hat! (*Giving him
hat*)
BRIG. (*putting on hat*)
    I'm overcome by your great kindness, sir.
    Oh, thank you, thank you, Mr Traveller.
    Words fail me! But I must not keep you here
    On this dark moonless night so cold and drear.
(*Brandishes his pistols*)
TRAV. No, do go on.
BRIG. All right. Then from our birth,
    Don't you agree, sir, till we leave this earth,
    Man's life with constant miseries is crossed.
    Take me: three brothers and three sisters lost,
    And then my purse, by stern policeman seized.
    I can't forgive Dame Fortune, whom it pleased
    To make me brigand without laws or creed.
    But not content with this, ah, cruel indeed,
    She has denied me one small boon, to wear
    A clean and decent doublet; yet I swear
    That's all I ask, so surely it's no sin.
    Though envy, I confess, has now crept in,
    To think of you possessing what I lack,
    Wearing that handsome coat upon your back.
    I long to have it, you may care to note.
    I still have got two pistols, let me say.
    Look!
TRAV. (*giving him coat*)
    Yes, I see them. Please put them away.
    And be so good as to accept this coat.
BRIG. I'm overcome by your great kindness, sir.
    Oh, thank you, thank you, Mr Traveller.

11

Through such fine generosity at last
My back will be protected from the blast.
But men are so ungrateful here below:
They are not quickly satisfied, you know.
And if you'd gaze on misery complete
Pray look at these vile rags around my feet,
And say if you have seen beneath the sky
A wretch so pitifully shod as I.
Ah, by this blade I swear, if I could find
Tonight some soul beneficent and kind
To offer me such footwear as is fit –
Yes. I will vow (and you may witness it),
A pilgrim's journey shall at once be mine,
To burn a candle at Our Lady's shrine.
Whate'er the jealous say, I'm pious too.
You can make someone happy.

TRAV. *I* can?

BRIG. You!

Oh, my dear sir, if Nature had allowed
That I should have the privilege so proud
Of bringing joy to some poor wretch's heart,
How gladly, nobly, I'd have played my part
And showered gifts upon him from my store!
But I have bare existence, nothing more.

(*Passionately*)

Look at your shoes, how splendid and how fine!

(*Fiercely*)

If you'd exchange them for these rags of mine,
One heart would beat in both our breasts, I swear.
I still have got two pistols, may I say?
Look.

TRAV. Yes, I see them. Please put them away
If shoes you lack, then please accept this pair.

BRIG. I'm overcome by your great kindness, sir.
Oh, thank you, thank you, Mr Traveller.
But I can't always take and nothing give,
For I'm an honest fellow, as I live,
Whatever lies folk tell – whom I will gag –
But what to give? I've neither purse nor bag . . .

(*Suddenly beating his brow*)

12

Ah yes, my cloak, so venerably old,
Which still protects my body from the cold:
More than his twenty cloaks a rich man's pride
I hold it dear. My father, ere he died,
– God rest his soul – bequeathed it me for life:
This cloak, together with his trusty knife.
Yet, though I cherish it, I'll not refuse
To give it you, sir – none of us can lose
(*Takes off cloak*)
By a good deed. So, noble hood, farewell,
In whom the hiving honey-bees did dwell;
Thou cloak once piercèd by a sword accurs'd.
Before we part, come, let me bless thee first.
(*Blesses cloak and gives it to Traveller*)
Brrr, but it's bitter. Sir, I greatly fear
That you may catch some ugly fever here;
Two cloaks will overheat you. If you're wise,
You'll take one off – this one, I should advise.
Heavens, it's cold! My coat's too thin, you see.
But I've still got two pistols, let me say.
Look!
TRAV. (*giving him new cloak*)
Yes, I see them. Please put them away.
Will you accept this extra cloak from me?
BRIG. (*putting it on*)
I'm overcome by your great kindness, sir.
Oh, thank you, thank you, Mr Traveller.
But listen, I am sure your wife must wait
Impatiently to see you, for it's late —
Or so I'd guess. One cannot be exact,
A minor inconvenience, in fact,
Of any wood. We've cuckoos all around;
In summer months you cannot miss the sound.
But since the hours these cuckoos do not chime,
They're no great help for telling me the time.
Nor was it Nature's will – aye, there's the rub –
To hang a clock on tree or bush or shrub.
My timeless state has often proved a trial,
So should I chance on chronometric dial,
It would be a most happy stroke of fate.

I have, of course, two pistols, did I say?
Look!

TRAV. (*giving his watch*)
Yes, I see them. Please put them away.
I hope this watch may cure your timeless state.

BRIG. (*taking it*)
I'm overcome by your great kindness, sir.
Oh, thank you, thank you, Mr Traveller.
Alas, for all the gifts you bid me take,
There is no recompense that I can make.
I cannot pay you save by grateful heart.
What boots it to have played a victor's part,
Defying the police on every hand;
What boots it now to roam throughout the land,
Spreading an honest terror, if one still
Lacks money wherewithal to eat one's fill?
We brigands, whom the ignorant accuse
Of living on mere robbery and ruse,
Are of course prompted to our bloody crimes
By natural desire to eat sometimes.
Great strength of will I need for instance, not
To make your wife a widow on the spot.
Oh, when I see that purse hang at your side
And hear it clink with gold that I'm denied,
You'd die at once unless I kept tight rein.

(*Entreating*)
Oh, save a soul, and help it to refrain
From blood-lust blind to kill a fellow-man!
Save it from the abyss, and sure you can
Boast all tomorrow of a deed so fine.
I've still got these two pistols, let me say.
Just look!

TRAV. (*giving him purse*)
I see them. Please put them away.
Accept, I pray, this humble purse of mine.

BRIG. (*taking it*)
I'm overcome by such great kindness, sir.
Oh, thank you, thank you, Mr Traveller.

(*Looking at watch which he has taken from* TRAVELLER)
Dear me, it's midnight. Really I must fly.

14

I fear, dear sir, that we must say good-bye.
The memory of your kindness I shall treasure.
So nice to meet you, sir.
(*Brandishes pistols*)
TRAV. (*hastily*) It's been a pleasure.

The play shows something of the boy's ability at fourteen, and
his father, of course, could help him to get ahead in his school-
work. Before he was fourteen, he had begun working for the
first part of his *Baccalauréat*, and he passed the whole examina-
tion very young, having started to specialize in mathematics.
Henri de Gaulle was an extremely devoted father, proud of all
his children, and he admired Charles's exceptional gifts, although
recognizing with some anxiety the dangers in the boy's character.
'Charles will go far ... very far. ... Pray God all goes well, too.'
Charles himself, despite being so reserved, pugnacious and even
domineering, was very fond of his parents and not ashamed to
show it: 'he is the most affectionate of the de Gaulle children,' it
was said.

In 1907, when the Jesuits were expelled from France, M. de
Gaulle sent him to study advanced mathematics at a Jesuit
college in Belgium; many of the boys there were from very
aristocratic circles conscious of their 'superiority'. Charles was
a most promising mathematician, and as he had settled for
a military career, his teachers urged him to try for the Poly-
technic (the Military Academy of Artillery and Engineering).
But he had also settled on the Saint-Cyr Military College,
and on the infantry, though this was less aristocratic than
the cavalry. When some expressed surprise at this choice, he
explained that in the infantry 'the field of action is infinitely
vaster'.

At the end of the first school year, in May 1908, there was a
week's retreat for the boys of the Jesuit college. One boy was
Joseph Teilhard de Chardin, brother of Pierre the future philosopher; and he has described the outstanding boy who was
called on to thank the Preacher at this retreat. The boy, Charles
de Gaulle, had long hair parted on the left, rather protruding
ears, and wore a bow tie with a high stiff collar. He began his
speech by saying: 'Those who go to Jesuit schools are accused
of having no personality. We shall prove there is nothing in this

15

accusation.' Pause. 'As to the future, it will be a great one, for it will be full of our works.'

The same year an Englishman some fifteen years older, Winston Churchill, confided: 'I sometimes feel I could carry the world on my shoulders.' Perhaps it is not surprising that young men with greatness in them should have this sense of what the future holds in store. At fourteen Victor Hugo wrote in his school diary: 'I want to be Chateaubriand or nothing.' And at seventeen, according to another fellow pupil of his at the Belgian college, Charles de Gaulle knew that he would be 'General and Commander-in-Chief'.

After three years in Belgium he returned to Paris and attended a special college to work for his entrance to Saint-Cyr. From a taste for mortification or the will to acquire self-mastery, he subjected himself to severe personal discipline. He was also greatly upset by the misconduct of one of the Jesuit teachers, and went through a spiritual crisis, nearly losing his faith.

The royalist writer Charles Maurras had recently turned the *Action Française* into a daily paper, and during breaks in class teachers and pupils debated, often with some passion, the Maurras doctrines of nationalism. Charles de Gaulle was not a royalist. Loyalty for him did not exclude awareness of realities, and the monarchy was a fading shadow. It belonged to the glories of French history, but French history was a continuing process. Henri de Gaulle was too old to make any concessions, and Madame de Gaulle too was shocked that her sons should be republicans; for the younger generation of de Gaulles, however, it seemed less and less likely that parliamentary democracy would be challenged again.

Moreover, the Republic was proving ardently patriotic. Governments passed away, but France remained, surviving them all. For the moment, in the eyes of Charles de Gaulle, the Third Republic had become part of the natural order of things.

By the terms of a law passed in 1905 officer cadets had to start by doing a year's military service in a line regiment. Charles de Gaulle chose the 33rd Infantry Regiment at Arras. Then at last, in 1910, he went to Saint-Cyr, where he underwent the usual rigorous training with crammed time-table, dashing from drill to gymnastics, from fencing to riding, attending lectures and taking tests in history, geography, administration and law, fortifications and artillery. Leaving Saint-Cyr in 1912 with golden epaulettes on his tunic and sword at his side, Second Lieutenant de Gaulle returned to the 33rd Regiment.

The young officer was deeply interested in politics, and to the dismayed surprise of his family he expressed his admiration for a parliamentary leader, 'the Tiger', Georges Clemenceau – 'the only statesman worthy of that name'. Before 1914 Clemenceau was generally regarded as a man of the left, hereditary enemy of priests and kings; but to de Gaulle he had all the really essential qualities. He was the head of government who had placed reasons of state above personal feelings, checking social agitation with the help of the army, despite cries of 'murderer' from the trade unions, his former allies.

This fierce fanatic, aggressive and dictatorial, arrogant, ruthless and indomitable, still believed above all in national honour and the interests of France. Like the royalist right, he had fought angrily and desperately against Jules Ferry's policy of colonial expansion, which he believed wasted the country's forces, a criminal policy when France needed all her soldiers and all her money in Europe. Clemenceau maintained that overseas expeditions were 'high treason', weakening the defence of the home country; the frontiers of France were on the Rhine, not on the Mekong, the Niger or in the Sahara. Charles de Gaulle, brought up on the prospect of revenge against the Germans, could only approve such ideas in the highest degree.

17

3

De Gaulle Comes under Pétain

A new commanding officer had just been appointed to the 33rd Regiment, Colonel Philippe Pétain. He was of farming stock, and had chosen a military career after the French defeat in 1870–71. Like Henri de Gaulle he was dominated by the idea of the great Revenge, and would not be seduced by the colonial conquests of the age. Many young officers hoped to win laurels in the campaigns of Tong-king, Dahomey and Madagascar, but Pétain was not of that school. His mind was never far from the vital Eastern frontier and preparations for war in Europe. (In fact, throughout their military careers neither Pétain nor de Gaulle ever served as an officer of the Colonial Army or of a regiment overseas.)

In the stern hierarchy of the regiment a commanding officer and a second lieutenant, although they had many points in common, would not quickly come very close to each other. But right from the start de Gaulle felt great enthusiasm for this crack officer, hard-working, clear-headed, and no respecter of persons: as far as promotion went, he had already been a victim of his intellectual independence.

There were thirty years between the two men. When Charles de Gaulle was born, Philippe Pétain was training at the Staff College. In 1900 he was appointed instructor at the National College of Musketry, where he at once abandoned the beaten paths of official doctrine, thus arousing unfavourable notice from his superiors. The orthodox line was that an area should be 'sprayed' with traversing fire, so as to provide more points of impact; cones of fire, with long trajectories spread over the target area, were also recommended. Pétain attacked those who supported this line to the neglect of individual precision and direct fire. It was a somewhat revolutionary approach, and infuriated the College's commanding officer, but Pétain refused to back down.

He was superseded, and from then on (until the war) his career was one of prolonged setbacks, with only brief periods

18

of success. Assistant lecturer on infantry tactics at the Staff College, he had difficulties there too, but did become full professor. Knowing his subject backwards, he was a brilliant instructor; yet his outspokenness soon made him unpopular again, since he remained the champion of military heresies.

A great believer in heavy artillery – 'gunfire kills,' he proclaimed – he rejected the call for all-out offensives which some of the general staff favoured as the best technique for modern war. There was Colonel de Grandmaison, for instance, who told M. Paul-Boncour that 'in an offensive, rashness is the safest policy'. In 1911 this Colonel ended a lecture at army headquarters by saying: 'We must prepare ourselves for the only method which can force victory, and prepare others for it by cultivating . . . everything which in any way bears the mark of the offensive spirit. Let us go too far even, and it will perhaps be not far enough.' (De Grandmaison was a general in 1914, and died bravely – following out his theories.)

It should not be thought that those who believed in offensives at all costs were showing elementary stupidity. They felt it was essential not to leave the initiative to the enemy; to conduct operations with such force and fury that the enemy was reduced to parrying the thrust. In this way you could be master, not slave, of events – as was expounded in an impartial analysis of theories by the military historian Colonel Bouvard:

'Since battle, the exclusive aim of all operations, is the only way to break the enemy's will, the commander's first duty is to plan for battle. He will apply his plan with tenacity, regardless of obstacles. He will therefore keep the enemy within the main lines of this plan, until success is achieved. He will plunge in headlong, ready to engage down to the last battalion, so as to destroy his adversary's fighting forces; he will thrust home the attacks and accept the inevitable heavy casualties. Any other conception must be rejected as contrary to the very nature of war.'

At the same period German military doctrine favoured offensives just as much, the only difference being that the Kaiser's armies were far superior in men and materials. They showed even more confidence in the doctrine, because they were expecting to meet an enemy they believed to be militarily and politically decadent.

So Colonel Pétain's warnings, like those of Colonel de Gaulle before the Second World War, fell on deaf ears. De Gaulle himself wrote in *La France et son armée*: 'For two years we had to attack without the arms we needed. ... The 75 gun would not do everything for us. Apart from the fact that wide belts of ground were outside its trajectory, it hadn't enough power to do effective damage to protected targets. ... Although in 1915 the High Command at last decided they must have adequate heavy artillery, this did not go into service until the beginning of 1917. Hence the vast losses ... we suffered so long as a result of our repeated assaults. In 1915, on the French front alone, we lost 1,350,000 men killed, injured and taken prisoner, in order to put out of action 550,000 Germans. Our country, so weak in manpower, had to pay for errors and delays with human lives.'

One of Pétain's cadets at the Staff College has recorded these impressions:

'The course drew the military *élite*. On days when Colonel Pétain was lecturing, the big hall was crammed and you could hear a pin drop. Many generals and staff officers joined the officers under training, so that some of the latter could not even find a place.

'Pétain would come up on to the rostrum, icy and impassive. He spoke without gestures or wasted words. A strong personality, he was not suited to interpreting the ideas of others. He had his own to expound, his laws of battle: the overriding importance of artillery; artillery alone made movement possible.

'"To attack", he would say, "is to constitute a line of fire in front of the objective. The important thing is to bring it nearer and nearer to the enemy so as finally, but only then, to charge at him with bayonets. We should try to think in terms of a new image, the fulcrum of a lever. The time is now over for artillery to operate in isolation. It is no longer possible for objectives to be decided without taking into account the progress of the infantry. But it is important to take the offensive? Certainly. Provided you produce gunfire powerful and destructive enough to clear the way for it."

'Colonel Pétain inveighed against the mystique of the breakthrough, and making it a point of honour not to surrender an inch of ground. His good sense told him that, on the contrary, positions must be abandoned when their defence proved too costly. He protested against the way defensives had been disparaged. Defensives were a necessary manœuvre when you had to spare your forces, conserve your resources, and gain time.'

'Pétain is a great man,' de Gaulle declared roundly. He was shocked by the way the 'old' Colonel was ignored and passed over. 'I was old as a lieutenant, as a captain, as a colonel, I have been old in all my ranks,' Pétain once said with a smile; but this superficial humour concealed a bitterness which was to come to the surface in his old age in the form of consuming ambition. In 1913 General Franchet d'Esperey gave him the acting command of a brigade, intending to appoint him brigadier general in the promotions of June 1914, so that he could then become full general afterwards. But the principal private secretary at the War Ministry told d'Esperey categorically: 'Pétain will never become a full general.' At this time Pétain was preparing for retirement, and had bought a little house in the country near Saint-Omer (Pas de Calais).

De Gaulle was struck by the originality and sound sense of Pétain's doctrines, which foretold the triumph of military equipment in a future war. In *La France et son armée* he wrote: 'Pétain insisted that gunfire kills and that gunfire must be made the foundation of every operation. Because of this insistence his career was "arranged" so that he should never be given important commands. While Germany was building a powerful heavy artillery, most of our experts categorically rejected any innovation of this kind. "You talk to us of heavy artillery," the representative from Army Headquarters replied in 1909 to parliament's Budget Committee. "Thank God, we haven't got any. The power of the French forces is in the lightness of its guns." And the War Minister confirmed the point: "It's unnecessary! With enough rounds from the 75 all obstacles are overcome." Even the growth of air power left many officers sceptical. Returning from a demonstration given in 1910 by military aircraft, the head of the Staff College exclaimed: "All that's mere sport. For the Army the aeroplane is nothing."'

So on the eve of the Great War, Pétain was a rock-like figure standing for a doctrine that was military but also potentially political, a doctrine which he never abandoned; not to launch an attack before the enemy was worn out. He was the man of the counter-offensive, a remarkable tactician. But he lacked one string to his bow: he was no strategist.

Certainly de Gaulle was greatly attracted by the character of this man who had sacrificed his future to his ideas; and the Colonel, who was a fair judge of people, took a liking to this second lieutenant, reporting on him in October 1913 as follows:

1st term: Passed out of Saint-Cyr 13th out of 211, has from the beginning shown himself an officer of real quality, extremely promising. . . .

2nd term: Very intelligent, loves his profession passionately. . . . Worthy of the highest praise.

Despite appearances both men were shy, and therefore much on their own. Both were proud, but in very different ways: Pétain had the sly pride of a countryman, de Gaulle an aristocratic pride *à la* Cyrano. Aware of their own worth, they cultivated a scorn of the common herd who did not understand them. They had mediocrity all round them, and were irritated by stupidity. De Gaulle flaunted his sense of superiority, so that at Saint-Cyr some called him the Cock or even the Peacock.

Pétain, on the other hand, instinctively concealed his pride, so that most people who had dealings with him found him modest, at times almost self-effacing, with rather the air of a simple N.C.O. In fact he was well above the average intellectually, even outside military matters; for instance, he could hold his own in a conversation about Bergson. His intellectual abilities, however, were far below those of de Gaulle, an all-embracing mind with an insatiable curiosity and very deep culture.

There were other big differences between the two men. Although educated at a Catholic school in Saint-Omer, then by the Dominicans, Pétain lost his faith early. He was an inveterate bachelor, who had dozens of *affaires*, no doubt flattering to his self-esteem. He flitted from skirt to skirt, and was fond of declaring: 'I love two things above all, sex and the infantry.' He liked puns, spoonerisms, funny stories. The stories were often rather blue and not in the best of taste; then he would descend to guardroom level.

He was certainly a personality, a 'card'. He may well have deliberately fostered the image of an officer not afraid of stand-

espectively by Charles Maurras and the socialist
t terrible of his party. Sembat's book was called
, or else Make Peace', and its message was that
not capable of waging a war. It wasn't created for
st either avoid war at any price, or else make way
tutions.'

ing up to superiors
'reds' (33rd Regime
the 'blues'. The bl
orthodox plan, and
who had prepared a
vres was furious.
said: 'One must on
Pétain. I call on hi
with the words: 'W

Having made a
churia and the B;
Suvorov that 'Bull
In the manœuvre
company took pa
October), the divi
deployed in the a
according to plan
three regiments, f
without a seriou
artillery; the 'R(
magnificent, with
parade-ground: (

When the man
turn to speak, he
'I am sure Gener
your minds, mus
mistakes which
paused. 'Let us f
wards we shall v

At the time, ir
with the aid of v
done in the lec
advance. A defe
wins ground, th

With war exp
Army, Pétain ir
mentary régime
danger. Lieuter
ments either, ar

reading list, i
Sembat, *enfa*
'Make a King
'this régime is
that; so it mu
for other insti

4

De Gaulle and His 'Chief' in the Great War

The war broke out, and de Gaulle saw with fury the results of ignoring Pétain's warnings: from the first days of August 1914, it became clear that the French Army's heavy artillery was woefully inadequate. The machine-gun was a new and unfamiliar weapon, of which the director-general of the infantry had said in 1910, at a gunnery school where exercises with it were being held: 'We have made some machine-guns to please public opinion. But take my word for it, this device won't make much difference to anything.'[1] The machine-gun indeed 'was not considered a *solid* enough weapon; suited at most to spatter the ramparts of a fort, but likely to break down in the field if inexpertly handled, and exhaust a battalion's ammunition boxes in ten minutes to no purpose'.[2]

So the old cadets of Saint-Cyr, in their blue greatcoats, and red trousers, with their white gloves and plumes on their shakos, were mown down by a rain of enemy fire. As de Gaulle later described it, 'the calm affected by the officers, who allowed themselves to be killed where they stood; the fixed bayonets of some stubborn sections; bugles sounding the charge; heroic last rushes by isolated individuals: such things had no effect. It was immediately obvious that all the courage in the world could never prevail against superior fire power.'

On 15th August de Gaulle himself was wounded at Dinant in a vain attempt to hold the bridge. He was evacuated to Charleroi and operated on at Arras. As the Germans advanced, he made his own way to Paris by taxi, where he had a second operation. But this was before the victory on the Marne, so to stay at Paris might mean being caught in a trap. He hired a car next day

[1] Quoted by Paul Reynaud in a speech to the Chambre des Députés (Jan. 1937) calling for special mechanized corps.

[2] From speech by Paul Valéry welcoming Pétain to the Académie Française.

and left the city, determined above all not to fall into enemy hands.

As to Pétain, he readily faced personal danger, calm and imperturbable at the head of his brigade. Paul Valéry, referring to the operations of 1914, had this to say when welcoming Pétain to the Académie Française (1931): 'One could reproach you, sir, with having needlessly exposed a commander's precious life, had this daring, in a man of your good sense and self-control, not signified something quite different from foolhardy impulse. With your distrust for mere theories, you were eager for the realities, danger or no.'

On returning to his regiment, de Gaulle was appointed adjutant to the colonel, but asked for the command of a company so that he could fight in the line. He was made acting captain in February 1915 (the promotion was confirmed in September), and took part in the trench warfare, where his tallness must have been a considerable handicap – he was always having to duck. But his physical courage was remarkable. One day he and two other officers were out on reconnaissance when they saw a shell coming. The other two threw themselves to the ground before the explosion. When they picked themselves up, de Gaulle was still standing there serenely unconcerned, and asked coldly: 'Were you frightened, gentlemen?'

In February 1916, following a second wound, he returned to the line at Verdun, where the 1st Army Corps had been sent as emergency reinforcements. In a terrible six-day battle his company was practically wiped out, he was wounded once more, and this time was at last captured. Pétain's citation reads: 'Captain de Gaulle, company commander, well-known for his high intellectual and moral courage, when his company was undergoing appalling bombardment . . . with the enemy attacking from all sides, led his men into a furious assault and fierce hand-to-hand fighting, the only solution he deemed compatible with his sense of military honour. He fell in the fray. An officer outstanding in every respect.' For the rest of the war Captain de Gaulle was in various prisoner-of-war camps, the last one being on the banks of the Danube.

After the ineffective 'Champagne offensive', which he severely criticized, Pétain had been relieved of active command until the beginning of 1916, when Joffre put him in command of the army formed to relieve Verdun, the town with which his name became inseparably connected. Thereafter he rose steadily; until in 1918, under Foch as Supreme Commander, he was entrusted with the general attack by all French forces. De Gaulle has given a character study of him at this time, which is incidentally very revealing of the writer's own ideas on the qualities needed by a military commander:

'As soon as a choice had to be made between ruin and reason, they promoted Pétain. Excellent at grasping the practical essentials in any situation, he accomplished his task by force of intellect, though also stamping that accomplishment with the imprint of his character. Between his lucid personality and the great intensity of action called for in modern war, there was such complete harmony that it seemed like a law of nature. Moreover, he was trusted as a man who had scorned the advantages of obsequiousness and had yet won through to high command. He had been saved from empty favours by the power of his critical spirit. Nobly independent, he yet obeyed orders; dominant in council, he was immune to outside pressures. He had the prestige of a deep reserve, intensified by a deliberate coldness of manner, quick sarcasm, and a pride which protected his aloofness.'

Pétain was very popular throughout the French Army. The ordinary soldier never classed him among the know-all theorists who gained their glory over a mass of dead bodies. He went on hammering home his messages: 'You can't fight with men against guns', 'as little infantry as possible, as much artillery as possible', etc. In a note on 'the attitude of High Command', he wrote: 'In the present war the murderous power of gunfire does not allow any experiments: the smallest operation demands a minute preparation for which the agreement of all honest minds is indispensable. However, once the preparation has been well studied, the decision taken and the order given, the operation must be carried out with a whole-hearted energy and firmness of purpose.'

He prepared his offensives carefully with methodical shelling. Soon the first tanks went ahead of the marching infantrymen. General Laure relates how during a conference at 10th Army Headquarters 'General d'Urbal asked each of his corps commanders how many grenades he felt he should have. "5,000," replied the most daring. When it came to Pétain's turn, he said quietly: "I want 50,000."'

Édouard Daladier, one of the prominent French politicians of the period between the wars, who had been a second lieutenant of artillery at Verdun, declared on the 45th anniversary of that battle: 'I have no great admiration for the military chiefs of 14–18. I shall surprise you, no doubt, by saying that if I make an exception, it is for Pétain, although afterwards I did not have a very high esteem for him. You may call him a defeatist. But he said: "We shall not move until we have enough arms and ammunition." And the guns, the machine-guns, the ammunition flowed in. This is a fact.'

Until the summer when Foch took victory in hand, Pétain combined as far as possible his military sense and his humanity. Before any attack he turned himself into an accountant, 'estimating costs'. His formula was attrition, not break-through, and he once observed: 'There are no longer decisive battles as there used to be.'

His 'humanity' was relative, of course, for he was essentially a realist about war, and did not feel any personal emotion towards his men; he would have considered this sentimentality. He looked at them with a clear eye, so as to decide the best use he could make of them in the supreme interest of the nation. The technique, in fact, was part of 'administration', department of 'human material': the head ruled the heart. 'An iron hand in a velvet glove' was a saying extremely apt in relation to Pétain: so was another maxim culled from the wisdom of the people, 'You catch more flies with honey than with vinegar.'

This technique helped to save France at the time of the 1917 mutinies. Indeed in the opinion of the British military expert Liddell Hart, Pétain was the only military leader of the war France could not have done without, the only one who enabled her to survive the crisis of 1917; the impetuous, fire-breathing Foch might have 'hastened her ruin instead of checking it'. Pétain was also carrying out a mission of self-sacrifice; for he was sent to cure an army suffering from a disease which seemed likely to be mortal, following slaughters caused by inadequate supplies. He took over responsibility for the mistakes of others. It was perhaps a sort of vocation, for as Clemenceau wrote of him afterwards: 'He was always ready for personal sacrifice.'

In June 1917 Henry Bordeaux accompanied him to one of the mutinous regiments where men were singing the International. Pétain asked Bordeaux afterwards not to talk about it, but 'how can I keep silent on his extraordinary success in changing these men? He walked up to them alone (I stayed a few paces away), with his splendid, majestic bearing. And he began speaking to them without familiarity or coaxing, but just as man to man. Yes, they had reasons to complain. The war was too long and too hard. But it had been imposed on us and we must win it. Let them be patient. He was looking after them, their food and wine, their leaves and reliefs. He guaranteed that he would not send them into battle unless they were well covered by artillery, that he had their lives at heart more than his own. Then his voice rose: behind them were their wives and children, their old folk, their region, their land. Without them, all would be lost and it would be slavery under the Germans. Let them be patient and resolute men. Let them believe in France and draw strength from her like the strength of those who believe in God. . . . The angry faces calmed down, and I saw tears flowing . . .'

Did Pétain himself conceal his softer side? An officer who arrived in 1918 at the General's headquarters, and accompanied him on his visits to the wounded in hospital, tells us: 'The terrible sights drew tears from many, but Pétain always remained imperturbable, withdrawn, as if indifferent – superficially anyhow, I cannot speak for his deeper feelings – like a great surgeon starting on his operations. This calm never left him. He reminded me of the commander of a besieged town who isolates himself, and refuses to see the population's sufferings, lest he should succumb to pity.'

'Strong emotions held in rein by an iron will,' diagnosed the future General Héring, chief of Pétain's staff in the early 1920s. 'He has a horror of sentimentality,' observed another officer attached to his headquarters in 1917, 'but whenever he passes an ambulance, he cannot speak without a choke in his voice'.

A further memory from that period is recorded by Colonel Henri Carré: 'Inspecting a front-line hospital one day, Pétain noticed a very young soldier, with feverish eyes, and a huge dressing over his chest, who was feebly moving his hand above his sheet, as if to call the visitor. At an inquiring glance from the general, the medical superintendent whispered: "Eighteen years old, both lungs perforated, no hope."

'The Commander-in-Chief went up to the boy, whose features lit up in a faint smile.

'"What do you want, my boy, can I do anything for you?"

'"I would like . . . to see my mother," the boy said in a rattling voice.

'"You *shall* see her, I promise." He turned to his aide. "Take a note of the address. Telegraph to the mother. Instruct all the authorities to let her pass. Keep me informed."'

Pétain himself once said: 'I am kind. I know this and distrust it. Luckily I have a mask of ice.' This is confirmed by the future General Serrigny, attached to his staff from the beginning of the war, who noted: 'At bottom, beneath his mask of rigidity, the man hides a sensitive soul.' And: 'Now that I know him well, I know he has a soul full of tenderness.'

But tenderness could become complete ruthlessness, when it was demanded by duty or what he believed to be duty. He admitted to the future Marshal Fayolle, in November 1914, that he had started by having shirkers shot; he had 'acted like a butcher'. Fayolle records an order of Pétain's in January 1915, to shoot twenty-five out of forty men with self-inflicted hand wounds. Next day, changing his mind, 'he merely had them bound and thrown from the other side of the parapet to the trenches nearest the enemy. "They will spend the night there." He didn't say if they would be left to starve there . . .'

Nevertheless, it must be admitted that Pétain gradually became an object of deep veneration to officers and men at the front. As a matter of fact he believed that a commander must cultivate his popularity so as to maintain the morale of his subordinates. Anyone who observed him very closely could see that he was instinctively an *actor* who adopted the character of a serene, fatherly old man.

Once he was changing trains at a big junction, where there were always a great many soldiers on leave coming and going. It was a cold day, and the ladies of the Red Cross were serving coffee, so he got into the queue. He was wearing an ordinary greatcoat without orders or stars, as he often did. At last his turn came. But the lady giving out the coffee failed to identify him and called out: 'Here, this fellow hasn't got his mug. Come on, the next man.' The General said nothing, as usual, but there was an officer escorting him who informed her of her mistake, so that the General was then served.

One of his most loyal officers agreed with Fayolle that Pétain 'liked showing off', and told me of his habit of inviting nurses to join him at a lunch-break on the roadside or in the ruins of a town. He would break up the ordinary army bread, share out the tins of food, and when it came to cheese would say: 'Please excuse me, I haven't introduced myself. I am General Pétain.' He would then enjoy the surprise and excitement caused.

The same officer also records that at one period he rode in a requisitioned Rolls-Royce. The figure on the radiator cap was mistaken by the ordinary French soldier for the figure of Victory; and on days when things were going badly, Pétain had it removed, for fear people should laugh at him.

Not that he was superstitious. As for religion, he was now completely agnostic, and confided to one of his officers: 'I used to be a believer, but no longer. I have nothing left of the faith of my childhood.'

Although sixty in 1916, he was still very vigorous physically, and still had many liaisons with women. Serrigny recalls the occasion when Joffre sent orders through at 10 p.m. for Pétain to leave at once for Verdun: Pétain was away from his headquarters that night, and when Serrigny eventually located him in Paris, it was at the Hôtel Terminus near the Gare du Nord – in a lady's company.

Serrigny also relates the following: 'One day I handed him the text of a radio message from the German Ambassador in Madrid to his government, which our Intelligence Service had given me in great secrecy. It contained the information that a mistress had at last been found for the French General with emoluments of 12,000 pesetas a month. I asked the General whether he suspected the identity of the lady chosen by the enemy, to which after some hesitation he answered that he did. I took advantage of this to warn him once more to be on his guard with women, and after that their visits to him became a little less frequent.'

Pétain also retained much of his independent spirit. For instance, before Clemenceau had become the architect of final victory, he was paying a visit to the armies in the field; on the day when he was expected at Pétain's headquarters, Pétain sent a message that he was too busy to see him. This may also have been evidence, of course, of increasing vanity, for Fayolle's diary, in January 1917, notes: 'Pétain believes himself a great man. He declares quite seriously that the Republic is afraid of him.' Raymond Poincaré, President of the Republic, refused to have him succeed Joffre because he saw Pétain as 'a would-be dictator'. This was no doubt because some time before, at a private dinner with Poincaré, Pétain had maintained that co-ordinating all government machinery was only possible through a dictatorship exercised by the head of state. 'But what about the Constitution, General?' Poincaré protested. 'To Hell with the Constitution!' said Pétain.

Pessimistic by temperament, the General became even more so as the war dragged on. He was determined to spare his soldiers' blood, and had a horror of mass slaughters. He was often reproached with accepting too easily the need to retreat, but for him retreat was an important manœuvre with its own principles and requirements. Serrigny quotes an occasion when he told Poincaré: 'You know, monsieur le Président, that great captains never become famous except by skilful retreats. I don't know if I shall be obliged to abandon Verdun, but if that measure seemed necessary to me, I should not hesitate to face it.' To which Poincaré replied at once: 'You mustn't think of it, General. It would be a parliamentary disaster.'

After the war the Inter-Allied Circle gave a dinner in honour of General Gouraud, who had commanded the French 4th Army in Champagne. After the dinner and speeches Pétain took Gouraud aside and told him: 'You know, I nearly had you court-martialled in Champagne. I had just arrived and said to you: "Retreat so as to avoid useless losses, then start attacking again later." You answered. "I am not in the habit of retreating." I told you: "It's an order." If you had not obeyed, I should not have hesitated: I should have sent you for court-martial.'

He remained more than ever opposed to the idea of offensives at all costs. Like his model from ancient Rome, Fabius Cunctator, he believed the country could be saved by avoiding battle; daring for him was 'the art of not risking too much'. He grasped very clearly the importance both military and economic of America's entry into the war, and was determined to wait for a mass landing of American soldiers; after this victory, could be driven home by force of superior arms, especially by mass production of the new arm, the tank.

But meanwhile pessimism was in the air. After a big break in the British front in March 1918 one French general thought there was nothing for it but to make peace on the best terms possible; and Pétain told Clemenceau: 'If we are beaten, it will be the fault of the British.' Clemenceau was horrified by Pétain's pessimism, and confided to Poincaré how Pétain had said to him: 'The Germans will defeat the British in the open country. After which they will defeat us too.' 'Ought a general to talk or even think like that?' asked Clemenceau.

However, Pétain was also the man who declared: '*On les aura*', who restored hope in the ranks of the army when morale was at its lowest, giving them new confidence in final victory. In 1917 France lost only 190,000 killed and captured, as against 430,000 in 1915, the year of Joffre's command. And Pétain had realized that France could only be saved by solving the man-power problem. Thanks to his policy and the saving of resources he achieved in men and materials, while waiting for the Americans to arrive, disaster was retrieved in the victory of March 1918.

He could be called, in fact, the organizer of victory. To quote once more from Paul Valéry's address on Pétain's admission to the Académie, 'in a few months, in Pétain's hands, the French Army became an instrument of power, precision and incomparable resistance. During the critical and decisive year, between the British Army, soon to be terribly tested, and the American Army, slowly growing and coming into action, this revived French Army was to be the essential agent of common defence and victory.'

Nor was Pétain always the man of defence rather than attack. Jean de Pierrefeu, author of *G.Q.G. Secteur 1*, writes: 'I watched a curious psychological phenomenon. Despite our need to re-build all our forces for a future effort, the more spirited elements on the general staff were already looking forward to a resumption of the offensive. The signal for advance and driving the enemy back must be given as soon as possible. The enormous pocket which his advance had just driven made him vulnerable. Everything was reduced to the following alternatives: either you wait for the enemy, although you might be beaten in the end; or you forestall him by attacking and defeat him. Now, according to common belief, even at G.H.Q., Pétain was for the first plan, Foch for the second. . . . Yet for three months and a half Foch stayed resolutely on the defensive, and at the time of the counter-attack Pétain was urging Foch to hasten the ending.'

It is certainly the case that he pushed Foch to the final 'rush'. 'We must not leave the enemy time to breathe,' he proclaimed; and called for a 'German Sedan'. Taking everything into account, de Gaulle was right: Pétain, despite the failings and weaknesses from which no one is free, had shown himself to be a great chief, who had proved to his former lieutenant 'what the gift and art of command are worth'.

If Pétain was the high command's cart-horse, so to speak, Foch was the thoroughbred, a military genius. He never had any doubts, and was undeterred by difficulties, however formidable. His officers said: 'When he *wants* something, no obstacle must exist.' 'Of course I'm prejudiced,' he declared, twirling his moustache. 'I always see things from the side of salvation, not the side of defeat. I eliminate objections.'

Certainly Foch did not like being contradicted. 'You would think that he too heard voices,' Clemenceau groaned. He drove on to victory with all his furious energy, which would have become dangerous had it not rested on good sense, intelligence and mature reflection on the lessons of History. He had no idea of tactics, but was the complete strategist. He admired Napoleon, Clausewitz, Frederick the Great. The Rrrrhine – as he pronounced it with the rolling Rs of his Pyrenean origin – was one of his obsessions.

He was extremely difficult to get on with, for he never deigned to explain himself. He considered generals all-important, the main factor in victory. 'As Napoleon said,' he wrote, 'it was Caesar, not the Roman legions, who conquered the Gauls; Hannibal, not the Carthaginian soldiers, who made Rome tremble.' Religion, however, set bounds to his immense egoism. 'Napoleon forgot that a man can't be God; that above the individual there is a nation; that above men there is morality.'

Although impulsive, effervescent, dynamic, Foch usually proved to have thought out his ideas rationally, to be arguing with sound logic. His judgement, admittedly, was by no means

34

infallible, especially outside the military sphere, and there were many besides Clemenceau who wondered whether he was not slightly mad. He was not at all convinced of the supremacy of the civil power; and when peace came, meant to write a book castigating the 'drones', i.e. the members of parliament. He demanded a government which governed, and a head of state worthy of the name. He was quite ready to do away with the constitution.

Proud and ambitious, he was passionately patriotic and had the faith which moves mountains. 'To win a victory,' he declared, 'the will to win is everything.' One of his more extravagant remarks was the famous: '*Mon centre cède, ma droite recule. Situation excellente. J'attaque.*'

Often these apparent supermen only seem mad to those who cannot see so far ahead as they can; and many would rate Foch as the greatest general the world has known since Napoleon. But such men are still human, and make mistakes; because of their greatness, the mistakes too are on an outsize scale, and may reach monstrous proportions.

'This time he *is* mad,' thought the staff officers of the inter-Allied command. Foch had evidently had a vision, and was gesticulating wildly, waving clenched fists, miming actions, rapping out staccato words and eventually exclaiming: 'The parrot . . . subtle creature . . . sublime creature.' No one dared speak, and the explanation only came a few days later, through former students of his at the Staff College, where this image had been used in a lecture. The subtle parrot climbs by advancing first its beak, then one foot, then both feet; then having achieved a firm base, it settles.

The French and Belgian tanks, coming out of the factories in their thousands, now helped to occupy these firm bases, while the Germans were far behind in motorization and armour. *Die Frankfurter Zeitung* said: 'Foch has tanks, and we have not.'

De Gaulle studied these problems in his prisoner-of-war camps. He kept himself quite up to date thanks to the German Press, which, unlike the French papers, rarely censored enemy communiqués. He also managed to procure Swiss papers now and then.

He followed the promotions of the great generals, and did not

35

hide his growing admiration for Pétain. Every time 'the Chief' received a higher command, he would tell his fellow officers: 'Good news, Pétain is forging ahead. He deserves it.' He liked recalling memories of his old colonel, and declared: 'Pétain is certainly the officer on the general staff with the greatest all-round ability. His ideas are sound. He at least did not prepare for the last war.'

De Gaulle was bored and frustrated as a prisoner. Captain at twenty-five, *chevalier de la Légion d' Honneur, croix de guerre,* three times wounded, he champed at the bit, wishing he could fight for his country, and either die for it or at least win his fair share of glory. He felt it unworthy of a regular soldier to remain a prisoner. Five times he tried to escape, but his tallness was a handicap and he did not succeed.

He took refuge in study, especially military study. Pétain's ideas had triumphed in the first stages of the war. Superiority in supplies was shown to be a golden rule, while those at the Staff College who had made a sacred cow of the 75 gun were completely discomfited.

De Gaulle gave lectures in camp. He had not yet seen tanks deployed in the field, but learnt about them from military articles he read. He already suspected, though without daring to assert it firmly, the full importance of these mechanical battering-rams, this *force de frappe.*

The signs of a revolution in the military field were becoming apparent. The armoured corps had first gone into action on the Franco-British side on 15th September 1916, day of the Battle of the Somme. At Cambrai, from 20th November till 6th December 1917, the experiment continued, with some preliminary disappointments and setbacks. The attacks were based on the surprise and speed produced by the masses of steel. For miles of front the Germans collapsed, taken from the rear or the flank. The breakthrough had succeeded, the bells rang in London – too soon. There was no exploitation of the ground gained. The method had not been perfected, and success was not turned into victory. The daring irruption of the steel giants petered out in uncertainty. All the same, the Battle of Cambrai was the proving point of the new form of war for the British tanks.

In 1918 the French hurled into the attack their excellent tanks, Renault, Schneider, Saint-Chamond. Foch studied a project for

36

a 'mechanized battle'. Churchill had advocated a grandiose plan: 10,000 tanks striking on a front of 200 to 250 miles, followed by the allied infantry and 1,000 tracked vehicles. At Soissons the French tanks, overwhelming the defence network, crossing the trenches, destroying the machine-gun nests, achieved terrific results (in 1940 the Wehrmacht used just such methods, assimilated and modernized). 'These were the first Stations of the Cross the German Army had to pass through,' wrote one of the German generals afterwards, 'leading to the November days of death.' The 'victory tanks' destroyed the morale of the Germans, who had scarcely realized their possibilities at all. In March 1918, referring to the first fifty tanks built in Germany, Ludendorff is said to have remarked: 'They probably won't do much good, but since they've been made, we too might as well use them.' Yet concerning the battle of Soissons Ludendorff was to write: 'Our troops were swamped by squadrons of assault tanks. It was the intervention of these tanks which ensured victory for the French.'

On the French front the famous Allied break-through stopped too soon, and the Kaiser's divisions were saved at the last moment from complete disaster. There are three invariable principles in war: surprise, power, exploitation. The French achieved the first two, but not the third.

In his prisoner-of-war camp de Gaulle went over the offensives for his fellow officers. He noted that in this war, whenever a break-through had succeeded, pockets of resistance had been established, so that the war of position was continually restarting. How, he asked, with the necessary arms and ammunition, could one return to the war of movement, of manœuvre, the Napoleonic war? Would the tanks' wave of assault at last make possible a decisive break in the enemy front? De Gaulle declared himself for complete motorization and the forming of a specialized corps of regular soldiers.

At the camp he was called *le Connétable* (the old name for a commander-in-chief), a nickname dating from his year in the ranks in the 33rd Regiment, when Captain de Tugny, commanding the 9th Company, remarked: 'Why should I make this boy a sergeant when he would only feel at home as commander-in-chief?'

There was a distinct aura of prestige round *le Connétable*.

Few of the officers were on familiar terms with him. Some appreciated him at his true worth for his outstanding intelligence, his boldness in facing the future, his sensitivity and courteousness. Others found him haughty, full of arrogance and ambition, lacking in humanity. For the rest of their lives the former could say, 'I have been a Gaullist since 1916'; the latter, 'I have been an anti-Gaullist since 1916.'

5

Back to Saint-Cyr

After the Armistice on the western front, Captain de Gaulle, released from captivity, took part in the operations against the Bolsheviks in Poland. His commanding officers reported on him as 'an officer of remarkable fearlessness', 'exceptional qualities of character and intellect', 'a glutton for work'. He was, of course, determined to make up for lost time; for he considered himself handicapped in comparison with those of his fellows who had been privileged to fight all through the war.

He returned to France in December 1920 to get married (early in 1921) – to a girl from Calais called Yvonne Vendroux whom he had met on leave in Paris – and became assistant lecturer in history at Saint-Cyr. His lecture course was on the period from the Revolution onwards, and he could hold the attention of the class speaking for the whole hour without a single note. Always smartly turned out, white gloves setting off the blue uniform, he stood out as a fine officer. The high black boots with spurs made him seem immensely tall; the sword hanging at his side looked like an absurd little dagger. The prominent Adam's apple went up and down under the high stiff collar of his tunic.

Sternly dispassionate when examining a class, he lectured brilliantly, with the fire and eloquence born of his own enthusiasm. An artist in choice of words, he excelled at recreating epic battles, capturing the continual movement of charging cavalry and marching infantry, so that a great heroic pageant sprang to life, with flesh-and-blood soldiers rising out of the darkness of the past. You could hear the clank of armour. 'You are beating your drum,' Clemenceau would have said, 'with the bones of the dead'; but de Gaulle and his pupils were oblivious of such reflections. Military glory was an essential part of their career.

When he came to the sad times of 1870, he could make the class feel the full weight of the disasters and dangers which overtook France, with Bazaine refusing to admit his unfitness for

39

command. The generals of those days had courage enough, but they lacked 'breadth of view, range of judgement, without which you cannot grasp the problems of war. . . . The generals who have not achieved the higher philosophy of their art which yields breadth of judgement, can never think far enough ahead.' The great defeat was not fatal, however, 'One might have thought that the bitter blows of fortune would have left us crushed. That would be to forget the secret strength which will always lift us from the depths.'

Captain de Gaulle leaned forward, concluding his lecture, and banged on the table. 'To your feet, gentlemen.' The class leapt to their feet. 'Atten-shun.' For the minute's salute to the French Army he stood rigid and solemn; then he paid homage to the soldiers of August 1870. 'In that war without consolations, we lacked neither men nor courage; the many proofs of this testified to the precious heritage, still intact, of our military virtues . . .

'These valiant men tried by sheer courage to conquer an evil destiny. They knew their duty, and joyfully answered the call to arms. On 14th August, when they were retreating towards the Moselle, they turned directly they heard French guns, and counter-attacked in a furious charge. . . . On the evening of the 16th . . . they could feel that the enemy was exhausted, beaten, ready to break; but they were held back themselves by an inexplicable lack of drive in their own command. Yet they shouted all along the line: "Forward, forward!"

'No defeat destroyed their will to fight. They fought at Saint-Privat as bravely as at Spicheren. Besieged in Metz, with disaster staring them in the face, they went into action at Noisseville and at Ladonchamps, as if they were still full of confidence. They fought skilfully with the arms given them, and against odds of two to one, overwhelmed by far superior artillery, they killed and wounded 58,000 Germans during the three great weeks of August, losing 49,000 themselves.

'They were loyal to the end, and suffered misery and humiliation to pay for the mistakes of others. Returning from the prisoner-of-war camps, they were loyal and disciplined enough to remove the barricades of the Commune and save the State.

'The unfair humiliations they suffered can never be forgotten or wiped out; they will remain a perpetual lesson for those who govern and those who command.

40

'Stand at . . . ease!' Pause. 'Thank you, gentlemen.'

For two seconds the class stood silent and spellbound. Time stopped. The lecture-hall seemed full of ghostly presences. Then the visions faded, the magic departed, and the class trooped out into the common light of day.

The First Empire was a happier subject, although de Gaulle deplored Napoleon as well as admiring him. But in the end the balance was tilted in favour of admiration:

'His glory had been great, and great was his fall: the mind boggles at both . . . Napoleon left France crushed, invaded, drained of blood and courage, smaller than when he took her over, condemned to unjust frontiers, which have never been rectified, exposed to the distrust of Europe, a distrust from which she still suffers after over a century. But on the other side there is the immense prestige he won for our arms; the knowledge which the nation gained once for all of its immense military potentialities; the power and renown, still felt today, which he brought to France: surely these must count for something? No one has shaken human passions more profoundly, has provoked more violent hatreds, more furious curses; yet what name stirs so much devotion and enthusiasm, so that one cannot utter it without kindling a smouldering fire in the soul? Napoleon exhausted the good-will of the French, abused their sacrifices, covered Europe with tombs, ashes and tears; yet those he made to suffer, the soldiers, were the most faithful to him; and even in our day, despite the time that has passed, the different emotions he arouses, and many new heroes to mourn, crowds still come from all over the world to pay homage to his memory, and near his tomb are overcome by the thrill of his greatness.'

On the reigns of Charles X, Louis-Philippe and especially Napoleon III, de Gaulle passed severe judgements. The underlying philosophy of his teaching was that the conquest of Algeria, the Crimean and Mexican Wars, all the overseas expeditions, by 'quenching the thirst for great enterprises', had ended by distracting the French Army from its chief mission, to guard the frontiers of France. France was entangled in American adventures when the Prussian army defeated Austria at Sadowa. 'How much blood and tears it cost us, that mistake of the Second Empire – letting Sadowa happen without bringing our army to the Rhine!'

He deplored the fact that 'from 1820 to 1869, 300,000 Frenchmen had died in war' – these heavy losses overseas had much to do with the surrender in 1871. He shared the state of mind of Bugeaud, as seen by Victor Hugo in 1841: 'The General was very annoyed with Algeria. He declared that this conquest was preventing France from having her full say in Europe.'

'No doubt,' said de Gaulle, 'to besiege Sebastopol and drive the Austrians out of Lombardy were limited tasks which our army carried out creditably. But by allowing the establishment on our frontiers of two new great powers, by contributing to the humiliation of Russia and Austria, the Emperor Napoleon III prepared all the conditions for a conflict in which France would have to defend unaided her soil and her future. To wage this great war would have required a different army. . . . In 1870 France was armed for a local war and hurled herself into a war of peoples.'

De Gaulle also belonged (like Pétain) to the 'Metropolitan' school, which maintained that in Madagascar, Tong-king and Morocco 'the army of Africa and the marines had lost sight of sound principles . . . even if the proof that French military valour was intact soothed the national sorrow and raised hopes. . . . It was a longing for past glories.' And again: 'France looks always towards the Vosges. To distract the troops from that is surely a betrayal of trust.'

Marshal Pétain (who had also got married, during the same year as de Gaulle) had become Vice-President of the Council of War. De Gaulle's admiration for his former 'chief' was as strong as ever, and he often went to the Marshal's headquarters in the Boulevard des Invalides. He was the disciple, Pétain the master, a 'guide, philosopher and friend'; so that when in December 1921 Madame de Gaulle gave birth to a son, the parents called the boy Philippe in honour of Pétain. 'The Marshal is godfather,' de Gaulle repeated proudly, although in fact he can only have been a sort of lay godfather; for according to family traditions Philippe was taken to the font by M. Henri de Gaulle and Mme. Jacques Vendroux, his maternal grandmother. However, above the cot in Philippe's room there was a fine photograph of the victor of Verdun, with dedication beneath to this effect: 'To my young friend Philippe de Gaulle, hoping that his life may show all his father's qualities and gifts. Affectionately, Philippe Pétain.'

One result of de Gaulle's visits to Pétain's headquarters was that he penetrated into the circles where the great statesmen and generals moved, men he had known before only by repute. They fascinated him, even if some of the greatest were already in decline.

Clemenceau, for instance, although seventy-seven, had still had boundless energy and dynamism at the end of the war – he thrust his head out over the trenches, brandishing his clenched fist at the Boches and shouting, amidst enthusiastic privates: 'Swine! Bastards! We'll get you in the end!' But after the war this 'Father of Victory', thrown out by the people he had saved, soon became a bitter disillusioned old man, dreaming of past glories, decrying parliament and democracy. 'How can you take seriously a parliament which drops its toys, then picks them up again? I no longer believe in the thing which once inspired me, democracy. . . . You will have a peace reeking of decadence. You won't suffer. It will be disgusting but luxurious, as when the Ancients opened their veins in a bath of milk.'

'I never really knew the French,' he declared on another occasion. 'They are a people of amnesics. They have forgotten everything: their griefs, their glories, the Germans. So much so, that if they had to be saved again, well, I would save them from force of habit, but it would no longer interest me.'

He was near the truth when he observed in melancholy mood: 'If I cared about my glory, I should die now.' Perhaps war heroes should be embalmed on the morrow of their triumphs, just as primitive tribes used to carry out a ritual murder of their chiefs. Jean Pottecher, before being killed in July 1918, wrote of Clemenceau: 'If he saves France, or rather acquires the reputation for this, he should be given infinite honours and afterwards immolated.'

Writing in his retirement, Clemenceau had a mixture of praise and criticism for Foch. He could not forgive Foch's insubordination – 'a soldier refusing to obey! Any trooper who behaved to his corporal as Foch did to me, would have been under detention at once.' On the other hand, he was between two men (Pétain and Foch), 'one who told me we were done for, the other who rushed round like a madman and wanted to fight. I said to myself, Let's try Foch, at least we'll die fighting. I let Foch the madman have his way, and he pulled us through.'

If Foch was a madman then, his madness increased after the war. Marshal Fayolle's *Cahiers Secrets* (not published until 1964) include these entries for 1919:

'May 14th. Have just picked Foch up at Mayence. He is delirious with joy after the grandiose reception organized for him by Mangin . . . I almost think Foch believes himself God's elect after the Kaiser!

'July 14th. Troops enter Paris. Foch and Pétain were in the Place de la République. Foch adopted absurd pose with his baton. That man disgusts me. Why couldn't he just behave simply?'

'September 24th, Paris. Saw Foch. Always the same air of craftiness and ambition.'

Such megalomania is a commonplace among victorious generals and statesmen. Equally common, of course, is the way in which war leaders, whether their country has won or lost the war, will quickly fall out in the peace – though Foch was prophetic enough to call the Versailles treaty 'not a peace but a twenty-year armistice'. An observer has supplied these notes from a conference at the Council of War presided over by M. Alexandre Millerand, President of the Republic:

'Like Napoleon's marshals, the great chiefs are quarrelling about their share in the glory. . . . The victorious generals of the Great War are appallingly conceited.

'Foch systematically contradicts Pétain. Pétain despises Gouraud for "having no ideas of his own". Franchet d'Esperey says practically nothing. Joffre and Fayolle produce sensible remarks when they speak, which is rare. When Guillaumat speaks, Pétain calls him names under his breath.

'These arguments get out of hand. The President tries vainly to reach clear decisions. The chief of the general staff asserts himself as best he can. Pétain abdicates, lets the discussion drift; he is afraid of Foch, who always opposes him, if necessary with untenable arguments. They all want to have their own way. Their pride is unshakeable.'

Disagreeing so often and so violently, these marshals were almost unanimous, however, in their dislike of government by parties. Their enthusiasm for the Republic was very slight, some indeed openly called themselves monarchists, and all of them might have welcomed the system adopted in times of crisis

44

during the ancient Roman Republic, of having temporary dic-
tatorships. Each would no doubt have assumed that he was to be
the dictator.

What did Captain de Gaulle think of these supermen? In his
prisoner-of-war camp he had studied German philosophers, including Nietzsche, and when in 1924 he published his first book,
La Discorde chez l'ennemi, he had this to say of the German
generals:

'The superman with his exceptional character – the will to
power, readiness for risks and contempt for others, which
Zarathustra attributes to him – appeared to these passionately
ambitious men as the ideal to which they should attain. They
chose deliberately to become part of the Nietzschean *élite* of
power who pursue their own glory, convinced that they are
serving the general interest: who constrain the mass of slaves
while despising them; and who do not stop in the face of human
suffering, save to acknowledge it as necessary and desirable.'

Instead of this attitude, what de Gaulle recommended for
France's future military leaders was a classical moderation,
harmony and sense of proportion. 'In a French park no tree
seeks to smother the other trees with its shade; the lawns accept
being geometrically laid out; you do not get the lake trying to be
a waterfall or the statues claiming that they alone must be
admired. Sometimes there is an air of noble melancholy about
such a park. Perhaps it comes from the feeling that each part, in
isolation, might have shone more brightly. But this would have
been damaging to the whole, and those who walk in the park
rejoice in the sound sense which has produced its present
splendid harmony.'

De Gaulle insisted that a nation's leaders must be inspired by
a higher philosophy of war. This, he said, summing up the
lessons of 1914–18, 'constitutes the surest guarantee of the
country's destinies'.

6

De Gaulle at the Staff College

De Gaulle left his position at Saint-Cyr in 1922 to go to the Army Staff College for the usual two-year course. The report on him after the first year said: 'Very lively intelligence, very extensive general knowledge, quick-thinking, good at assessing situations, gives clear orders, decisive, very hard-working.

'Strongly developed personality, great self-confidence. Should achieve excellent results if he makes concessions with a little better grace and listens to argument more readily. Has succeeded very well in all branches of the army.'

The second year, following staff manœuvres, his file contained the following notes under 'detailed appreciation' : 'An intelligent, knowledgeable and conscientious officer; brilliant and talented; full of character.

'Unfortunately mars these indisputable qualities by his excessive self-confidence, unwillingness to listen to the opinions of others, and his attitude of "a king in exile". Appears, moreover, to have more aptitude for general, synthetic study of a problem than for studying practically and in depth how its solution is to be carried out.

'Was in command of the Army Corps during the first period of the manœuvres; showed decision, calm and powers of command, but also a lack of balanced judgement; adopted solutions somewhat unsuited to the situation, as, however, he frankly acknowledged.

'Afterwards, although slightly out of touch with his colleagues, carried out satisfactorily the functions of head of the Army Corps' operations branch and divisional chief of staff.'

This report (for May 1923) was signed by Colonel (later General) Moyrand, chief lecturer in general tactics, who commented on these notes at a later date : 'De Gaulle was an interesting, difficult and delicate case. He clearly had great qualities, and was an unusual personality. I rated him far above average. He mixed little with the other officers, and almost always arrived at the lecture hall by himself.'

Colonel Moyrand's reserves in praising de Gaulle are partly explained by a general difference between the two men in matters of tactics: de Gaulle's approach was much more empirical and flexible than the Colonel's. Also Moyrand did not himself care for contradiction, and an incident in June 1924, during that year's staff manœuvres, illustrates the clash of temperaments. It is described by Captain Chauvin, one of de Gaulle's contemporaries at the College:

'De Gaulle was being put through his paces. He was given the command of an army corps, and all of us, under his orders, were fulfilling the functions of his most important subordinates: divisional commanders, chiefs of staff, etc.

'All day Colonel Moyrand was making realistic modifications to the manœuvres, so as to give the officer being tested a variety of situations to face, making him foresee what would happen in each case and take decisions accordingly. Our man made an excellent showing, carefully studying the problems, calmly working out the appropriate solutions and translating them into lucid, concise, effective orders, proving both his clear-headedness and his keen sense of practical action.

'In the evening we all met in a local school for the criticism of these manœuvres. The Colonel presided on the rostrum, while de Gaulle sat opposite him, his long legs looking very cramped under the school desk. Next to de Gaulle sat Captain Château-vieux, his chief of staff for the occasion.

'The questions asked and the rather sarcastic aggressive tone which the Colonel adopted made it seem like a severe cross-examination in a law-court. De Gaulle, however, maintained his calm and self-control, answering with restraint, explaining methodically; he showed no signs of temperament, whatever the provocation.

'But the more serene he appeared, the more it irritated the Colonel, who saw all his traps skilfully avoided. A last absurd and irrelevant question seemed almost an admission of defeat: "Where are the supply services of the left-hand regiment of your division on the right?"

'Barely turning his head towards his chief of staff, de Gaulle said: "Châteauvieux, please answer."

'"But I asked you, de Gaulle," said the Colonel furiously.

'"Mon Colonel," de Gaulle replied calmly, "you entrusted

me with the responsibilities of an army corps commander. If I had to assume those of my subordinates as well, I should not have my mind free enough to fulfil my assignment satisfactorily: *de minimis non curat praetor*. Châteauvieux, please answer the Colonel."

'The Colonel just managed to control himself, then concluded very tersely: "All right. We knew you considered many tasks were beneath you. I now know where I stand."'

The end-of-year staff manœuvres were the deciding factor on how trainees passed out of the Staff College; so the honour of commanding an army corps was a perilous one. But de Gaulle, as always, was like some great forest oak standing alone defying storms. Like Pétain, his model, he seemed careless of the effects his independence might have.

Captain Chauvin also recalls an earlier incident, during a visit to a fortified region near Metz, where a solo turn of de Gaulle's was better received:

'We had to cross the battlefield of Saint-Privat. Luckily we had with us the assistant lecturer in history; and this made some people ask General Dufieux to stop us where our troops had fought so bravely in August 1870. He agreed, and called on the lecturer to talk about this battle. Taken unawares, the unfortunate historian did his best, but kept on stumbling over names, times, the number of a unit. When he hesitated too long, we heard a muffled voice in our rear prompting him. The gaps in his knowledge became more and more frequent, until in the end we literally pushed the helpful prompter, de Gaulle, to the front . . . he gradually took over from the lecturer and treated us to a dazzling account of the battle, making us follow the action regiment by regiment, casting a clear light on every detail. I saw the amused but admiring expression on General Dufieux's face, while the displaced historian took it very well and was obviously appreciating this virtuoso performance in his own subject. We could not refrain from applauding our brilliant brother-officer.'

Unfortunately, many of the lecturers and instructors on the staff of the College showed little sympathy with the ideas of the officers they were instructing. A tank officer with a new conception of the use of tanks was told by one lecturer: 'Have fun with your toys, young man.' According to Chauvin, analysing the differences of approach at that time, the staff of the College still treated war as being wholly a matter of gaining ground. Strategy on a broad front was barely considered.

'Our lecturers and instructors were mostly colonels who had spent the four years of trench warfare on tactical missions which as a rule they had carried out very ably. They were past masters in tactical combination of forces, infantry, artillery, tanks, etc. But when we entered the Staff College, we expected to find a new spirit, guided by the past, of course, but capable of facing the future boldly. For us the future meant essentially strategy, i.e. the study and application of principles from physics such as mass, speed, points of pressure, levers. So it was a great disappointment to find we were still kept on the sterile tactical chemistry of trench warfare. We realized before long that our High Command was more concerned to perfect us in mistaken principles and practice than to show us how to avoid such mistakes. So there soon developed a fatal and obvious conflict between the staff and ourselves.

'We had too much respect for their integrity and experience, and were also too well-disciplined, to express our disagreement openly, unless there was a free discussion and we were definitely called on to give our opinions. On these occasions Captain de Gaulle quickly acquired a reputation for saying what he thought with great frankness.'

In the circumstances it is no wonder that some of the staff indulged in sly digs at the 'king in exile' and took every chance to put him in his place. How did he behave towards his fellow officers under instruction? 'There's a man who thinks a lot of himself,' was the first impression registered by Captain André Laffargue; for certainly in his immaculate blue uniform, holding himself so stiff and erect and proud, with a rather strutting walk, de Gaulle looked self-conscious, a man to stand on his dignity.

But Laffargue, who was drafted to the same section, came to feel, through daily life in close proximity to him, that this first impression was false. 'He was never scornful, arrogant or domineering. He could show originality and had his high-spirited moments, and on return from an exercise I can remember hearing his sepulchral voice joining in some bawdy chorus as lustily as the rest.

'I noticed, though, that he seemed to lack a sense of proportion, was sometimes out of touch with the real world, and could then be incredibly obstinate. He was one of those who try to solve all problems with a ready-made system of their own. If the solution happens to square with the facts, all is well. If not, they refuse to accept the facts, and then things may go wrong.'

Captain Chauvin found a personal magnetism about him, but observed that he made friends with difficulty and few close ones. He was more interested in things than people, and seemed to live an intense inner life; but was too keen on action to indulge in sterile introspection. When he withdrew into himself, he was no doubt brooding on great plans for the future or else on sweeping views of the past. For he confided to Chauvin: 'I have a passion for history' – and certainly he had an amazing grasp of it. He seemed to have an answer for everything, as if he had studied every problem, military or otherwise; and would produce apt analogies to illustrate his points, often seasoned with sardonic humour. He expressed his opinions with deliberate conciseness, perhaps to stress how firm and unchallengeable they were; and generally found an excuse to break off arguments that were too long drawn out.

Politically, he favoured some sort of autocracy. In the general election of 1924 an anti-clerical left-wing *bloc* came to power under Herriot. Poincaré retired into private life. In an atmosphere of economic crisis, the socialist Renaudel cried, 'We'll take the money where we find it'; and Herriot spoke eloquently of attacking 'the wall of gold'. But the officers at the Staff College were afraid the politicians were losing the peace; and during discussions de Gaulle sometimes declared in his grave, even voice: 'As for me, I can't help being a monarchist – by family tradition.'

'A king in exile,' Colonel Moyrand noted. One day Chauvin and de Gaulle were sent out together to study an offensive supported by tanks. In the evening they sat in a clearing on the edge of a wood, leaning against a tree, smoking dreamily as they watched the sun go down. 'I broke the silence,' Chauvin recalls, 'and to my own surprise heard myself saying: "You know, old chap, I'm going to tell you something that will probably make you smile. I have a curious feeling that you've got a very great destiny ahead of you." I waited for a laugh or a dig in the ribs to teach me to make such predictions; but there was no reaction. Surprised at this, and curious to see how he had taken my remark, I turned my head towards him. He sat quite still, gazing into the far distance. Then in a low voice he spoke the four words I can still hear today: "Yes, so have I."'

The great destiny had a temporary setback, however. Officers passed out of the Staff College with a classification in one of three categories, *Très bien*, *Bien*, and *Assez bien*, the last being equivalent to a mere pass. De Gaulle came into the second category, and some of the lecturers and instructors would have liked to put him in the third. They all recognized his remarkable qualities, but as against that there were his touchiness, obstinacy, over-confidence, refusal to listen to others' arguments.

The Director of the Staff College at this time was General Dufieux, who had different views on tanks from de Gaulle's. He believed that tanks should protect and cover infantry forces, joining in an infantry break-through; but he never envisaged their being used on their own as a strategic weapon. However, he taught that concrete cases were more important than theoretical knowledge, that it was important to develop powers of judgement and decision so that commanders could quickly adapt themselves to an unforeseen war situation; and in this teaching de Gaulle was very much with him.

Marshal Pétain had no great love for the Staff College: after all, his career had nearly stopped short there on account of his intellectual unorthodoxy, his heretical insistence that 'gunfire kills'. When he heard that his protégé, Captain de Gaulle, rising hope of the younger generation, was being discussed unfavourably by the College staff and was in danger of passing out in the lowest class, he brought the full weight of his influence to bear. General Dufieux in any case saw the Captain's worth clearly enough to insist that he was classed '*Bien*'; although this was far from satisfying the Marshal.

As for de Gaulle himself, he was furious, mortified, deeply wounded at an unfair verdict. He could be heard proclaiming in the College's main court: 'I shan't come back to this miserable dump till I'm Director of it. You'll see how things will change *then*.' Beyond this understandable imprecation on the College, the other officers caught a glimpse of an unsuspected 'great destiny' or at least great ambition.

7

Three Lectures

De Gaulle had earlier been hoping for a lectureship at the Staff College, but these hopes now had to be abandoned: only those who passed out in the *Très bien* class could obtain such an appointment. At one point he even contemplated leaving the army altogether, but never reached what would have been a fateful decision. He was drafted to army headquarters as a staff officer in the supplies and rations department, with special responsibility for food storage – a position which was no doubt intended to mortify him. After a few months there, he had a further few months in the same department at the headquarters of the Rhine Army, after which Marshal Pétain, Inspector General of the Army and Vice-President of the Council of War, recalled him to be on his personal staff.

Pétain continued to see a good deal of his maltreated protégé, and brooded on revenge, for himself as well as for de Gaulle. Immediately after the class lists were out, he had tried to obtain a reversal, but this attempt was frustrated by the College lecturers in a semi-official *démarche* to General Dufieux, the Director.

In 1926 General Héring became Director of the College. A man of fine intelligence, wide general knowledge and breadth of vision, 'the sworn enemy of all conformity', he foresaw that a future war would be mostly a war of movement, with the intervention of tanks and air force. He had been four years on Pétain's staff at the Council of War. In 1926 the Marshal told him: 'The more I think about it, the more I feel this de Gaulle business was as monstrous as a miscarriage of justice.' And the following year Pétain thought of a way to teach the professors a salutary lesson: Héring was to organize a series of three public lectures to be given by de Gaulle at the Staff College, with the Marshal presiding. Everyone was amazed at the Marshal's action: it was unheard of to invite a junior officer from outside the College to give such lectures. Clearly he took an exceptional interest in de Gaulle's career.

The day of the first lecture was 7th April 1927. All the staff assembled in an office near the lecture-hall. The Marshal arrived, accompanied by General Héring. The little gathering prepared to join the officer trainees. There were a few preliminary remarks made, and the Marshal, turning to the lecturers, said: 'I have never entered the lecture-hall without considerable nervousness.'

Everyone moved back to let the famous soldier go in first. He called to de Gaulle: 'The honour is yours. It is the lecturer's privilege to lead the way. And after entering the hall he is entitled to teach what he wishes. This principle is sacred. That is how I applied it myself, expressing ideas different from those of my time.'

The strange procession filed solemnly in, like the characters in some formal drama or pageant; led by de Gaulle, in full-dress uniform, three long bands of glittering braid on his sleeve, followed by the Marshal with his seven stars, escorted by the Director, the Assistant Director, the lecturers and instructors. The hall was packed. De Gaulle went up on to the platform; with slow, deliberate gestures put his cap down on the table in front of him, placed his sword beside it, removed his white gloves. The backcloth was a blackboard and a sort of frame with pulleys and ropes to help illustrate military operations. Pétain opened the session with a few terse words: 'Gentlemen, Captain de Gaulle is going to express his ideas to you. Kindly listen to them attentively.'

Now stiff as a statue, facing his audience, now pacing up and down, de Gaulle began his lecture, going straight into his subject with an attack on inflexible preconceived plans: the subject was military leadership.

'Military action has an essentially contingent character. The result it aims at is relative to the enemy, who is always a variable factor: the enemy may appear in any number of ways; the exact strength of his forces is unknown; he may carry out his intentions in many different forms.

'Moreover, the ground is never constant: events take the action first into one area, then another; whatever the ground, it provides a wide variety of conditions, depending on the direction, speed and method of the forces engaged. The means at one's disposal have no absolute value: the effectiveness of arms and the morale of troops vary enormously according to the circumstances. These include atmospheric conditions, which may alter continually and will exert their own influence. So the combatants are perpetually faced with a new situation, which is always at least partly unforeseen.

'. . . What has happened before will never happen again, and whatever the action, it could quite well not have taken place or have taken place differently. This contingent character of military action is what makes it so difficult and so great a thing to master. Superficially it seems very simple, but it sets the human mind the most exacting of problems; for to resolve them one must leave the beaten tracks of conventional thought.

'In the well-known pages serving as introduction to *Creative Evolution*, Bergson describes and analyses for us the uneasiness of the intellect when it makes contact with the changing reality of life. It is the nature of the intellect to grasp and consider what is constant, fixed and definite; so it tries to avoid what is changing, unstable, divergent. "The intellect feels at home," Bergson tells us, "as long as it is left among inert objects, more especially solids; for our concepts have been formed on the image of solids, and our logic is above all a logic of solids. We have a strong sense that none of the categories of our thought apply exactly to the things of life. In vain do we push what is living into one or another of our frames; all the frames split: they are too narrow and above all too rigid for what we would like to put in them. Our reasoning, so sure of itself when dealing with inert objects, feels ill at ease on this new ground."'

De Gaulle produced these and other long quotations, very fluently, from memory. He went on: 'As Bergson has shown us, to make the direct contact with realities which is indispensable for action, man's mind must acquire intuition, by combining instinct with intelligence.'

As to instinct, 'The great war leaders have always known the important part it plays. Surely what Alexander called "his hope", Caesar "his fortune", Napoleon "his star", is merely a strange faculty giving these men close enough contact with realities to be sure of always mastering them. Often, for those who are richly endowed with this faculty, it shines through their personality. Without their words or actions containing anything exceptional, the people who meet them feel a natural force which

54

suggests they are in control of what happens. Flaubert expressed this feeling when he portrayed Hannibal as a boy, already clothed in "the indefinable splendour of those destined for great enterprises." '

But to make the impulses of instinct effective, an essential instrument of the intellect is needed: method, which 'assesses in order of importance the different things to be done, sees how they are best carried out in time and space, and links the various operations and phases so that they fit into a coherent whole'. Pétain must have recognized a latent allusion to himself here, for de Gaulle often declared in private: 'The Marshal has a genius for method and the art of putting things in their right place.' The Marshal listened impassively, the hall was even more hushed and intent, as the lecturer turned to the leader and his prestige, 'divine element of authority':

'The essence of prestige is the impression produced by the leader that he is someone extraordinary, with a mysterious indefinable quality which is peculiar to him. In fact every leader whose prestige is recorded for us by History had this common factor: he always managed somehow to remain impenetrable to his subordinates, thereby maintaining their morale through a belief in his ability to improvise.

'They all inspired this impression, each in his own way. There is very little similarity of temperament between such men as Alexander, exuberant, histrionic, magnificent; Hannibal, simple, austere, reserved; Caesar, shrewd, subtle, eloquent; Turenne, cold, distant, taciturn; Napoleon, passionate, tormented, familiar. Yet all seemed superhuman to their armies. Their prestige doubtless depended first of all on their exceptional talents, but also on a psychological effect which they carefully reinforced by their appearance and behaviour.'

This passage was followed by further indirect homage to Pétain: 'Powerful personalities, organized for conflict, crises, great events, do not always possess the easy manners and superficially attractive qualities which go down well in ordinary life. They are usually blunt and uncompromising, without social graces. Although deep down the masses may obscurely do them justice, recognizing their superiority, they are rarely loved and in consequence rarely find an easy path to the top. Selection boards are inclined to go more on personal charm than merit.

'It is difficult in our day,' de Gaulle concluded, 'to train and choose military leaders. Men have been tried too hard in recent times, and as a result wills are relaxed, characters depressed, morale is weakened. A military career has lost its appeal, and even those with the firmest sense of vocation are disturbed. There can be few men in the army who have not sometimes wondered: "Why am I here?".'

The lecture over, the officers of the two intakes dispersed through the College, discussing what they had heard. Opinions were sharply divided. Some praised the elevation of thought, the remarkable philosophy, the nobility of spirit, the mastery of language. Others inveighed against the man's condescending tone, his arrogance and conceit. 'What did he teach us? Nothing. . . . Incredible the Old Man should have encouraged such a performance. He must take us all for morons.'

In Héring's office, or in his quarters at Neuilly, the high officers were inclined to share the latter view, and some even objected that de Gaulle was pronouncing a panegyric on himself. 'Nonsense,' said Héring. 'You've completely missed the point. It all referred to the Marshal. Although his face gives nothing away, you could make out how pleased he was.'

'But you force this de Gaulle on us, mon Général, when he's obviously a megalomaniac who thinks he's Napoleon.'

Héring threw up his hands. 'He certainly has a very good opinion of himself, but so have all great men, or those who aspire to greatness. Otherwise do you really think they could fulfil their destiny?'

During the lecture de Gaulle had quoted by heart authorities ranging from Socrates and Lucretius to Comte and Bergson, from Pericles and Caesar to Frederick the Great, Napoleon, and Scharnhorst, from Goethe and Tolstoi to Victor Hugo and Anatole France. On this one point, if on nothing else, everyone who heard the lecture was unanimous: they were amazed by the man's prodigious memory. (Pétain himself, who as early as 1917 is recorded as worrying about failure of memory, said how lucky de Gaulle was 'to have received such a gift of Heaven'.)

A week later, with Pétain presiding once more, de Gaulle gave his second lecture. The subject this time was 'Character', and he opened by discussing a basic weakness in the French Army after 1815; implicitly he was deploring the fact of so many expeditions

56

overseas. 'For half a century the army followed a route with no guiding star ahead. True, its devotion never failed. The troops who conquered Algeria, took Sebastopol, crossed Italy, and meanwhile carried our flags in Spain and Greece before Antwerp, at Ancona, in Syria, Mexico and China, at Rome, showed great valour. But they did not have the final impulse which would have galvanized their efforts. In 1870, in a war of unforeseen conditions, facing an enemy inspired with the ardour of a new nation, leaders and troops alike could only respond to events with a sturdy resistance, a courageous resignation.'

The man of character was not only a fighter, he was like a gambler, who paid his debts with his own money: if need be, that is, with his life: 'Faced with action, the man of character has his own resources. His impulse is to take the action on his own shoulders, make it his business. Instead of sheltering behind his superiors, retreating into textbooks, covering himself with lengthy reports, he takes a firm stand and confronts the situation.

'Not that he wants to ignore orders or neglect advice, but he is eager for decision and action. He is well aware of the dangers and does not disregard the consequences, but he assesses them honestly and accepts them frankly. Still more, he embraces action with the pride of a master, for he is involved in it, it is part of him. He enjoys success if this is his due, and will bear the full responsibility for a defeat. . . . In short the man of character makes action noble. Without him it is the drudgery of a slave, through him it becomes the glorious mission of a hero.

'He makes stern demands on everyone, including himself, when a great effort is called for. His subordinates sometimes feel they have much to put up with, and they may mutter about his arrogance, his exacting standards. But once it comes to action, the critics fall away. All wills and hopes are drawn towards him as to a magnet. When the crisis comes, they follow *him*. He lifts the load with his own arms, though the arms may be near to breaking, and carries it on his back, though the back should crack under the strain. He is ennobled by the confidence he inspires in lesser men, and feels under an obligation to justify their faith. He is as firm as ever, but has also a kind of benevolence, for he is a natural protector of the weak. If the enterprise succeeds, he gives generous shares in the fruits of success; if there is a reverse, he accepts the blame himself. In return for the security he gives, he is rewarded with high esteem.'

While he spoke, de Gaulle often kept his eyes fixed on the Marshal, who possessed so many features of this 'man of character'.

'In the ordinary run of events he is at a disadvantage with his superiors. Being sure of his judgements and aware of his powers, he makes no concessions to the desire to please. He is firm and resolute because that is his nature, not because he is under orders; and this often makes him less ready to give unquestioning obedience. He believes that, having been given a job to do, he should be left master in his own house to do it. Many in the hierarchy are too much absorbed in trivial detail and formalities: they find such a demand intolerable. They are afraid, too, of his dynamism, because it pays little heed to the requirements of routine or a quiet life. They do not realize that strong personalities are likely to have their rough side, that you can only lean on something which does not give, and that firm uncompromising people are more worth while than those who are slack and malleable.

'But if there are grave events and imminent danger, if strong action is suddenly needed for the common salvation, the perspective changes at once, and a sort of ground-swell pushes the man of character to the fore. His advice is taken, his gifts are praised, his ability is relied on. He is naturally given the difficult assignment, *he* must make the main effort. Everything he suggests is adopted, everything he asks for is granted. Moreover, he does not abuse his position, and answers the call, bearing no grudges. He has no time to savour his revenge on those who have kept him down; for he is completely absorbed by action.

'Those who have accomplished something great have often had to disregard orders: like Pélissier at Sebastopol, who put away the Emperor's threatening telegrams, to read them only when the battle was over; like Lanrezac, saving his army after Charleroi by breaking off the battle against orders received; like Lyautey, who retained the whole of Morocco in 1914 despite instructions from the government. After the Battle of Jutland Lord Fisher, First Lord of the Admiralty, receiving Admiral Jellicoe's report, wrote regretfully: "He has all Nelson's qualities except one: he does not know how to disobey."'

Once more Héring met a running fire of questions from the stunned members of the staff. At the first lecture they had been expecting to have at least an address from the Marshal; now they had listened to another *ex cathedra* statement from this upstart captain. Nor did they accept that de Gaulle had Pétain in mind: Pétain was not arrogant, and come to that, had he so much 'character'? Héring refrained from answering these points, but reminded them that de Gaulle, quoting twelve famous examples from the lives of great men, had included Pétain.

The third week saw a third performance. The Marshal listened as impassively as ever, unlike many others, who were infuriated by de Gaulle's self-assurance and professorial tone. This time he returned to the subject of prestige:

'The old nations have succumbed to a decadence which is affecting authority. This phenomenon is a consequence of the decline in the moral, social and political order. Conventions are collapsing. . . . Such a crisis can only last for a time. Fundamentally men cannot get on without being directed, any more than they can get on without food, drink and sleep. These political animals need organization, which means order and leaders.

'If the foundations of authority are shaken . . . sooner or later, for better or worse, others will appear in the natural course of events . . . and they will be based on the superior powers of a few individuals.

'All the credit that the masses once accorded to office or birth, they now give to the only people who have been able to assert their authority. What legitimate prince was ever obeyed like some dictator rising on nothing but his own boldness? What established power ever left such a deep mark on an enterprise as some engineer's invention can do today? What conquerors were acclaimed like our athletes who gain their successes by their own unaided efforts?'

A change was taking place in society, silently and almost imperceptibly. 'This transformation of authority cannot but affect military discipline. In the army, as elsewhere, it is said that "respect is disappearing". Rather, it is shifting. The man who commands . . . must rely more on his real worth than on his high rank to bring him obedience. Power and its attributes must no longer be confused.'

59

Seniority and the number of stars weighed less than the commander's personal prestige. 'He does not, of course, reject all discipline, for he was moulded by it. Men do not change so quickly or completely. . . . But in an unsettled age, in a society with shattered framework and traditions, the conventions of obedience are also weakened, and the leader's personal prestige becomes the prop of command . . .

'The fact is that certain men, almost from birth, spread an air of authority, the secret of which you cannot analyse; which can astonish you even while you are feeling its effects . . .

'First of all, prestige cannot come without mystery; we have little respect for what we know too well. All the religions have their secret shrines, and no man is a hero to his valet.

'Therefore such a man's plans and impulses and manner must contain an element which the rest cannot grasp, which intrigues and excites them, keeps them in suspense. He does not, of course, have to shut himself up in an ivory tower, ignoring his subordinates and remaining inaccessible to them. Far from it: command over other people means you must observe them keenly and make each one feel you are taking special notice of him. But the man of character, while watching everyone else, will systematically avoid revealing himself to others; he will deliberately preserve some secret element of surprise which can be brought into play at any moment. The latent credibility of the masses will do the rest. . . . He wins their confidence because they believe that, as well as being capable in familiar spheres, he has mysterious powers peculiar to himself.'

De Gaulle went on to deal with the importance of what to-day we should call '*image*'. . . . Military experts have never neglected the importance of creating an impression. . . . Flaubert in *Salammbo* describes the effect produced on the hesitating soldiers by Hamilcar's calculated appearance. Every page of Julius Caesar's *Commentaries* shows us how carefully he worked out his public actions; and Napoleon was equally careful to appear always in the most impressive conditions.

'. . . The leaders of men are either politicians, prophets or soldiers. While rationally we may sometimes blame them, emotionally we cannot help being thrilled by them. . . . Of course these heroes, even if *sans peur*, are by no means *sans reproche*. But in the long run, in terms of History, how little weight is given to unfortunate incidents! Some men who have really done nothing but incite to revolution and excesses, still keep a sort of grim glory in the eyes of posterity, when their crimes were committed in the name of a noble cause.

'The hero cannot hope for the happiness of the common herd: he must fight, first of all against himself. He must make up his mind, and the choice is cruel. A state of contentment, inner peace, deliberate serenity, which is conventionally called happiness – this is incompatible with personal dominance. The leader of men always has a conflict within himself, "more or less severe according to his temperament, but tormenting him at every hour of the day . . ."'

Alas, much of what de Gaulle said passed over the heads of most of his audience. The officers in the lecture-hall included some brilliant minds, but they were first of all professional soldiers, and they found all this high-flown eloquence on the subject of character and prestige inappropriate, not to say out of place, in the Army Staff College. Colonel Nachin, a loyal friend, speaks of de Gaulle's disappointment:

'He was well aware that despite their receptivity the officers making up the audience had only partly understood his train of thought. They may have been held by his extraordinary brilliance, but the training they had received, the mentality imbuing them, their present environment, produced not only lack of comprehension but a sort of latent hostility, a state of resistance to his teaching. They and de Gaulle were really not on the same level.'

After the third lecture was over, General Héring had to listen to more arguments in his office over de Gaulle and his three 'performances'. One of the hostile critics, with the air of saying the last word on the subject, declared that de Gaulle was 'just a crib on Pétain'.

8

Battalion Commander

In the same month as de Gaulle gave the three lectures (April 1927), he published a historical work called *Le Flambeau* (The Torch) dealing with the period from the Revolution to the Restoration of the Monarchy. It took the form of a dialogue between three soldiers, a sergeant, a captain in the revolutionary wars, and a Saint-Cyrien – a future field-marshal. In 1826 the captain, placed on half pay, was recalling the desertions of Napoleon's generals in the year before Waterloo and by contrast the faithfulness of the ordinary soldiers. Some of these had joined up to serve the king, others had enrolled for the Revolution and the Republic, but all ended by following the Emperor and if necessary giving their lives for him. 'And now whom will you serve?' the Captain asks the Saint-Cyrien. 'Captain,' the latter answers, 'we shall serve France. Men pass, one régime succeeds another. But France remains.'

Yet the Saint-Cyrien deplores the wretchedness of the times, where everyone is weary of war and therefore 'forgets the army'; he quotes the Marshal de Saxe a hundred years earlier: 'We soldiers are like the cloaks which people only remember when the rain comes. At present it is not raining. But come the storm, and they will need us. We are the cloaks of France.'

In the autumn of 1927 de Gaulle obtained permission from his superiors to give his three lectures again at the Sorbonne before an audience of politicians, academics and intellectuals. The lectures were sponsored by an important Discussion Circle closely connected with *Action Française*. Left-wing students tried to heckle, but de Gaulle dealt with them in masterly fashion. Yet dazzling as his performance was once more, he found the civilian audience no more enthusiastic about his ideas than the military men had been.

Still, some of the army leaders recognized his quality; they could not very well ignore a man so obviously under Pétain's wing. 'I am placing a future commander-in-chief,' General Matter, Director of Infantry, confided to a friend. He sent de

62

Gaulle to command the 19th Battalion of Alpine Rifles, a crack unit in the army occupying the Rhineland, stationed at Trèves (Trier) on the Moselle. The Army Corps there comprised a cavalry division, an infantry division, an artillery regiment, an engineers' regiment and various supply units.

Arriving at Trèves in December 1927, de Gaulle kept his battalion very busy with manœuvres, alerts, firing practice, field operations, parades, competitions; understandably, they reached a very high standard of training. There were also plenty of leisure activities in the way of sport and entertainments. The battalion commander took his social responsibilities very seriously, concerned himself with troops' welfare, and showed a keen interest in all his officers. To improve their intellectual standards, he had every officer give regular lectures on historical subjects. This was all right for the products of military academies, but came hard on those who had worked their way up from the ranks.

He himself began giving a series of lectures outside the battalion at Trèves, Mainz and elsewhere. On reaching the platform he had an unvarying ritual of putting down his cap, sword and white gloves on the table; then he would deliver the lecture, lasting for an hour or an hour and a half, and, as always, without any notes.

Lecturing to nearly 200 officers at Trèves, he spoke of the statesmen of the *ancien régime:* 'Their policies were empirical. They were realists who avoided abstractions and preferred the expedient to the sublime, opportunism to idealism. They looked for a practical solution to each problem. They were not too scrupulous over means, but achieved greatness by keeping the right balance between the end willed and the forces available to the State.' And of Louvois, Louis XIV's great War Minister, who gave France her standing army: 'Persistent in his plans, he could yet show suppleness. He made his preparations with fierce drive, but knew how to bide his time. Without scruples over means. . . . Aloof but approachable, listening to all reports and advice, then making up his own mind – he had enemies and supporters, but no friends.'

Consciously or otherwise, there seemed to be something of a self-portrait here at least. For the battalion's officers almost all felt admiration for their commander, despite his air of aloofness.

Always impeccably turned out, he looked a fine figure, and although on the shy side had a courteous, affable manner – 'aloof but approachable'. The aloofness was partly deliberate, for as he told his officers, 'there is no true command without prestige, and no prestige without a certain isolation'.

Once in an address to his men on the barrack square, with his officers all round him, he quoted from Ibsen: 'Why are you climbing that hill, plainsman? To get a better view of the plain, was the answer. I have only understood the plain since I saw it from the hills.' He continued on this elevated note, with scarcely anyone understanding a word of what he was saying. In the officers' mess some wit referred to Major de Gaulle's *Ibscenities*.

But although or because he had his head in the air, he sometimes had a longer vision than most. In 1928 there was trouble in Germany. Accused of treason by the nationalists and Nazis, Stresemann asked the Allies to evacuate the whole of the Rhineland; Poincaré refused this. De Gaulle wrote to a friend, ten years before Hitler marched into Vienna: 'The force of events is destroying all that is left in Europe of accepted and precious barriers. We must realize that the *Anschluss* will come quite soon, then Germany will recover willy-nilly all that was taken from her and given to Poland. After which she'll demand Alsace back from us. This seems to me to be written in Heaven.'

De Gaulle led a modest and humdrum life in Trèves, devoted to the training of his unit, to his studies and his family. In the evenings it was Madame de Gaulle herself who washed the famous white gloves which, with his immense height, made the battalion commander immediately recognizable. In the morning he would walk to the barracks, almost invariably accompanied by a particular officer who lived in a villa near his. They had to cross the Moselle bridge, and he often stopped for a moment or two on the bridge, looking over the ancient town, dominated by the cathedral.

As a soldier de Gaulle was non-conformist in big things and small. On parade he wore his beret turned down to the left instead of the right, which was customary, and the battalion had to adopt the new style. A show of independence on a larger scale occurred during the winter of 1928. That autumn he had organized an operation, in which the whole battalion crossed the Moselle near the Luxemburg frontier. He intended to repeat this in midwinter on the ice-covered river, after first establishing from soundings that the ice was safe. The companies, wagons and mules were all ready to move off, but then an about-turn was ordered; the Trèves headquarters had heard of the operation and vetoed it.

De Gaulle was furious, and soon afterwards decided to show the high-ups what his men were capable of. The battalion were out on a long march with two stages still to do. He handed over the command, and rode off on horse-back, escorted by two cyclists, to investigate conditions. The battalion followed, and when they reached a certain crossroads, their commander rejoined them, the usual cigarette in his mouth. There was an hour's stop, during which he had summoned the officers, informing them: 'We are returning to Trèves tonight.' The Medical Officer was afraid it might be too much for the young recruits. The captains objected: 'We're in a divisional column of march. The Supply Corps have fixed up the billets for tonight. Shouldn't we get authorization from the General?'

'I take full responsibility, and I'll give you written orders,' de Gaulle told them curtly. 'We are making a forced march.' The troops' equipment was lightened, their kitbags put in the wagons, and the march started.

Long after nightfall the 19th Battalion marched through Trèves to their barracks. Not a man had broken down. But de Gaulle had committed a double breach of discipline: an unauthorized forced march and returning in the middle of the night. The authorities of the occupied town complained, and his officers warned de Gaulle he would get a fortnight under arrest at least. 'You'll see,' said de Gaulle. 'I think things will calm down all right – luckily I have a friend at court.'

His forecast proved correct. The General commanding the infantry division investigated the complaints, and against all precedent refrained from taking any action against the offender.

The winter of 1928–29 was an unusually cold one, and an epidemic of influenza caused 143 deaths in the Rhine Army, thirty of them at Trèves. The country was deeply concerned in case there had been negligence among the military authorities, and there were vigorous protests made in parliament: the food out there was inadequate, besides which it was criminal to send young men from the South of France to regions of such extreme cold. Poincaré's Government even seemed in danger, and quickly set up a parliamentary committee to make further investigations. One of its members, Colonel Picot, gave evidence which included the following:

'There have been a great many deaths in the 19th Battalion of Rifles. But they are certainly not due to the way the men are treated. This battalion is admirably commanded.' After enumerating all the precautions taken, Picot continued by quoting from one of the battalion's recent orders:

'The battalion commander, de Gaulle, regrets to announce the death of Rifleman Gouraud . . . of the machine-gun company . . . on the 3rd March. The whole company will attend the funeral. All officers will be present. Walking-out uniform, without swords. Since Rifleman Gouraud has no family, the battalion commander and the company commander will go into mourning.'

True to his word, de Gaulle wore a crêpe arm-band on his uniform for a month, in memory of this young private soldier without a family, whose death had moved him.

One morning he was crossing the bridge with his usual companion, when the other man said: 'Mon Commandant, I know how sensitive you are. Yet very often, if you don't mind my saying so, I find you not inhuman but a-human.'

De Gaulle gave this remark some reflection, then nodded slowly and answered: 'You may be right, my friend, you may well be right.'

Yet from the beginning of 1928 he was deeply touched as a human being by a terrible private grief: on New Year's Day his wife had given birth to a Mongol child. Beneath a mask of ice he was bitterly unhappy and often near despair. Madame de Gaulle wrote to one of her friends: 'Charles and I would give anything, health, all our money, advancement, career, if only Anne could be an ordinary little girl like the rest.' Throughout her short life the parents lavished on her immense tenderness and love – a proof of the father's 'human' side which was not often shown to the world.

Amidst prolonged applause from parliament, the government decided to send Marshal Pétain, with his great prestige and reputation for 'humanity', on a mission to the Rhine Army to restore morale. De Gaulle, of course, was delighted; everyone knew that the Marshal's favours extended to being godfather to young Philippe de Gaulle (it was naturally believed that he had actually stood as godfather at the christening).

When Pétain visited the 19th Battalion of Alpine Rifles, he found everything in good order. But soon after he had gone, it transpired that many men in the unit, wanting to escape from the rigours of an occupation force and the severity of winters in the Rhineland, were asking their *Députés* to get them moved back to France – using private influence if they could. This process reached alarming proportions, damaging to discipline and training.

De Gaulle drew up an order to be read at the daily roll-call: any man who took such steps to get drafted away from the unit would be punished. Shortly afterwards he received a telegram from the war ministry notifying him that one of his men was to be transferred to a different Army Corps. It was later established, apparently, that the man had written to his *Député* before the battalion commander's order was issued. Instead of sending him on his way, de Gaulle had 'the offender' given a fortnight's detention.

Understandably, the *Député* concerned made a strong complaint, and Paul Painlevé, the War Minister, was obliged to investigate. On the face of it there was a flagrant breach of discipline, and de Gaulle, summoned to Paris, seemed likely to get sixty days of close arrest at least, and possibly suspension as well.

On arriving at Paris, he presented himself at the Marshal's headquarters in the Boulevard des Invalides. 'I've had a bit of trouble,' he told the staff officers there. 'It's rather a tricky business, so I've come to see the Boss.'

Pétain received him, called the Minister, with whom he was on the best of terms, and closed the incident, which might have had the most serious consequences for de Gaulle's career. 'I got him out of a real scrape,' the Marshal observed. Not many people at headquarters knew the inside story, but those who did began to remark that this man de Gaulle, so exacting over discipline in others, was somewhat lax over his own conduct.

Back in the battalion, he continued to command with a firm hand, and with a readiness for innovation. He was intent on improving the unit's high standards still further, and formed cadres for special manœuvres in which each officer in turn was in command of engineers, artillery and tanks. It would be wrong to think of de Gaulle as a great pioneer in the use of tanks; he was still at the stage of studying them in theory and practice, comparing notes, thinking about their potentialities. Without having any revolutionary ideas about them, he was convinced of their future importance. On one occasion his battalion was taking part in an exercise with a tank battalion. The officer commanding it showed little grasp of the wide scope open to tanks, and de Gaulle remarked to one of his officers: 'One must use technicians – but not pay too much attention to them.'

He was grateful to Pétain for his recent intervention, and at this date, of course, he still considered Pétain a great man – but even then the scales seem to have fallen from his eyes. He advised one of the young lieutenants at the battalion: 'In the next war, my lad, if you become a marshal of France, don't hang on too long. Retire after hostilities.' To the ordinary observer Pétain still had all his powers, but there were disturbing lapses and weakness, which de Gaulle claimed to have noticed already. Some allowance must be made for hindsight, no doubt, since the claim was made only in later years, but at any rate he told the writer Georges Duhamel in 1951: 'In 1925, when I was on his staff, I saw the first appearance in him of two equally strong features which worked against each other: senile indifference and senile ambitions.'

9

Pétain's Speech to the Academy, and Two Books from de Gaulle

At the end of 1929, his term of command having expired, de Gaulle left the 19th Battalion, and was posted to the staff of the army in the Levant. This was a disappointment to him, since he had hoped to go back on Pétain's staff. In particular, the Marshal having been elected to the Académie Française on Foch's death, de Gaulle hoped to be the 'ghost' who would write his speech on admission. The Marshal wrote very little himself by then, but was anxious to preserve his reputation as a writer, especially in the eyes of the outside world. So he was scared of being let down by a 'ghost', and listened to members of his entourage who warned him: 'De Gaulle is too keen to parade his own literary talents. He won't be discreet enough, and he'll want to show everyone that *he* wrote the speech.'

The speech presented special difficulties anyhow, since part of it had to be in praise of Foch, his late rival, and for Pétain this went against the grain. Foch had 'understood nothing of tactics', and in strategy he had relied excessively on the General's will-power and dynamism, the heroism of the troops, to the neglect of more prosaic advantages. Moreover, Pétain still considered Foch guilty in 1918 of 'laying down his sword before the enemy was destroyed', 'sparing the proud German Army a humiliating disaster', and allowing it 'to go back across the Rhine unmolested'; in short, Foch should never have signed the Armistice on 11th November. (Foch's answer to such charges had been that he did not feel he could sacrifice more lives by prolonging operations; besides, Germany was then in chaos, and he had feared the French Army might be contaminated by Bolshevism.)

The officers helping Pétain prepare his speech pointed out that he had so far been wholly critical of Foch. He told them to manage as best they could for the 'obituary part'; and they devised something more or less adequate. Meanwhile he traced

69

out the general lines for the rest of the speech, to be worked up afterwards by two officers specially selected. In it he meant to set out his fundamental ideas, and it would also 'contain an indirect refutation of "Fochism"'.

'Good morale,' Pétain declared in his speech, 'far from being the result of exhortations and orders by the general, essential though these are, is founded on more concrete factors, such as adequate arms, mutual confidence between officers and men, proficiency in training, professional ability of the special units, and also the troops' physical condition. A commander can only arouse confidence, main lever of the fighting spirit, by attending whole-heartedly to these factors. And to maintain confidence, which may be diminished at any moment by the contingencies of battle, he must show not only intelligence, imagination and character, but a rarer quality besides, the sense of what is possible. This is a quality which gives proof of real basic humanity.'

He developed a thesis common to him and de Gaulle, on the dangers of military thinkers 'going to sleep': 'At the beginning of the 1870–71 War the army made a series of heroic but vain improvisations. This was the result of an inertia beforehand which left it helpless in face of an army bred on strong military doctrines.'

And for the period before the Great War the Marshal recalled in passing the neglect of previous warnings by the High Command: 'On the eve of war, closing its eyes to the lessons of the Transvaal, Manchuria and the Balkans, the French Army leaders were still proudly self-confident. They felt strong enough to overcome the stresses of battle through the flame of patriotism. They had only one idea: to attack.'

Pétain did not mention that he himself had given these warnings, but the implication was no doubt obvious to all those who heard his speech, delivered to the Académie in January 1931. So were his other latent criticisms, and Paul Válery, director of the Académie, in his reply welcoming the new member, spoke of the Marshal implicitly making important points, which 'one feels are supported by all the facts'.

Meanwhile, de Gaulle was in the Levant, where he felt that France's general position left much to be desired. 'We've been

70

here ten years,' he wrote to Colonel Nachin, 'and my impression is that we've scarcely penetrated at all; the people here are as much strangers to us as ever, and we to them. . . . They have never been satisfied with anybody or anything, but submit to the will of the stronger, so long as that will is expressed; and the mandatory power has not yet decided how to carry out its mandate. This makes for chronic uncertainty, which is to be found, as a matter of fact, throughout the region.'

In the Levant he continued his literary work, revising his lectures to the Staff College and adding two supplementary chapters. After a year and a half he returned to Paris, and in 1932 the whole work was published as a monograph entitled *Le Fil de l'épée* (The Sword's Edge). In the extra chapters he stated the case once more for empirical realism, and against dogmatic, 'metaphysical' theories of generalship, which always fought the last war but one, and in 1914 had been obsessed with an offensive regardless of the difficulties. 'We know the tragic consequences of such metaphysical principles, the cruel losses which our infantry suffered, all the more cruel for the courage with which they fought in their hopeless battles.'

In the first supplementary chapter de Gaulle quoted Pétain three times, and never mentioned Foch. At one point, indeed, he implicitly criticized Foch and justified Pétain's so-called 'defeatist' attitude at the end of the war. 'The same principle of adaptation to circumstances could be seen in our defensive of spring 1918. Were we to attack the enemy while his forces were superior to ours, although in the summer we knew American reinforcements would arrive and we could attack from strength? Preconceived ideas would have counselled immediate attack, empirical realism opposed it – and was proved right by the final victory.'

There were new references to the French Army's primary duty, from which it must not be distracted. 'Under Louis Philippe's "July Monarchy" and the Republic of 1848, the army was absorbed abroad in the conquest of Algeria and at home in suppressing revolts: it had too many excuses for not thinking about the main war (in Europe).' De Gaulle even sounded a Bismarckian note, recalling the Iron Chancellor's intention that 'the hegemony of his country should exercise a salutary and impartial influence in Europe. . . . Germany would be making the

71

worst possible mistake if one day she took sides in these questions of the East which have no special interest for her.'

The second supplementary chapter, called 'Politics and the Soldier', stressed the supreme importance for politicians of controlling opinion. 'They apply all their skill to winning people over, dissimulating their own views according to the circumstances and making no statements except as expediency dictates. . . . At last, by countless intrigues and speeches, they gain the control they need. Can they now act without pretence? No – they must still seek to please, convince prince or parliament, flatter passions, keep private interests wondering.'

Politics being like this, there should be no political meddling in the army. 'Everything which comes from the parties – parading passions, outbidding each other in policies, choosing or excluding men for their opinions – can quickly corrupt the army, whose power depends above all on its integrity.'

On the other hand, the soldier must not leave the framework of the State. He must wait for circumstances within the State to bring him to the fore. In a national crisis it is a military leader's duty to take a stand – like Foch who was even prepared to rebel against Clemenceau's civil power. But once called to power, great military leaders could prove equally successful in politics. 'Alexander, king and general, conquered Asia within ten years. Rome instituted dictatorship for times of great danger. Frederick the Great established his State, directed diplomacy and led his troops so that everything should fit into the general plan he had conceived. Napoleon brought equal genius to the military art and to government.'

And the chapter concluded: 'Nothing great can be done without great men, and they are great because they have willed greatness. In his boyhood Disraeli was already learning to think as Prime Minister. While Foch was still obscure, you could see in his teaching the future commander-in-chief.'

Le Fil de l'épée was published in 1932, and the author sent a first copy, printed on special paper, to his own 'great man', with a hand-written dedication: 'Homage from C. de Gaulle, in deepest respect and devotion.' There was also an official dedication:

'To Marshal Pétain. This essay, Monsieur le Maréchal, could only be dedicated to you, for nothing shows better than your glory how clear thought can lead to correct action.'

When the Marshal opened his private copy and read the dedication, he took his pen and crossed out the words 'better than your glory'. Some saw this as modesty, others as a sort of inverted pride – like that of Clemenceau who had written shortly before his death: 'My pride demands nothing less than the glory of refusing glory.' This copy of the book, incidentally, was to escape the vicissitudes of the war and the occupation; and after the war, when Pétain was imprisoned on the Isle of Yeu, off the Vendean Coast, he re-read passages from it with satisfaction. His widow later presented it to a friend.

When it first came out, the book was not very successful, except in a small circle of the war ministry and the army, where it caused a distinct stir. One of the reviews said: 'Only a bold man would have expressed all his ideas at once at this high level, and he sustained the effort with admirable consistency. But such a man will all too probably have to embody these ideas in practice; he will contract a moral obligation to represent their living reality. Major de Gaulle has the stature to assume this responsibility.'

On his return from the Levant de Gaulle was posted to the general secretariat of the Higher Council for National Defence, created on Marshal Pétain's initiative. Here he studied French plans in case of war, in relation to the world's military forces, a study which later came under the heading of 'logistics'. He worked very hard, and had a long article on 'Economic Mobilization Abroad' published in the *Military Information Review*. This article included a passage on Italian Fascism:

'As if to compensate [for Italy's poverty in raw materials], the Fascist régime allows the public authorities to extract from existing resources all they can possibly give. Measures of national defence are very much easier to carry out with the imperious subordination of private interests to those of the State, the discipline demanded and obtained from all, the co-ordination imposed on the various departments by the *Duce's* personal action, and finally the latent exaltation which the people feel under Fascism for anything concerned with the country's greatness.'

Although this might suggest that de Gaulle at that time approved of the Fascist system, he went on to say: 'A very interesting study published in the *Belgian Bulletin of Military Science* by Lieutenant-Colonel Giron, head of the country's mobilization services, shows us that efforts made in a free country may often be fruitful too.'

In 1933 he was promoted to Lieutenant-Colonel himself, and at the end of that year had a book published entitled *Vers l'armée de métier* (Towards a Professional Army), in which he remarked that 'as seeing a person's portrait may suggest an impression of his destiny, so the map of France reveals our fortune, whether good or bad.... What haunts us is the security of our *hexagon*.' (The first use of this word in de Gaulle's geopolitical writings.)

For the first time also he expressed a wistful hope which he did not see brought nearer to fulfilment till over twenty-five years later: 'The Franco-German frontier is the lip of a wound ... Frenchman and German may recognize each other's worth, so that one dreams sometimes of the great things they could do together.' But alas, the differences of temperament and history kept the two peoples in a constant state of mistrust, and de Gaulle drew a portrait, half critical, half admiring, of his own countrymen:

'This Frenchman, so orderly in mind and disorderly in action, a logician who doubts everything, solemn but frivolous, a stay-at-home who settles in colonies, an ardent formalist and lover of pomp who can yet sing lustily and "let himself go", a Jacobin who shouts "*Vive l'Empereur*", a soldier defeated at Charleroi who can still attack on the Marne – in short this people so changeable, uncertain, contradictory ...'

In face of the Germans he was sceptical of the aid which the Allies might bring France in case of a new conflict: 'There is nothing to show we should again have world support such as enabled us to win the last war.'

He developed once more his favourite ideas on military leadership and exceptional personalities: 'Ambition gives a keen incentive. . . . Glory is only given to those who have always dreamed of it ... [such a personality] must not be animated by a passion for rank and honours, which is mere careerism; but he may indeed have the hope of playing a great part in great events.'

The virtues of pragmatism were praised again with illustrations from classical times: 'In Xenophon's *Anabasis*, in Caesar's *Commentaries*, there is not the slightest allusion to [military] principles, but simply an account of the circumstances.' Then followed new homage to independence of thought *à la* Pétain: 'It is remarkable that the leaders in the Great War who showed the best all-round ability considered themselves very little bound by orthodox teachings. Of course, they had a good knowledge of methods, and also an extra intuition based on wide experience. But the creative spark rising in each special case did not come to them from set rules. The mainspring of their actions was within themselves.'

In some paragraphs on technique, which seemed to extend beyond the military sphere, he stressed the advantages of surprise, which had to be carefully and subtly organized. 'Those who make plans and decisions must of course keep secret all statements, orders and reports, and must mask their preparations; but they should also lay on a thick veil of deception.' Of course the enemy might get hold of important information, but this was just where he could be confused still further. 'If we are ready to make changes in our own plans, deliberately misleading the very men we are intending to use, spreading wrong ideas by all the media which in these days allow one side to know what is going on in the other's camp – then we shall be able to hide the truth behind the falsehood. . . . Cunning must be used to make them believe we are in places where we are not and have intentions that we do not have.'

10

Tanks, Air-power – and Two Crises

Unlike the two previous works, *Vers l'armée de métier* was dedicated not to the Marshal but to the French Army. De Gaulle realized that Pétain, who was now increasingly distant towards him, did not at all share his views on a professional army of 100,000 men and on mechanization. De Gaulle in 1934 was the spiritual heir of the Pétain of 1914 – who no longer existed.

Why was the book given the title it was, instead of *Vers l'armée motorisée*, which would have been a better summary of its contents? Some thought this a grave psychological error, since all the left would be roused against the mere principle of such a large professional army. Others maintained that he was deliberately trying to cause an outcry, in order to draw attention to a plan of vital interest to the country.

In his writings before the Second World War, de Gaulle often paid homage to those who had first put forward the ideas he was reviving or rediscovering; and it was the same with his championship of armoured divisions. No military genius in France, Germany, Russia, Britain or anywhere else, had invented a complete doctrine for the use of armoured divisions; the man with the best claim to be called 'father of the French Tank Corps' is General Estienne, who showed remarkable far-sightedness in a lecture delivered in February 1920:

'In comparison, gentlemen, with the mass armies of the recent past, think of the strategic advantages which an army of 100,000 men would have, capable of covering fifty miles in a night with arms and baggage, in any direction and at any moment. They would only need 8,000 trucks or tracked vehicles and 4,000 armoured fighting vehicles, carrying 20,000 shock troops. For the sake of clarity we will still call them infantry, artillery, cavalry; but all these soldiers will in future make up a single army, with the essential characteristic that it can fight at close quarters, attack the enemy vigorously and always with the advantages of a surprise attack.

76

'Here, first of all, are the heavy tanks, of 50 or 100 tons perhaps, which roll straight on, scorning détours, under cover of night or a thick fog (natural or artificial), crushing all obstacles, gutting houses. The armoured infantry and escort artillery follow them, taking advantage of the track that has been made; the first enemy lines are soon broken, and then the light tanks charge forward like the old-time cavalry to complete the victory. At the same time powerful guns trained on railways, guided by observers in the air, will use their vast range to destroy the last enemy soldiers on the battlefield.

'With the tank in pursuit the enemy cannot re-establish his position; he is irreparably defeated. . . . And some days later, brought up to strength in personnel, tanks, ammunition and petrol, our 100,000 men are ready for a new attack sixty miles further on.

'They will be halted somewhere, no doubt, but probably too late to affect the issue of the campaign. That will be decided within a few months.'

The same theme was developed in July 1927 by Colonel Doumenc, lecturing to the Centre of High Military Studies:[1] 'The first day of mobilization has been fixed for D-Day at Zero Hour. At Zero Hour plus 6, the armoured corps which was in the Bordeaux area is on the Seine. At Zero Hour plus 10, it is at the Eastern frontier.' For an hour he sketched the launching of attacks with armoured regiments 'spitting fire, scaling hills and crossing waterways, spreading panic through a stunned, harassed, mutilated and defenceless enemy. . . . There, gentlemen, you have a bird's-eye view of the future.' The following year he submitted to the general staff a blue-print for an armoured division, like the one which was later established by the Germans.

In Britain, where the first tank was developed – under the name of 'Peppermint Cream' – General Fuller, former chief of staff of the Royal Tank Corps, declared: 'The supreme lesson of the war is that petrol has made possible a revival of armour, and armour a revival of the offensive.' Captain Liddell Hart, the famous military critic, also foresaw the increasing use of armour in war.

[1] Quoted in *Mirages et Réalités* by General Weygand, who introduced Doumenc to the Centre saying: '*Voici mon sorcier.*'

In Germany Guderian was working methodically to perfect the *Panzer* divisions. He read with professional interest the new book by de Gaulle, in his eyes one of the few Frenchmen who understood the problems involved, and quoted and discussed it. But the German tank experts were developing a strategy on their own, in the light of Franco-British experiments in the First World War, at a time when the German High Command did not believe in the effectiveness of the new arm. Guderian had learnt from his own experience as a young officer on the Western Front, when he saw the German lines breached by tanks, which were given ground support by the 1st Air Division of the French Army (created on 14th May 1918). This division with its twenty-four squadrons of eighteen planes (432 Spad, precursors of the Stukas), machine-gunned the ground troops and pounded the battlefield. The combination of tanks and planes conceived by his enemies was the new factor which struck Guderian so forcibly, and was to lead him towards decisive victory a few years later. 'I obtained my information,' he told a French officer, 'from the use of tanks in 1918 by your army, in liaison with the air division.'

De Gaulle did not discuss this combination in his book, although in one place he said that 'ground troops, specially armoured ones, will receive valuable help for their camouflage from the air force. Smoke-screens spread from the air will conceal vast expanses of ground in a few minutes.' In a new edition published after the war, however, he added: 'But above all by itself striking at direct range and in depth, the air force becomes *par excellence* the arm whose shattering effects combine best with the advantages of break-throughs and the exploitation of large mechanized units.' Paul Reynaud, however, who defended in parliament the proposal to create a powerful mechanized and armoured corps, and relied on de Gaulle for the technical part of his speech, did not say a word about air-power in combined action with tanks.

De Gaulle was interested enough in the use of air-power, but he did not appreciate its complexity, nor did he grasp the importance of the part which would be played by parachutists. This is not so surprising; after all, Foch had said in 1910, having watched an air display: 'All very fine for sport, you know. But the aeroplane's no use to the army.' There was a considerable

technical revolution going on all the time, and however brilliant
de Gaulle's mind, he could not be expected to follow up every
new development.

He did, however, ask for a meeting with Colonel Rougeron,
chief engineer in the corps of naval constructors, who had
written books and monographs on the value of fighter-bombers
and dive-bombing, air attack on tanks – in short, shock air-
power, which was very much favoured in Italy and the United
States.

De Gaulle's book was translated into several languages; the
English translation was called *The Army of the Future*. In
Russian and in German the book had a greater success than in
French – in Russia it sold 8,000 copies in 1935, three or four
times as many as in France. In Austria that year General von
Eimannsberger, who had no doubt read *Vers l'armée de
métier*, published at Munich a book on tank warfare, in which he
wrote: 'In the summer of 1918 the British and the French were
preparing an attack for spring 1919, which was to be led by
10,000 fighting tanks, followed by 10,000 supply tanks; so how
can people still refuse, fifteen years later, to see the profound
change in warfare brought about by the tank?'

So in the German High Command as well as the French there
were quite a number of good minds who failed to realize the
revolution that was taking place. Hitler imposed decisions on the
German generals, who for the most part remained faithful to the
tactics of tanks moving 'from visible horizon to visible horizon'
in protection of the infantry, according to the rules which had
triumphed in 1918.

De Gaulle simply took a clearer view than most French
military thinkers. He was no more the inventor of the tank than
Pétain had been the inventor of artillery in 1914, but he saw the
tank's virtues as well as its weaknesses, and went straight to
essentials. He recalled the basic principles of the military art,
'surprise, power, exploitation' – and how in 1918 the Franco-
British forces had failed in the last after their successful break-
through.

Of course some people pointed out that de Gaulle's books
contained little in the way of technical details. This was true
enough, but then he was not intending to write a manual. At
that time he was still mainly a theorist who took wide-ranging

views and expressed them with eloquence, a military philosopher, not an expert technician.

Some officers called him a mere journalist, but if his ideas had been put into practice, and France had had the armoured corps he recommended, it might well have changed the course of events in the great crisis of 1936 when Hitler reoccupied the Rhineland. Having preached for so long in the wilderness of high political and military circles, de Gaulle was in despair over what happened. He wrote to one friend, the day after the Germans marched in: 'We should have acted with surprise, ruthlessness, speed.' These three words sum up de Gaulle's whole approach to war and diplomacy.

He confided to his intimates: 'It is a disaster, probably an irreparable one. The general staff and the government hesitated. They refused to resort to general mobilization. If we had had my professional army and my tanks, mobilization would not have been necessary. We should have advanced and the Germans would have retreated. If we had done our duty, peace would have been assured.'

For him and many other Frenchmen, France lost the war on 7th March 1936. Surprise, ruthlessness, speed: faced by an immediate counter-stroke from France, Hitler's troops would have faded away. He had not yet built up the powerful military force he was working towards. This seems to be confirmed by considerable evidence, including Guderian's declaration after the war, on being questioned by officers of the Army Historical Branch: 'If you French had taken action in the Rhineland in 1936, we should have collapsed and Hitler would have fallen.'

Had de Gaulle been chief of the general staff or War Minister, he would have answered the Nazi bluff with counter-bluff. He certainly believed in trickery in such a context: for the country's safety. In his eyes, the end justified the means. In war you must deceive and win or be deceived and defeated; stratagems are an essential part of strategy at all times. A military leader has only one objective, to win battles and the war at all costs.

Pétain, unlike de Gaulle, had failed to move with the times: small wonder, perhaps, for in that year of the German march into the Rhineland, he had his eightieth birthday. He seemed to have forgotten Napoleon's precept that 'tactics change every ten years'. The far-sighted leader who in 1917–18 demanded 3,000 tanks still clung to a doctrine out of date in a motorized age: 'The defensive is a situation infinitely superior to the offensive, because fire kills.' For Pétain, to plan a tank onslaught would have been like repeating the murderous folly of the all-out offensives in 1914.

Was Pétain becoming senile? De Gaulle had thought so for some time, yet many people who had an interview with the Marshal found him in full possession of all his faculties. One of his generals, however, confided to Pétain's old friend Colonel Bouvard, just returned from Indo-China: 'His memory is going. He remembers things in the past perfectly, but doesn't assimilate new ones or not very well.' Pétain himself was well aware of the danger, and told a former colleague his fears of losing his sense of realities.

But he also succumbed to a form of egoism, natural enough at his age, shown towards the individuals around him and the events taking place under his eyes. It was extremely sad for de Gaulle to watch the advance of senility in perhaps the only living man he had sincerely admired. Pétain, who had once been the epitome of strong character, was today 'eaten away' by the onslaughts of old age. The most typical feature was the frequency of mental blackouts, short at first but growing longer. After them a veneer of lucidity would reappear; hence the illusion maintained towards the outside world. Only those who knew him well realized the underlying changes. 'The Marshal,' de Gaulle observed, 'is all withered inside. . . . He has no generous feelings or resolve left. Gone are the days when he showed uncompromising independence, when he would send the highest authorities packing, without any concern for his career or advancement.'

Major Loustaunau-Lacau, who succeeded de Gaulle in the 'writer's' chair on Pétain's staff, also watched the decline of a great man. There were days, he said, when you could have written on Pétain's face: 'Closed owing to old age.' He also found Pétain 'un-interested' in the things of this world. 'He had seen so many men and things, joys and misfortunes, heights and depths, grandeurs and trifles, that the arrival of the car he was waiting for interested him as much or as little as the fall of a ministry or the death of a man he knew. Life leaves its mark on even the straightest shoulders.'

But there was no question of Pétain completely losing touch. Admittedly he could not escape from the original conception of the use of tanks, as held in 1918: he was mainly concerned with the infantry and its protection; the tank was just an auxiliary. But on the other hand he foresaw the importance of the air arm; increasingly, in fact, he gave planes priority over tanks. In April 1935, when presenting the *Légion d'honneur* at the Staff College, his speech – written as usual by a 'ghost' in uniform, but approved by him – gave a picture which would not be disowned by a de Gaulle:

'Mechanized units are capable of giving operations a rhythm and scope unknown till now.

'The plane, by bringing destruction to the most distant of vital centres, expands the framework of the battle, which was once limited to the range of artillery attacks, and changes the conditions of strategic action. The essential rules of the military art are likely to be deeply affected by it. One may even wonder whether the plane will not dictate its own rules in the wars of the future.

'So it would be strange if this arm, with its power and prestige increasing daily, did not become the object of the most thorough study at this College.

'Indeed the victory will go to the one who first discovers how to make the best use of the special properties of modern devices, and how to combine their action, at whatever level, so as to destroy the enemy's means of carrying on the struggle.'

Colonel de Gaulle had just taken over the command of the 507th Regiment of Fighter Tanks at Metz, in November 1937, when the Cagoulard conspiracy broke out. It was mastered, but systematically minimized from the start, by the President of the Republic and Daladier, the War Minister. They were anxious to avoid a new Dreyfus affair in the French Army, when the dangers on France's frontiers were so menacing. The Cagoulards were fiercely anti-German, but favourable to Franco and Italian Fascism. There proved to be large numbers of conspirators in the army, under the cover of the anti-communist struggle; and a field-marshal, no doubt from the best patriotic motives, allowed himself to become involved. Three generals with regional commands, also from fear of subversion inside the country, were affiliated to the 'Secret Committee for Revolutionary Action'.

The chief conspirator, Eugène Deloncle, was an extremely ambitious man, who saw himself as the head of the French State. He had succeeded in instilling his ideas into the minds of several influential members of the general staff, persuading them that from 'Red Spain in her death-throes' the U.S.S.R., via the Komintern, was preparing to spread the flames into France: at any minute dozens of Russian bombers would leave Barcelona to land at French aerodromes. However, in the night of 15th–16th November, while Paris was asleep, the great conspiracy collapsed.

Suspicions arose in police circles that de Gaulle was one of the army officers involved, but in fact this suspicion was without substance. Since March 1936, when Charles Maurras had taken up positions in foreign policy which de Gaulle condemned, he had broken completely with the old nationalist leader – to whom he had dedicated his first book, *Discorde chez l'ennemi*, 'in respectful homage'. In any case the war in Spain had made many people change sides. Colonel Morel, who had been a history lecturer at Saint-Cyr at the same time as de Gaulle, went to the socialist, Vincent Auriol, and told him: 'I am a monarchist of *Action Française*, and I tell you: a king of France would make war on the side of the Spanish Republic!' De Gaulle's views on foreign policy seem to have been much the same, and he soon afterwards became a contributor to *Amis de Temps présent*, a Christian-democrat and anti-fascist weekly. As far as *Action Française* was concerned, it was widely read among army officers, and right up to the war its military page demanded a mechanized army – in line with de Gaulle's ideas.

Maurras at this time had said: 'We must bring Pétain to power, and he will restore the king.' Certainly the Marshal detested parliament and the parties, but according to General Héring, to whom he gave his political views, 'The Marshal appears indifferent to the form of régime: republic, monarchy, empire, it's all one to him. What interests him vitally in the structure of government is unity of command and stability. And above all, no "stop-go" ministers who will do anything for popularity.' To his close friend, the Senator Lémery, Pétain said: 'The government is like a military command. One leader at the head, with capable ministers. When that no longer works, they are replaced. But only one leader. The powers of the chief of State and head of government must be merged.'

His ideas, indeed, do not seem to have been very clear, but in the main he probably supported a form of presidential government. However, during a railway journey in 1938, he was in the dining-car with a Member of Parliament, and spent an hour inveighing against 'politicians', then discussing very fluently the reforms of the constitution he felt necessary. The other man said: 'You will become Prime Minister, Monsieur le Maréchal.' To which Pétain replied: 'I can only work three or four hours a day.' The campaign launched in a journal called *La Victoire*, 'It is Pétain we need', irritated and annoyed him; he asked for it to be stopped.

The same year, a woman who was a close friend said to him at lunch: 'Yesterday I visited the Malmaison Museum. I would like to have stolen the First Consul's portfolio on your behalf.' 'My dear friend,' the Marshal replied, 'I wouldn't mind your stealing it if only you could take fifty years off me.'

On the other hand, still in 1938, when the daughter of one of the generals involved in the Cagoulard conspiracy asked him to try to obtain special treatment in prison for her father, Pétain said: 'It is possible I may have a part to play. I cannot be compromised in this business.'

He saw a grave national crisis developing and war imminent. After all, he was the last survivor of the famous Frenchmen of the Great War, in which he had reached all the heights except that of being supreme commander. He could still render immense services to his country, and perhaps even save it, as in 1917.

Not only did he have great support; there were many people on the left who were prejudiced in his favour because they shared his attachment to defensives. Léon Blum in *Le Populaire* called him 'the noblest of military leaders'. He was a 'republican marshal', and far outside all military factions. 'I'm told the socialists speak well of me,' he remarked in the presence of Colonel Bouvard. 'I must say I wonder why.' As for Blum, 'He is the man who has undermined the French Army. And Herriot? That man! His place is not in politics. In the Académie at most.'

The successive officers on his personal staff over ten years, though all very devoted to him, held different opinions about his character. Some thought him hard beneath an apparent good nature, declining more and more into egoism and ingratitude towards his most loyal colleagues, friends and even his wife. The others said: 'He is barricading himself in deliberate insensitivity. He represses affectionate impulses from fear that any kindness will be considered a sign of weakness in him. He has a very kind heart, but doesn't want anyone to see it. Did you know, for instance, that he is secretly paying a young man's fees at a missionary college? He is an unknown quantity really, with two different sides to his character. The kind-hearted side is always trying to take over.'

Curiously enough, Pétain himself, encouraged by his staff, made the same charge against de Gaulle as de Gaulle had levelled at Pétain: 'De Gaulle? Completely heartless.'

That year de Gaulle was in conversation with a great Catholic author, who had discovered in Burgundy a curious municipal plaque saying: 'Rue Bernard de Clairvaux, statesman'. Some historians claimed that St Bernard sometimes sinned from lack of charity, and de Gaulle asked: 'Do you know if Bernard de Clairvaux had a kind heart?' When the author hesitated before answering, de Gaulle went on: 'If you said "no", that would not condemn him in my eyes.'

Clairvaux, St Bernard's foundation, was not far from Colombey-les-Deux-Églises, where de Gaulle often stayed with his family. A long Calvary had led him to this humble village. He had bought a house in a big park, where his daughter Anne could live; the soothing climate of these wooded regions had been recommended for her. She was mentally deficient without the power of speech. Her parents had refused to be parted from her, to have her put in a home. Whenever such a course was suggested, de Gaulle answered: 'She did not ask to come into the world. We shall do everything to make her happy.'

And Anne found her happiness in her father's military cap; the sight of it had a magical effect on her. A gleam seemed to come into the lifeless eyes. He would take her in his arms, rock her, then lay her down. He clapped his hands, and her face lit up. He slapped his thighs, danced about in his boots, sang little songs to her, performed little pantomimes, dandled her and swung her about. Anne brought out articulate sounds, which showed her joy, and in the end a laugh that was almost human. Then, tired but happy, she would go off to sleep, with her hand in her father's.

The stern face of Charles de Gaulle relaxed at last – in tears. He removed the mask and wept, as his heart demanded, in this quiet lonely place.

11

Reactions to Impending Disaster

On the eve of the Second World War de Gaulle had a strangely mixed reputation in military circles. Many admired him greatly, and were fascinated by him; rather more ridiculed, slandered and disparaged him, no doubt partly from jealousy. 'I have never seen an officer so detested,' said a general who was one of his supporters. 'His prestige is so great,' said another, 'I would follow him to the ends of the earth.' 'I am keeping his letters,' said a third. 'Something tells me this man has a great future ahead of him.'

A military critic wrote in an important literary magazine: 'It is difficult to be as polite as one would wish in assessing ideas which border on delirium. Let us just say that M. de Gaulle was forestalled a number of years ago by Jarry's famous character, Père Ubu, who was also a great tactician with modern ideas. In due course, he used to say, we shall use physics to invent a wind machine for transporting the whole army.' In the same vein one general compared de Gaulle to Alcibiades 'cutting off his dog's tail to get himself noticed', and sneered that 'De Gaulle has bought a gramophone: Paul Reynaud.'

To all the criticisms and vexations, the coalition of mediocrities against him, de Gaulle reacted with a steely contempt which was often unfair. He was so conscious of his intellectual superiority that he treated all who questioned his opinions as either fools or knaves; he ignored the fact that the French Army leaders included a good many men of intelligence and integrity. His pride, of course, was not concerned merely, or even mainly, with his own reputation; he was immensely ambitious for the French Army and its crack troops. When foiled in his plans, he suffered something like the pangs of a crossed lover.

His defenders, in any case, could say that it was surely not pride to be aware of your worth and wish to serve your country to the best of your ability; that a certain harshness, which might offend the soft and half-hearted, was only the reverse side of a strong character; that de Gaulle was certainly no careerist, since he was always fighting against the Establishment and upsetting the general staff by his outspoken criticisms. As to ambition, he had himself written (in *Le Fil de l'épée*) of the outstanding men of ambition who 'see no other reason for life save to make their mark on events; from the shore where routine keeps them, they dream only of the great waves of History'.

When he was sent to Metz in 1937, the then War Minister remarked to him: 'You've given us enough trouble with your paper tanks. Let's see what you make of the metal sort.' It turned out that the metal tanks were subjected to extremely stern tests, so that at one point the supplies branch almost reprimanded him for excessive zeal. He was no administrator colonel who sat on his bottom; he had to be always on the move, looking into everything – he was sometimes known as 'the Spider'. In the routine of regimental life he shook everybody into constant activity, opening up tank sheds and sounding night alarms, organizing inter-arm exercises, driving in parades at full speed at the head of his throbbing steel monsters.

De Gaulle's tank regiment was attached to an infantry division commanded by a brigadier general who was favourable to him; and the division was part of an army corps commanded by General Giraud, who was not. Nevertheless in 1939 the former got Giraud to put de Gaulle's name on the list of those suitable for promotion to general. Once when a manœuvre was held on a plateau above the Moselle, de Gaulle sent his tanks some miles ahead, to the disgust of the infantry, who felt they were unprotected and would be mown down by machine-guns. De Gaulle maintained that 'when the tanks have gone past, there will be nothing left'.

Nearly 500 officers were present at the criticism. The brigadier who had directed the manœuvre was convinced that de Gaulle was right; not so General Giraud. As tall as de Gaulle, he stood very erect in front of the assembly, pointed a finger and began: 'As for you, mon petit Gaulle, so long as I am commanding this army corps . . .' Then he demolished the tank operation, defending the infantry's attitude. De Gaulle went pale with fury, but had to sit through it.

With the catastrophe approaching, he found it agonizing that the War Council and most of the generals should ridicule the ideas he believed in so fanatically. In the political world, too, the Communist leader Maurice Thorez poured scorn on 'certain theorists, notably Colonel de Gaulle', who 'envisage a small motorized army, a super-army with which they plan to tour Europe. . . .' But less far to the left de Gaulle had made some converts, such as Blum and Marcel Déat, as well as on the right – Paul Reynaud and a *député* for Paris, Frédéric-Dupont. The latter visited General Gamelin on behalf of the Parliamentary Committee on the Army, who were worried by the extent of German motorization, and asked the General's opinion of de Gaulle's ideas.

Gamelin replied: 'I don't believe in Colonel de Gaulle's theories. They aren't sensible or realistic. We need tanks, of course . . . you can make a useful diversion on the wing, carry out a spectacular operation, destroy an enemy control post, yes. But you cannot hope to achieve real break-throughs with tanks. The tank is not independent enough. It has to go ahead, but then must return for fuel and supplies. As to the air force, it will not play the part you expect. . . . The air crews will destroy each other, and finding new planes will be a much quicker business than finding new crews.' Gamelin made a lavish gesture to sum up both tank and air offensives. 'It'll be a flash in the pan.'

Pétain showed irritation at his former protégé's political activities behind the scenes. 'De Gaulle is getting too much mixed up in politics. It's not a soldier's business. He is incredibly vain.' Yet the Marshal himself could call politics 'amusing', and he had been very flattered when at the age of seventy-eight he was given the War Ministry in the 1934 Doumergue Government. Since then he was somehow attracted by the idea of a political career, a career devoted to his country's service.

In 1936 he agreed to see the historian Jean Martet, who asked for an interview on behalf of *Le Journal*. But Pétain started by saying: 'Monsieur, I don't really know what you expect of me, and I am surprised, in fact, that my doors have been opened to you. I have made a firm rule never to accord an interview and not to go in for politics.' However, the interview proceeded, concluding with a statement from the Marshal that 'We are like sailors without a pilot or a rudder. That is what we have to fight against. We must rediscover a mystique, call it what you will – a mystique of patriotism or simply tradition. Without that there is no salvation. We come after millions of people who have laboured and suffered so that we might become what we are. They have the right to demand of us that at least we continue with their task.'

'How would you sum up your ideas in one phrase, Monsieur le Maréchal?'

'*Rassemblement national.*'

The following year Pierre Laval said: 'We are moving towards catastrophe, the dismemberment of the country. But we'll have Marshal Pétain. He will be our banner; we'll get him going.'

At the beginning of 1939 Georges Duhamel asked Pétain at a lunch held by the Inter-Allied Circle: 'Do you expect to do anything in the present crisis, Monsieur le Maréchal?' He replied in a furious voice: 'Nothing! First because I have not been asked to do anything; next because I am too old. I can work for fifteen days, not for fifteen weeks.'

In March 1939 the government nominated him as Ambassador to Spain, giving him the task of re-establishing relations with General Franco's Spain, which had been exceedingly strained. De Gaulle considered this a devaluation of the Marshal's prestige: 'Poor Marshal! He's accepting the position of ambassador. He's so far gone in senile ambition he would accept anything. It's terrible and pathetic. He's no longer in a condition to take on responsibilities.'

In Spain the phenomena of old age grew more pronounced. His colleagues, both civilian and military, noticed on many occasions that he would forget everything from one day to the next. As to new facts he remembered them with difficulty and in a fragmentary way. Not that he was completely senile, for he could still show extraordinary lucidity; but there were fewer hours a day when he was 'all there'. His physical condition was excellent, and he was like the 'old man of the sea' later described by Hemingway: 'Everything about him was old except his eyes and they were the same colour as the sea and were cheerful and undefeated.' Perhaps 'undefeated' is too much; at any rate Pétain had become the old man who refused to let go.

To the outside world, the fiction of a Pétain still at the height of his powers was maintained, though his entourage was secretly very worried. Captain Bonhomme, one of his aides, confided in private; 'The old man has been successful in everything, but now I'm scared stiff that he may be carried to power – there's a strong movement to take him there. He is a passenger now, he ought to stay quietly enjoying the sun on his property in the South of France. We can't even tell him anything. He can make the most appalling diplomatic blunders. The man is finished – sad, sad.'

On 3rd September, when war broke out, he was extremely pessimistic. He no longer believed in the virtues of his countrymen and found Allied preparations inadequate. A week later he wrote to his close friend at Paris, the Senator Lémery, Vice-President of the committee for foreign affairs:

'My dear friend,

Thank you for the souvenir brought to me this morning by M. Martinez. Here one feels so far away from France. The papers reach us late. One thing strikes me, the extension of Bolshevist propaganda in France, despite the measures taken against their agents. I often ask myself this: is the delay in launching real operations more favourable to the Allies or the Germans? My answer is that it will be favourable to us if we can successfully maintain morale at the front and safeguard it in the rear. France continues to gain ground progressively, but the Spanish Press is still subject to German influence. We are going to make a big effort. But the Germans live hard and have vast resources for keeping in with the Press.'

There was a curious little incident early in October, during an official ceremony organized by the Spanish Government which was attended by the whole diplomatic corps. The German Ambassador bowed to the French Ambassador because the latter was a famous old soldier. Pétain held out his hand to the German Ambassador. His aides were shocked and at first thought he must have been victim once more of a lapse of memory. But he told them afterwards: 'Everybody will believe I made a mistake. I once gave the Germans a good drubbing. I can allow myself to shake this young man's hand.'

Shortly afterwards Senator Lémery arrived in Spain, having been invited by the Marshal's military advisers. The following dialogue took place, as recorded by Lémery:

Pétain: 'What am I doing here? Nothing. I would like to return to Paris.'

Lémery: 'You have all the more reason to because they will soon have to call for you. The information I possess on the state of the army is such that we can expect very serious developments. You must prepare yourself for power, so that you can form a cabinet and carry on the war, like my former chief Clemenceau.'

Pétain: 'The war, yes. But in politics, as far as I am concerned, you must be joking. Running a government is not my trade.' A pause. 'Besides, I know practically nobody in the parliamentary world.'

Lémery: 'I can prepare a cabinet for you, Monsieur le Maréchal.'

Pétain: 'A cabinet? Can you, though? Let's see.'

Lémery: 'You know men you respect: Pietri, for example.'

Pétain: 'Yes.'

Lémery: 'Take *him*, then. You also know Alibert.'

Pétain: 'Yes.'

Lémery: 'And Adrien Marquet, who was your colleague at the Ministry of Labour in the Doumergue Government. And Pierre Laval. Give him the Interior.'

Pétain: 'Where does *he* get his fortune from?'

Lémery: 'Leave Maurras to ask that.'

Pétain: 'You haven't considered the point that a Prime Minister is questioned continually on agricultural matters, the merchant navy, salaries, etc. I don't want to make a fool of myself in front of parliament.'

Lémery: 'You can appoint a government spokesman.'

Pétain: 'They'll say I'm not up to it.'

Nevertheless, by the end of the conversation, there was a 'shadow' Pétain Government formally approved. Only, the Marshal closed the proceedings by stating: 'In no circumstances shall I accept power.'

M. Lémery returned to Paris and continued his campaign for bringing Pétain to power. In January 1940 Pétain paid a visit to Paris, and went straight to the Senator's house. 'I have come to ask you urgently to stop your campaign. I don't know Gustave Hervé, so I can't stop him calling for my presence in the government. But you are my friend, and if you persist, they'll spread the rumour that the campaign is being organized with my consent. I don't want power, not at any price.' M. Lémery yielded.

At Madrid the Marshal's financial adviser warned him in very diplomatic terms: 'Don't accept anything. Politics is a very hard life which will be beyond your physical capacities.' Nobody mentioned his mental capacities.

In May 1940 the Marshal was very critical of the way the war was being fought, and it was no surprise to him when Reynaud called him to the government as a Vice-Premier: he had expected the call to come. When it came, he accepted it; before that he would not put himself forward. As an old infantryman he believed in the principle of 'never sticking your head out of a hole too soon'.

12

An Authors' Quarrel

To Colonel de Gaulle, commanding his tank regiment at Metz, the Munich agreement of September 1938 was a disaster, peace with dishonour. He fully supported the comment of Paul Reynaud, then Finance Minister in the Daladier cabinet, to General Gamelin, the Commander in Chief: 'The only thing for you now is to find thirty-five divisions.'

Meanwhile de Gaulle's own ideas for improving France's preparedness went almost unheeded. 'After practical experience,' he wrote to his friend Colonel Nachin, 'I am more convinced than ever of the soundness of the ideas I have tried to spread, which, alas, have been followed by the Germans much more readily than by our compatriots. You can't carry out ground manœuvres or make attacks without tanks. The age of the infantry is over, except as a defensive arm. The artillery retains its relative value, but from now on must be used above all in supporting the tanks. We have first to recognize this, then reorganize the French Army accordingly, by producing an instrument for manœuvre and shock tactics based on tanks: that is to say, an armoured corps.'

And to another friend: 'The turn which events have taken is forcing us to carry out [the ideas on tanks] bit by bit. But we shall no doubt go on doing things too little and too late, while the Germans under our very noses apply intact the system we have rejected.'

Five days before the Munich agreement de Gaulle had written this letter to Reynaud: 'On Tuesday a book of mine was published by Plon entitled *La France et son armée*. I am sending you a copy. It is a summary of a thousand years of our country's history, our fighting, suffering and triumphant country. I hope, perhaps rather presumptuously, that you will find a little time to have a look at it.

'My regiment is ready. As for myself, I see coming, without surprise, the greatest events in France's history, and I am confident that you are marked out to play a leading part in them. Let me assure you that in any case, should I survive, I shall be resolute in your service if you feel you can use me.'

This book, which Reynaud read with enthusiasm, was the cause of a decisive rupture between its author and Pétain; but to call de Gaulle its author is perhaps to beg a question going back fifteen years, which was the origin of the quarrel.

In 1922 the Marshal had the idea of writing a book on the French soldier through the centuries under all the different régimes. It was to be a lofty philosophic tome to which he could put his name at the end of a long life, and it would finish on a very high note, showing how the crisis of morale in 1917 was overcome.

Various officers on Pétain's staff began to do preliminary work on the book, Colonel Bouvard, Captain de Gaulle, Captain Barthe. A doctor of law who was a clerk at the War Office, a young corporal called René Pleven (destined for future political prominence), was transferred to Pétain's staff to assist them. Colonel Duchêne, the Marshal's chief secretary, welcomed him in these terms: 'We are going to introduce you to Captain de Gaulle, who will one day be one of the great leaders of the French Army.'

The months passed, several staff writers were moved on to other work, and quite soon de Gaulle became solely responsible for the first draft; before he left the staff, four chapters had been completed. 'Read what de Gaulle has written,' the Marshal would often exclaim. 'What a style the man has, what magnificent language he uses! He is brilliant at finding the exact word or phrase.'

Pétain himself never wrote anything these days – except for letters. Malicious critics said he was too lazy, but more probably he just had no gift for literary composition. As it was, he regarded writing as a subordinate's duty, and got a 'ghost' to draft everything he put his name to, not only speeches and articles but military directives and orders of the day. Even during the war there were articles 'of his' which were written by a member of the Académie, Louis Madelin; and the book he published in 1929, *La Bataille de Verdun*, was ghosted by one of his colonels.

There was nothing very unusual in this; it was a point in common with Joffre, of whom one author says: 'The victor of the Marne . . . never wrote. Occasionally he consulted a file, but he much preferred that one of his assistants should provide him with a concise account of the situation.' A captain on Joffre's staff recalls that Joffre told him: 'You'll put this, this and that,' and quietly developed three or four ideas. Another officer who had served on his staff said: 'Joffre was extraordinary. He had very sound judgement, but never did anything by himself. You had to suggest something to him, prepare him a plan – and he would weigh it up and decide.'

So Pétain did the same; but he was not inactive on the literary front for all that. A pencil carefully sharpened by a sergeant-major was put on his desk every day, and the officers would sometimes say: 'Ah, the pencil's doing its stuff tonight.' He ticked a phrase or sentence, struck out another, lopped and pruned and grafted. Captain Montjean, who finally 'produced' the speech he delivered on admission to the Académie, has described his technique:

'The Marshal went through a draft line by line, stop by stop. He fought shy of adjectives, which weighed down the expression, he said, generally without adding to the thought if the noun was well chosen. He rejected adverbs or interjections like "alas", "unluckily", "luckily", and as often as possible removed conjunctions like "for", "well", "however". Ideas, he declared, have no need of these little words to link them up. He was very keen on the *mot juste*, especially with verbs. The French language is rich, he always stressed. There is only one word to express what you want to say. That word must be found.'

He gave a little lecture once to Major Loustaunau-Lacau: 'One must be simple, and sparing of words. Here is what I want: a central idea which holds the text together all the way through. Not many paragraphs, and those in proportion to their importance. For sentences, subject, verb, complement. Adjectives are ridiculous, they are like the silk sashes worn by officers in comic-opera armies. Few adverbs, and exact when you do use them. Extra words hide poverty of thought. The semicolon is a bastard of punctuation.'

He liked quoting examples: 'If you tell a woman "I love you",

that is enough. You don't need to say "I love you very much".'
A purist, he was very regular and conscientious in attending the
Académie's weekly sessions on vocabulary. When touching up
articles and speeches, with a cut here and an alteration there, he
obtained a distinctive smooth style of his own, cool and dispassionate, which became vivid and colourful through well-coined
phrases. He delighted in slogans, original turns of speech, terse
comments which captured the imagination. '*On les aura*' (we'll
get them) was one example, although he had at first raised
strong objections to this catch-phrase, declaring that it was 'not
French'.

For his literary stable Pétain had chosen a 'favourite' with the
same characteristic. 'You know,' de Gaulle would sometimes
remark, 'when I have hammered out a good literary formula, I
can't help bringing it out, even if it does not exactly correspond
to the *nuances* of my thought.'

After leaving Pétain's staff, de Gaulle continued writing the
book on his own, in the Rhineland and the Levant, and used in
his lectures the chapters on the era before the Revolution, the
First Empire, and the war of 1870. He was still writing it officially on behalf of Pétain, who held at his headquarters a copy of
the early chapters, carrying the mark of that evening 'pencil-
work'. The *magnum opus* on France and her army was to be
signed Philippe Pétain, although from first to last it was
obviously written by de Gaulle.

Some time round 1930, when the question of publishing the
first chapters in book form came up, de Gaulle claimed the
right to be associated with it. Pétain was very annoyed at this
presumption, taking the same view as Joffre on this matter.
Joffre had completed the second volume of his *Memoirs* in
1928; he considered that the officers who had written it for
him were honoured by the privilege of doing so. Staff writers
working at marshal's headquarters were a sort of literary
batman, who naturally remained anonymous. In Pétain's case,
moreover, his sworn enemy, Marshal Lyautey, was known
to be making sarcastic remarks in society about the proposed publication: 'Apparently M. Pétain is going to publish a
book. That's a good one. It can't be his own work, he couldn't
do it.'

Highly insulted, Pétain put his copy of the manuscript away in a drawer; while de Gaulle added other chapters and brought it to completion. The next step occurred early in 1936, when M. Daniel-Rops was commissioned by the publishing house of Plon to collect and edit a series of books by well-known men on their careers. He had met de Gaulle the previous year at a discussion group, and now asked if he would write a volume for the series. De Gaulle agreed to produce a book entitled *L'Homme sous les armes*, but later said he would not have this book ready for a long time owing to his military duties. M. Daniel-Rops continues his account as follows:

'He had, however, another book to suggest to me, which was more or less complete already. It was a sort of history of the French Army, or rather a philosophy of that history. He had undertaken it, he told me, on the request of and in collaboration with Marshal Pétain, when he was serving on the Marshal's staff. For a reason I have never heard, the Marshal decided not to go on with the work after the first chapters. But he had authorized Charles de Gaulle to complete it. Which had been done.

'It was in this way that the book *La France et son armée* appeared in my series. The question of the authorship came up: should the Marshal figure on the cover or not? There was a period of confused negotiations, but Colonel de Gaulle did not feel it necessary to involve the publishers or myself in the details. One day, however, an approach having been made to Plon by an officer on the Marshal's staff, with the obvious though unadmitted aim of stopping the book being published, Colonel de Gaulle telephoned me from Metz, and told me with his characteristic calm: "The Marshal and Co. are getting very worked up. But don't worry, I'll see him and it'll all be settled."

'In fact a solution was found, in the form of the dedication on the first page of the original edition, whereby the Marshal's collaboration on the book was formally indicated, without his name appearing at all on the cover. If I remember rightly, this dedication was kept in three successive editions. It was taken out in the new editions after 1945, which I regretted: it could be put in historical perspective merely by the date – it appeared on 27th September, 1938.'

The dedication was as follows:

To
Monsieur
le Maréchal Pétain
who wanted this book to be written,
who directed with his advice
the writing of the first five chapters,
and thanks to whom
the two last are the history
of our Victory.

On receiving a copy of this dedication three weeks before the publication date, Pétain wrote to de Gaulle:

'My dear de Gaulle,
You will find enclosed a draft dedication which could be printed on the front page of the first volume and would serve as a foreword. This dedication does not need any explanation or commentary.
I have tried to spare your feelings, and allusion is only made in this draft to "advice" in the "preparation" of the work.
Please give me your opinion or acceptance.
Very cordially,
Pétain.'

Draft dedication: To M. le Maréchal Pétain – who was kind enough, during the years 1925–1927, to help me with his advice in the preparation of Chapters 2 to 5 of this volume (Ancien Régime, Revolution, Napoleon, From One Disaster to Another) – I present my grateful homage.'

The book appeared, however, with its original dedication, and the following week Pétain wrote to the publishers in complaint:

'Dear Sir,
You have just published a book by Colonel de Gaulle entitled *La France et son armée*.
This officer, without first applying for my authorization, has used staff papers which he wrote according to my directives in 1925–1927, while he was under my orders. These papers have been incorporated into the present book intact: they are Chapters 2 to 5.
At the beginning of August, when I was sent proofs, thus

presenting me with a *fait accompli*, I at first intended to forbid Colonel de Gaulle to make use of staff papers which did not belong to him. Then, in a spirit of good-will, I finally authorized the book's appearance, but on condition that it was preceded by a printed dedication, the text of which I gave on 5th September 1928 . . . [1]

The dedication which has been printed is quite different. It contains two inexactitudes: (1) I did not "want the book to be written", since I first of all opposed it; (2) I had nothing to do with the writing of the first chapter. The dedication which has been printed must really be considered a breach of trust by Colonel de Gaulle.

Consequently, I asked him to remove it and to substitute for it the text indicated in my letter of 5th September 1938.

It was on this condition that I authorized its publication, and I have not changed my mind.

Veuillez accepter, monsieur le Directeur. . . .'

The publishers answered with a polite negative, and there was nothing further the Marshal could do. De Gaulle treated the matter phlegmatically. 'The old man is losing his sense of proportion,' he declared with a touch of pitying indulgence. 'He gets very tired, and has lapses of memory more and more often – he isn't himself any more. Think of it, he's eighty-two. I have watched him since 1925, and alas, from that year, when he was only sixty-nine, it has been one long decline. He forgets what we decided by common agreement. And there are people round him busy working him up against me.'

One or two of the Marshal's intimates *were* indeed ready to pour oil on the flames. Being 'writers' themselves, they insisted that rules were rules, that an officer from the Staff College knew what his obligations were: to work for his chief, anonymously. Such was the invariable principle in staff-work, and why should de Gaulle be exempt?'

To which de Gaulle's supporters would retort: 'It wasn't a matter of staff papers in the proper sense. The Marshal's part in it has been acknowledged, so why the fuss?'

Pétain could never forgive de Gaulle. 'That turkey-cock,' he would explode when the name of his former favourite was

[1] As on p. 99.

mentioned: and often went on to make some unpleasant remark about Madame de Gaulle too – for the rupture between the two men extended to a family feud.

Disgusted at de Gaulle's vanity, Pétain did not seem aware of his own tendencies in that direction, and there were many who still thought him the most modest and forbearing of men. He often told his staff: 'I consider pride the most detestable and baneful of faults.' But he may have been in the same case as Marshal Lyautey, presented in a well-known anecdote. Anxious to make a confession before death, after thirty years cut off from God, the great colonizer of Morocco sent for a village priest. The holy man, much moved by the mission with which Heaven had entrusted him and not really knowing where to start, suggested to Lyautey that he should just go through the seven deadly sins – 'How about pride, for instance, Monsieur le Maréchal?' 'Oh no, not that one,' Lyautey answered. 'I've always underestimated myself.' And the story ends with the priest himself falling on his knees in prayer.

Certainly de Gaulle was distressed and shocked by the old man's decline. 'Nothing and nobody,' he observed, 'will stop the Marshal on the road to senile ambition. His pride is immense. He can no longer control the demons inside him, as he once could when he gave us an example of the man of character.' De Gaulle was fond of a saying of Chateaubriand's, which he quoted frequently in connection with the Marshal: 'Old age is a wreck.'

As to the book's own fortunes M. Daniel-Rops writes: 'It was not very successful when it appeared. The first edition was not exhausted when war was declared, although it had a good press, specially an "oral press" (I remember Paul Reynaud talking to me enthusiastically about it when I met him at lunch one day). Whether by accident (because they forgot it) or design, the Germans did not put it on their black list, and the edition was available until it sold out in 1943. It was reprinted during the autumn of 1944; and we may note that although the dedication had disappeared, the author had not changed a word in the portrait of Marshal Pétain which it contains, and which is among the finest things Charles de Gaulle ever wrote.'

13

Moi, Général de Gaulle . . .

During the 'phoney war' the postal censors through whose hands de Gaulle's correspondence passed were surprised by the large number of letters he addressed to political personalities. At the end of January 1940, still commanding the tank brigade of the Fifth Lorraine Army, he sent a memorandum through Generals Gamelin, Weygand and Georges, up to Daladier the Prime Minister and his old supporter Paul Reynaud, then Finance Minister. In this he stressed the part which planes could play in combined action with tanks, thus rectifying an error in his 1934 book *Vers l'armée de métier*. In 1934 he believed that 'the era of great conquests is over'; but from the brief campaign in Poland he had learnt more of the possibilities of total war.

The memorandum was not well received by the military. One high officer called him 'a colour-blind man talking of colours', and another asserted: 'France is not Poland. Here the armoured divisions will be nailed down at once.' A third pooh-poohed the idea of dive-bombers. 'They're like artillery batteries which can only fire one round.' De Gaulle fulminated against the 'imbeciles', 'idols of mediocrity', the 'tired old men of the Supreme War Council'.

He exploded with fury on receiving the order to detach a tank battalion from his brigade in order to protect the infantry. He had long proclaimed that 'to create a specialized corps is to tip your spear with fire. To dilute your mechanized forces is to put a pincushion there instead.' He agreed with Guderian, who recommended 'Mass your armour, don't scatter it'. He blamed the errors on the typical preconceived ideas taught in the Staff College; and as Guderian was to say later: 'We thought up a daring stroke which shattered the French with their methodical Cartesian brains!' The vanquished of 1918 became the victors through the techniques formerly tried out by their adversaries.

However, Paul Reynaud had become Prime Minister at the end of March 1940, and early in May, just before the German armies started their break-through on the Western front, de Gaulle wrote him an urgent letter:

'Events in Norway, following those in Poland, prove that military enterprises today are impossible except through mechanized forces. Operations may very soon be extended to Swedish territory, then to the Ukraine, then to Belgium, and finally to the West, whether against the Siegfried positions or the Maginot Line. If they are, the same fact will be proved once again.

'Now, the French Army is conceived, organized, armed and commanded, in opposition on principle to this law of modern war. Radical reform of the whole system is the most vital and immediate necessity. . . . But reform, on which victory depends, is becoming all the more difficult, the longer decisions and actions are postponed.

'The military establishment, let me repeat, are naturally and inherently conformist: they will not reform of their own accord. Reform is a matter of state, the first priority, and a statesman is needed to bring it about.

'Because of your post, your personality, and the position you have taken in the matter – taken for six years without any support from others – you are the only man who can carry out this task. I might add that by making it your government's most urgent business, you will change the atmosphere at home and abroad, gaining many immediate advantages. At present, the value of these ideas is proved every day that passes, every event that occurs – at the same time, alas, as the enemy puts them into practice.

'I could aspire to no greater honour than that of serving you in this vital work, as soon as you decide to undertake it . . .'

At the beginning of May he was still commanding the tank brigade. But on 15th May, before he had a chance to demonstrate his theories on the battlefield round Laon, he was appointed brigadier-general in command of the 4th Armoured Division, a completely improvised division without even a radio set at its headquarters and with some crews who had not been at its tanks more than three hours. Such a division, hurled into the Battle of France, admired and feared their commander, though without feeling any affection for him. But his prestige was overwhelming. 'He will dash to any point where things are going

103

badly. If an attack is to be launched, he listens to no objections, even though apparently well founded. He never tires, and you see him everywhere, that leather jacket and peaked helmet and the invariable cigarette. . . . He is not an easy man to be with. He's aloof and serious, doesn't talk much, and if questioned will shake off any tiresome questioner with "You don't ask a brigadier-general questions" or "Whether captain or major, you have the same opinion as your brigadier".' He showed amazing physical courage, and some even found him a shade histrionic, the way he refused to duck when bombs were dropping and blasted with his scorn those who flung themselves to the ground.

No doubt he knew fear inside, like anyone else under bombardment, but he maintained this impressive, Olympian calm. He was tough, ruthless, inhuman, letting nothing and nobody count for him outside the battle: he was the spirit of decision personified. Nobody criticized him – this statue of self-mastery inspired complete confidence.

But of course his division could not alter the course of events, although in the national disaster it showed itself *sans peur et sans reproche*, and at the end of May the Germans fled before it in disorder near Abbeville, abandoning all their baggage. On 7th June its commander departed, to enter the new Reynaud Government, and took his leave of the division with these words: 'As from today I am giving up the command of the 4th Armoured Division, in order to take up the duties of Under-Secretary of State for War. I wish to tell everyone, officers, N.C.O.s and privates, how proud I have been to have commanded them in the victorious battles fought by the division since 15th May. I am confident that the division will follow up its successes and will be a vital element in the final triumph of France.'

Privately his last words were: 'The only hope now is to buy Russian tanks. Provided we can hold out till they arrive.'

One of his colleagues in the government was Marshal Pétain, who had been appointed Minister of State. Pétain was not at all pleased to see him there, and took care to inform Reynaud of the business about the book *La France et son armée*. Paul Baudouin, Secretary of the War Council, confirms that Pétain disliked having de Gaulle take part in deliberations and that the two men scarcely spoke to each other when they met.

As a matter of fact, the Marshal rarely opened his mouth in

this government, any more than he had done in the military councils and committees he had served on during the past ten years. Daladier had 'noticed, since 1938 at least, that you could talk to the Marshal for half an hour or three quarters, but after that his mind would no longer follow'. Albert Lebrun, then President of the Republic, described the scene on 9th June, after General Weygand had given a full statement on the situation: 'Atmosphere of great gloom. Marshal Pétain said nothing. He seemed half asleep, exhausted. "Won't you give your opinion, Monsieur le Maréchal?" I asked. "These gentlemen are anxious to hear from you." "I have nothing to say," he replied.'

New blows from the German Army followed hard on each other. Among many other problems the government was beset with difficulties about communications. Tank units found it almost impossible to keep in touch, since radios broke down all too readily: while the German columns were happily signalling away to each other, often without code. A general commanding the 2nd Armoured Division caught an uncoded message: '*Die Richtung ist Calais, die Richtung ist Calais.*' Many of the French units, for want of any other equipment, returned to the old-fashioned system of signalling by flag. Even carrier-pigeons were still used in 1940, as they had been in the 1914–18 War: during the battle of Verdun one besieged commander had remained in communication with Pétain by carrier-pigeons throughout his heroic resistance.

The Marshal evidently kept his nostalgia for those days, as is shown by the following scene, recorded by M. Laurent-Eynac, then Air Minister: 'The President of the Republic turned to the Marshal as high military authority: "Monsieur le Maréchal, how do you explain this unprecedented disaster (the breakdown of communications)?" M. Lebrun had thus asked the key question. We became even more attentive. This question raised the whole strategic problem of the war. I can still hear the Marshal's answer: "Perhaps we have developed electrical transmissions too much. They have been cut. Perhaps we were too quick to give up the use of pigeons. Perhaps we ought to put a pigeonry in at base through which General Headquarters could remain in permanent communication." We looked at each other incredulously.'

However, the Marshal had seven stars, and nobody protested.

In any case, as has been said, he rarely contributed to a discussion, except for occasionally muttering gloomy prognostications; mostly he seemed in a state of torpor. De Gaulle certainly had no illusions left about him: 'The poor Marshal died in 1925. His body is there, his mind is gone. But the Victor of Verdun is in position. He will not let go. At his age you don't let go, do you? In fact he aims even higher. It's his crisis of second childhood.'

But at other times he would call the Marshal a traitor, his patriotic soul offended by any hint of defeatism. He went himself to the other extreme, even as he received shattering news through the long days and nights, telephoned in from a captain at headquarters. 'It's not true,' he would rage, on hearing that the Germans had made a new advance, had captured some new place. 'But this is my information, mon Général. I'm afraid it *is* true . . .' 'Be quiet, do you hear! You have no right to say that.' Shades of Foch, who used to insist: 'On principle I eliminate the hypothesis of defeat.'

At one point de Gaulle was confiding to his wife: 'If the government yields and sues for an armistice, I shall have no choice but to take a new field command and die at the head of my troops.' Madame de Gaulle had been evacuated to Brittany. He had given her letters from Gamelin, Pétain and military leaders, telling her to take them with her at all costs. 'Things are going very badly indeed,' he warned her that first fortnight in June. 'If the armistice is signed, take the boat with the children straight away. I shall not surrender.'

He had tried to induce Weygand and Reynaud to let him defend the Marne, the Seine or Paris with his armoured division. In the end Reynaud agreed to let him establish his defences round Bordeaux, and the seat of government was moved there. But he was now fighting virtually alone, Reynaud resigned, and the armistice was signed by the new 'chief of the French State', Marshal Pétain. Madame de Gaulle heard the news when she was out shopping in Brest. A few days later, on 18th June, her husband made his famous broadcast: 'I, General de Gaulle, at present in London . . .' – the first official appearance of *Moidegaulle*.

'I alone know what it cost me,' he said later of his decision to go to London. A few days after his arrival Maurice Schumann asked him: 'Did you tell yourself that even if all was lost duty was still duty and right was still right? That the last word would not remain with Germany, and the place of France must be secured in the allied camp at the final victory?' 'I told myself all of that and none of it,' de Gaulle answered. 'It was really more simple: I saw treason before my eyes, and my heart refused in disgust to recognize it as victorious.'

Certainly France was down for the moment, but he already foresaw Russia's entry into the war together with the United States. (As far back as January, when dining with Léon Blum at Reynaud's house, he had wondered about the possibility of the Germans attacking eastwards 'to reach Moscow'.) In June 1940 his vision was based on his remarkable grasp of history and of contemporary information as well. He knew his de Toqueville backwards, but had also read the files built up, partly through his work, at the National Defence headquarters: files showing the exact proportions of economic and industrial forces in the world. It should be said that there were others at the National Headquarters who expressed the same confidence in final victory, that France had lost a battle but not the war.

Among all the men of the forces who reached London at this time a very small number heard de Gaulle's appeal. They wanted to fight, obeying an elementary reflex: not to surrender. René Mouchotte, a future French wing-commander, wrote in his diary: 'Once I had given up all hope of soon seeing my poor mother again, of coming to her aid morally and materially in the terrible time she was going through, my heart became fuller every day, and the longing to teach the Boche a lesson gripped me like an obsession.' But while men such as Mouchotte took up arms in this spirit, de Gaulle gathered his inspiration from a personified France. His philosophy of history was like Michelet's: 'Britain is an empire, Germany is a race, France is a person.' De Gaulle would often talk of 'notre dame la France'.

Many people who dislike de Gaulle have said that he seized his chance in the country's misfortune. But apart from considerations of a moral order, which are always to some extent subjective, the evidence of history is all against this version. Privately and publicly de Gaulle did everything a man could do to get the leading politicians of the Third Republic to join him, in order to establish outside continental France a political power under whose authority he would place himself. He appealed to all the military leaders of the Empire; and one with great prestige, General Noguès, governor of Morocco, arbiter of the fate of Africa, declared himself 'red with shame' when it came to giving up the struggle, but saw no other choice.[1] And in any case almost all the leaders bowed before the Marshal's seven stars: a choice of honour there also, and of obedience.

Of the politicians, too, many judged that it was their constitutional duty to remain at the side of the President of the Republic. If de Gaulle seized his chance, they failed to seize it, in a tragic dilemma, for equally honourable reasons.

After this, however, de Gaulle was no longer on the level of brigadier-generals. He was Under-Secretary of State, and being the only representative of the French Government in London, he became the government. He took the mantle of France on himself – he *was* France. The *élite* had failed. 'The groundswell of History carries the ambitious leader forward. No false modesty. At the first flash of the swords, the old order of values is overthrown.' Here was the terrible crisis, and here the man of character who 'lifted the load with his own arms', who bore the country on his shoulders, to redeem its sins. The hero is always a redeemer, it is his glory and his virtue. Some said he took himself for St Joan, but he had long declared his faith that 'History is the meeting of an event and a will', had long felt it as his destiny 'to play a great part in great events' – to save his country.

Sixteen years before, he had written: 'The men of power mould themselves. Destined to leave their own mark . . . they construct, in the secrecy of their inner life, the edifice of their feelings and ideas and will. That is why in the tragic hours when the storm sweeps away conventions and habits, they alone remain erect and thereby essential. Nothing is of more importance to the state than to promote and encourage within its cadres the exceptional personalities who at such times will be its last resort and refuge.'

So de Gaulle held the power, which for the rest of the war he was never to let go: 'I, General de Gaulle, at present in London . . .' And to this power he attached the principle of legitimacy. This was no *folie de grandeur*, it was forced on him,

[1] See Appendix 1.

by almost instinctive logic, in confronting Marshal Pétain. Without legitimate power 'I de Gaulle' would be a mere rebel, and the whole system would collapse. As it was, there were even cases where British officers and officials encouraged French soldiers to go back to France or discouraged them from leaving it – and 'deserting their legal government'.

De Gaulle waited impatiently, with growing exasperation. He had expected to be joined by the men of the Staff College, by the members of the Académie, by France's military men and her Catholics. Apart from a handful of aristocrats, a nucleus of regular army officers, a few diplomats, officials, technicians, and some minor clergy, the Frenchmen who landed on British shores were mainly humble people, fishermen – and Jews fleeing from persecution and death: the France of the synagogues, not the cathedrals; of the métro, not the châteaux; the common herd whom de Gaulle had been inclined to despise. Those from whom he had hoped the most, had let him down.

A captain arrived with his arm in a sling. 'What am I going to do with a one-armed man?' de Gaulle growled at him as a greeting. When after this preamble the captain proclaimed his confidence in the future, de Gaulle railed against his countrymen, who were like sheep. 'Look at the few people who've come over to me. Ah, well, we'll see.' The last officers were hesitating on British soil: they found his attitude alarming and almost forbidding. 'Unless you join me, you're traitors,' he told them.

At Vichy some were predicting that Britain would 'have her neck wrung like a chicken within six weeks'. Even in Britain not everyone had Churchill's lion heart. Mr Maisky, then Soviet Ambassador to London, has given his impressions of an interview with Joseph Kennedy, American Ambassador (father of the future President), who was admittedly a notorious defeatist: 'He is in complete panic himself and regards Great Britain as utterly helpless against Germany. The war is irretrievably lost, and peace should be made with Hitler as soon as possible.'

De Gaulle, on the other hand, still foresaw the inevitability of the German defeat, in common with René Pleven and Jean Monnet and another handful of Frenchmen in London – and of a great Italian in exile, Carlo Sforza, who had written to the King of Italy on 30th May: '. . . The world will shake itself. In the long run the United States will enter the conflict. They cannot do otherwise, because there as well, Germany's ambition for world hegemony will have aroused too much fear. . . . America will astonish the world by military and economic preparations which will make everything fall before them in the end.'

And again: 'Where our Prime Minister is deceiving us, where you are deceiving yourselves, is in believing that Great Britain will imitate France and collapse after a brief resistance. No, England has her back to the wall: but not only will she resist, not only will she and her dominions astonish the world by their tenacity, but in London itself a resistance will be organized so heroic that the world will perhaps have never seen its like.'

De Gaulle indeed had a dazzling clairvoyance in grand strategy, although he was less far-sighted in technical matters. (For instance, he took no interest in the precious stocks of hydrogen, destined for use in atomic research, which were saved by Paul Reynaud and the Armaments Minister, M. Dautry.) But he gave a masterly assessment at this period of what could have been done and of future prospects in the war:

'While there was still time, the General Staff should have brought together our thousands of tanks and machine-guns scattered through the different armies, counter-attacked the Germans, disorganized their rear, cut their lines of communication; and at the same time prepared to withdraw to North Africa the 500,000 men who filled the depots, sent there the troops from Narvik and any other forces in Europe, diverted to Casablanca the transports of American equipment, preserved all our navy, merchant navy and air-force personnel, worked out a world strategy free from the narrow limits of the mother country. Pétain and Weygand were too old to imagine this overall conception. There's the tragedy: too old.

'Yet in this world conflict it is only a matter of time before the United States intervenes on Britain's side. As to the Russians, I prophesy they will not remain indifferent for long. It is highly probable, in fact, that they will join in before the Americans.'

He drew his prognosis from the facts of history and geography. Since Peter the Great, Russia had always tried to extend her sway over the Balkans. Germany was overrunning eastern Europe as well as western; she would want to secure the indispensable resources of the Caucasus and the Ukraine. The clash was inevitable. Communism was only 'the proletarian vehicle of eternal Russia'.

Free France derived from the grandeur that was Rome. De Gaulle was like a reincarnation of the Roman magistrate who taught his son: 'We and our ancestors have increased the power of Rome, by always putting our country before our fathers and our children.' The General admonished those who objected to his policy: 'You tell me that Frenchmen will go hungry and cold. What counts is *la Patrie*.' Where France was concerned, de Gaulle was certainly 'inhuman'. Yet even in his inhumanity he could inspire the people around him. 'He is mad, quite mad,' said one Free French colonel. 'But who cares? We follow him all the same. We would fire our last rounds with him.'

Free France was also an act of resistance directed against the Pétain régime, which de Gaulle made responsible for the defeat. At this period some quite prominent people among the Free French spoke on the B.B.C. to condemn the armistice, while at the same time recognizing certain merits in the régime the Marshal was establishing. On the subject of the Third Republic and Vichy, de Gaulle was to write in a statement published by the underground papers in June 1942: 'One régime abdicated in defeat, after becoming paralysed through abuse of liberty. Another, emerging from a criminal surrender, is exalting itself in personal power.' And in a speech made in July 1952 he said: 'Vichy had spoilt, among other things, the idea of a political revival, by caricaturing it.' At the time, however, in 1940, he told one questioner, admittedly a man of the right: 'There's some good at Vichy, except for the Germans.'

He showed interest in the principles of the 'national revolution', but mocked at the Marshal draping himself in the banner of Work, Family, Country. 'Country? The man who saved Verdun has become a traitor. Family? He never wanted children, he's an old libertine. Work? He lost the habit long ago.'

But if anyone, whether officer or civilian, criticized Pétain's role in the 1914–18 War, hoping thereby to curry favour with de Gaulle, he was quickly put in his place. And in private conversations, away from the public statements and vehement harangues demanded by the new leader's image, de Gaulle would speak about Pétain, to his earliest comrades of the Free French crusade, in less harsh terms:

111

'It is terribly sad. Old age is like a shipwreck, and with it weaknesses are monstrously magnified. Poor old Marshal! Once he led France's armies to victory, without even really expecting it, and here he is now, having led them to surrender. He's eighty-four. If only he had gone in time! But at his age you don't *go*, you hang on. He's in the grip of senile ambition. Pathetic outer shell of a past glory, he has been hoisted on the shield of defeat, for want of anyone better. He is deceiving the French people on the reality of the armistice. His character has been eaten away by the years. He's nothing now but a piece of dead wood. A Marshal of France turns himself into a grumbling old country constable.

'I have taken up a position against him. It was very hard for me, very hard. But it was a national necessity. "I weep for you and for myself, but it had to come to this," said Corneille's Curiace. Between France and the Marshal one could not hesitate.

'You see, Pétain is a great man – who died in 1925. He is now a sly old dotard dominated by selfishness. He will be able to tell any number of lies. He's an old trickster, believe me. I know him well. He loves power. He is flattered that they should have come and pulled him out of his retirement to put him back in the saddle. It's only human. But all the same he had been quietly preparing for it.

'His attitude is not as disinterested as he says. It is the attitude of an old man who wants to get the reins in his hands. And that's why he is dishonouring himself in this adventure. . . . Ah, but he won't get me, he won't get me.'

Sometimes the old admiration came through in his remarks. 'All his life Pétain has been kept back. On the eve of the 1914–18 War he did not support the ideas of the day favoured by the Staff College. He was the victim of an intellectual ostracism, as I was between the two wars. He had sacrificed his whole career to unorthodox teaching. The War Ministry refused to make him a brigadier-general. They said he hadn't got it in him. This was an abominable denial of justice. He has never forgotten the check to his proud ambition. Such feelings come to the surface in the long run. Ambition is the last passion of the old.

'Pétain was a pioneer in the use of artillery, as I was with tanks.

112

'His greatest fault is that he has always been inclined to a certain pessimism. And pessimism for a soldier is defeatism.'

He recalled the last stages of the Battle of France. 'The Marshal did not realize that in this war the Marne was the same scale as the Mediterranean. He completely misses the war's global aspect. He tells himself: we lost in 1870, we won in 1918, we have lost again in 1940. This is the third round, we'll wait for the fourth.

'His perspectives do not go beyond the traditional Franco-German antagonism. He sees the past wars being repeated. On top of that – sprinkle a mixture of social conservatism and the fear of communism; and you have Vichy.

'Ah, it's one thing to be defeated, and another thing to be defeated in certain conditions.'

He realized the personal element in Pétain's attitude to himself. 'He has never forgiven me for putting my name to *La France et son armée*, although in fact I was its author from first to last line. I take back nothing of my praise of Pétain in that book. But consider the chapter carefully in its whole context. I was essentially bringing out Pétain's role in the 1917 crisis. He really was the great man necessary for one year: 1917. For 1916, was he the true victor of Verdun? I don't know. But those who criticize him so readily from a military standpoint couldn't hold a candle to the Pétain of the great days.

'He avoided disaster in 1917. He saved France. Afterwards I showed how Foch was in 1918 the man of victory. I haven't a comma to change.

'Today, here is the Marshal in the purple of surrender. If he had been still himself, he would never, I am sure, have accepted this disgrace. He is no longer himself. He is no longer in possession of his powers. In the country's most disastrous days, he displays merely his limitless pride.'

In France's greatest national tragedy de Gaulle was separated from Pétain by emotions which Racine once expressed:

'Oh, I have loved him too well not to feel hate for him now.'

14

Moi, Philippe Pétain . . .

On 18th June 1940 the most famous living Frenchman was Marshal Pétain. He had his feet on the ground, while de Gaulle's head was in the air. He gave Frenchmen hope, while de Gaulle gave hope to France. France for de Gaulle was an entity, for Pétain it was the land. Perhaps he still felt in his hand the plough his ancestors had wielded. To emigrate would be a form of nomadism which was beyond his understanding. His patriotism was earthy. When you leave the familiar fields at that age, who can be sure of seeing them again? An old man rarely agrees to leave his little piece of land; Pétain's piece of land was France. 'If we leave France,' he told General Laure, 'we shall never come back to it.' At forty-nine it was easier to be de Gaulle than Pétain at eighty-four: at that age it is hard to see a distant wood for the mass of trees.

The plebiscite was held, and 80 per cent to 90 per cent approved of the armistice. 'Tomorrow morning,' wrote the playwright Jean Giraudoux, 'I shall have to change my will. I had a great heritage to leave my son: a country which was one of the most beautiful in Europe, a nation bright with glory. This evening before I go to sleep – for even tonight one goes to bed and to sleep – I must put in some special clauses.'

Pétain addressed the country, and produced striking phrases and slogans, which became famous: 'I make France the gift of my person . . . I hate the lies which have done you so much harm.' (For four years, at Bordeaux and then at Vichy, the Marshal's speeches were always drafted by others. According to his custom, he revised the text and made it more concise. The 'writers' soon picked up the Marshal's 'style'.) As to the content, the few officers who had been long on his staff murmured sceptically: 'Hm, we have never seen the Marshal make anybody the gift of his person.' Was it the cry of supreme sacrifice or of extreme pride?

In 1918 the Marshal had the joy of writing the magnificent words 'closed owing to victory'; he had borne the victor's cross of honour. Now he bore the cross of the vanquished. A quarter of an hour before the official request for an armistice the mask of impassiveness was lifted, and he groaned to Paul Baudouin, the Foreign Minister: 'It's appalling. . . . I who commanded the French armies to final victory. . . . Ah, where is that final order of the day to the troops, "You have covered your flags with immortal glory"?'

But like de Gaulle, Pétain had read the maxims of Colonel Quinton, the philosopher soldier,[1] and could quote on his side: 'The hero is willing to suffer; he is proud of suffering. . . . Heroes love defeat, because it offers them great duties and gives them the initiative in overcoming it.' So the Marshal would be the Redeemer, redeeming 'the sins of the Popular Front'. 'How could you expect Richelieu's policies with Léon Blum's army?' was the sort of remark heard in his circle. At times he even seemed to take a bitter pleasure in playing the martyr hero. After his summons by the National Assembly he was taking his leave of General Franco, who has recorded his 'unique chance of witnessing the great soldier's agony of heart':

'"My country has been defeated, and they are calling on me to make the peace and sign the armistice. You were right. Here is the work of thirty years of Marxism. They are calling on me to take over the nation, and I have come to bid you farewell." The old Marshal's eyes were blurred with tears. A loyal friend's advice came to my lips: "Don't go, Marshal. Make your age an excuse. Let those who have lost the war liquidate it now and sign the armistice. You are the victorious soldier of Verdun: don't give your name to what others have lost." "I know, mon Général, but France calls me and I owe it to France. It is perhaps the last service I shall be able to render her." He embraced me with great emotion and left for the sacrifice.'

'They only call me in disasters,' sighed Pétain at Bordeaux. Yves Bouthillier, Minister of Finance in the new government, noted: 'Like a king on coronation day the Marshal ascended to power, surrounded by respect and gratitude, invested with an immense authority, acknowledged even by those he was replacing in the management of affairs.'

'Moi, Philippe Pétain, Maréchal de France . . .' General

---

[1] *Maximes sur la Guerre*, published in June 1930, formed part of de Gaulle's inspiration for *Le Fil de l'épée*.

Héring asked his chief if one might congratulate him. The Marshal took aside his old friend from the Staff College and told him: 'Only as a martyr.'

To sign the armistice, Hitler's plenipotentiaries met those of France in the forest of Compiègne at Rethondes, on the same spot and in the same railway coach as that in which Foch had handed his terms to the Germans in 1918. General Weygand confided privately that the Marshal's attitude reminded him of Erzberger's, the leader of the German delegation in 1918. 'He behaved with dignity, but you could somehow see in his face a certain satisfaction, as if he were telling himself: they came for me, and no other, in the country's distress. I personify my country.'

At seventy-eight Pétain had become, briefly, a Cabinet Minister; at eighty-two an Ambassador; and now at eighty-four Deputy Prime Minister, then Prime Minister, Chief of State, and – crown of crowns – Saviour of the Country. Here was the idol of France. Foch had robbed him of the supreme command, but here he was now, at an even higher peak, holding all the commands, civil as well as military, with the halo of a great mission. I alone can save something, he thought. With my prestige I alone can take a stand against the Germans and spare my country the worst. He believed himself an infallible judge of the situation; in consequence he could and must begin an exciting new career.

The *éminence grise*, Senator Lémery, came to join Pétain. He still remembered his last interview with the Marshal that January, and the words 'I don't want power at any price': he was very surprised to learn that the Marshal had now accepted it. Lémery was appointed Colonial Minister, and faced the photographers at the side of the Marshal, who on one occasion whispered to him: 'You see: these affairs start with flashlights firing at you and end up with machine-guns doing it.' 'I shall be shot,' Pétain soon began prophesying. 'They will put all the blame on me.' A high official claims to have heard him declare: 'In sacrifice one must be able to face even the risk of personal dishonour.' But he forgot that if he was personifying France, the dishonour would also be France's.

In practice he seemed to envisage events developing very slowly, whereas General Bineau, his chief military secretary,

analysed the situation in these terms: 'There are only two alternatives: either Great Britain still has a very powerful air force, in
which case the British attitude is ignoble: they hid their reserves
from us and are going to negotiate a compromise peace behind
our backs. Or else, they have nothing – as I believe – and by the
15th October His Majesty's flag will no longer be waving over
the Tower of London. England is done for.'

Pétain said little on this subject. He seemed to attach no
importance to Reynaud's warning that Hitler was a new Genghis
Khan. For him Hitler was a new Bismarck, one Chancellor
succeeding another. He feared the Soviet Union, whereas de
Gaulle with his world view saw it as the representative of
eternal Russia, an indispensable ally in defeat, to whose ideology
he was indifferent. Pétain was expecting the Americans, as in the
First World War; but with memories of that war he carried on
an old grudge against the British, reproaching them for having
withdrawn their groups too quickly. De Gaulle, on the other
hand, approved Churchill's action in recalling the British
fighter squadrons in preparation for subsequent resistance.

In privy council Pétain spoke of de Gaulle's decision in these
terms: 'He has tried a big bluff. Politics aren't like that. One
must look at events, sound them out, understand them. But to
take up a position out of the blue, as if one were above the
battle – it may succeed, and if it does, all right. But suppose it
doesn't? It's a gamble – and you can't gamble here.'

His prognosis to Lémery was: 'The Americans won't be ready
for four years. It's going to be hard. We shall have to pocket our
pride. Our contract with the Germans is for "present circumstances". Well, the victor always calls the tune.' In fact he was
reverting to his method, which had once caused so many con-
troversies at the Staff College, of pragmatic adaptation to circumstances. He had no firm line of policy except for two fixed
ideas: 'I shall never declare war on the British. I shall never
detach myself from the Americans.' The adaptation, of course,
produced its own principles: 'On the sea there is an ebb and
flow. One must know how to wait. The Germans reproach me
for keeping afloat. I am building a raft – so that France may keep
afloat and survive. . . . What is to be done? To rob Germany of
the fruits of victory without a clash! To endure, brace ourselves,
hoping to emerge with the least damage possible. It is no

solution to abandon the national territory. Forty million Frenchmen must have the chance to live.'

How hard it is to liberate oneself from the past! Pétain was led to the Armistice of 1940 by the Armistice of 1918. At the end of the First World War he was bitterly disappointed when Foch gave the Germans an armistice, instead of completely crushing the German Army. If Foch had listened to *him*, 'there would have been no Hitler to come and tell the tale that the German Army was never defeated.' He often declared: 'November 11th was a day of mourning in which we lost the war!' Now he hoped that the 1940 armistice would produce the same effects the opposite way, at the expense of the Germans.

At Bordeaux he told his colleagues: 'The harshest blow we can deliver Hitler is to sign the armistice, while preserving our fleet and our lines of communication with the Empire.' And again in the same sense: 'The Germans are making a mistake by giving us an armistice. Hitler wants to wipe out the German humiliation of 1918. He wants his revenge for the armistice railway coach. Well, that Rethondes coach will save us.' He seemed satisfied to escape total collapse, whereas in the Rethondes terms the German general staff was merely trying to prevent the French fleet regrouping in British ports and Africa breaking away.

As to the latter point, the Marshal had returned from his post in Spain convinced that the Spanish Army, exhausted by the civil war, would be unable to oppose the German divisions should Hitler try to cross to the peninsula. 'If it wished,' he said, 'the *Wehrmacht* could celebrate Christmas at Casablanca, Algiers, Tunis, and perhaps even at Dakar and Cairo.'

De Gaulle was very often in the Marshal's thoughts. He expressed the same ideas to his colleagues as he had done shortly before the armistice to General Spears, who was to take the future leader of the Free French to London in his plane: 'He thinks he knows everything about the mechanics of war. His vanity has made him believe that the art of war has no secrets for him. He might have invented it. I know everything about him. He served for a time on my staff and wrote a book – at least I explained to him how he should write it. I gave him the main lines for it, then I corrected it. In fact I annotated it with my own hand. When he published it, he did not even mention my contribution to the book's construction. He is not only vain, but also ungrateful. There's nothing surprising in that, for he gives the impression of looking down on everybody.'

Then the Marshal might remember happier things. 'Think of it. I am godfather to his son. I saw the young lieutenant arrive at the 33rd Infantry Regiment. . . . I know his qualities better than anyone. I have brought them out in my notes. He is very much the individualist, very ambitious. He also has a strong character, and a remarkable intelligence. I was the one who insisted on his lectures being given at the Staff College. I said: "I will preside over them. All the staff and all the college will be obliged to attend." He was the most brilliant officer of his intake . . . and he was not treated as he deserved. He should have passed out first. I wanted to give him public evidence of my esteem. In the lecture-hall he really cut a fine figure, resting his hands on his sword, standing like a statue. Oh, he knew his stuff all right. He was an officer I liked and admired.

'But there you are, he recognizes no limits to his ambition. He will do harm with the best intentions.'

More often, however, Pétain kept harking back obsessively to the book. 'He had prepared it for me, but brought it out under *his* name. It's not right. He shouldn't have acted like that towards me, who had been his chief. It was disrespectful. His individualism was already getting out of hand. . . . The book ought to have appeared with the preface I myself prepared for it. . . . He is mad with ambition. It was quite unprincipled. I had given him the framework, corrected the chapters. . . . Oh, yes, he'll give me a bad time if he can. He would be quite capable of getting me court-martialled. He doesn't like me, because he took offence over that manuscript.'

At other times he would change his mind again, and say: 'De Gaulle's the better man. We shall come together again. I shall have a reconciliation with him when the right moment comes. I shall settle things at the last minute. . . . I am his son's godfather. What a brain he has . . . and what a memory! Poincaré's the only other man I can think of who had a memory like his. He writes his own speeches, but never reads them. His brain photographs all the pages.'

As evidence that the Marshal retained some of his old affection, he gave Major Bonhomme, his aide, a highly confidential

119

mission: to find out whether Madame de Gaulle was in France with her children, and if so whether she was getting her husband's assignment of pay. In fact she had already come to England from Brittany during June.

His admiration for de Gaulle's memory was heightened by awareness that he was losing his own. In his good hours he still showed remarkable lucidity, which contributed to the illusion that he was lucid all the time. Externally too, he remained impressive, walking like a young man; his face was kept youthful by light massage. 'That's the terrible thing,' groaned General Bineau. 'The Marshal's all the more dangerous because he looks as if he could climb stairs four at a time.'

Bonhomme confided in distress: 'It may last for years like this, but the Marshal won't survive it. He can't carry the load any more. He used to be a superman who could work fourteen or eighteen hours a day – until he was sixty. At seventy-five he worked four or five hours a day, at eighty – three or four hours, at eighty-four. . . . Until he was eighty he signed documents in bed but took responsibility. Since then . . . he'll be a mere ornament. It's what Laval wants. . . . It's incredible Frenchmen still go on thinking of the good old Marshal, when he's no longer "good old" anything as *they* mean it. As the years pass, disasters slide over him. But then that may be a strong point. Only people who have had a very old man living with them can understand. Alas, the Marshal won't recover. He's too old.'

On 19th June at Bordeaux Bonhomme had given this warning to one of the Vice-Premiers, Camille Chautemps: 'I know that your policy, which is so far also the Marshal's, is to bring about the union of all Frenchmen and to maintain our republican institutions. Well, I have come to warn you that you are going adrift. You are acting towards the Marshal as you would with an ordinary political leader. You forget that he is a Marshal of France, accustomed to being flattered and having a large staff round him, that he is also an old man, rather weak, and sensitive to the influence of those who know how to work their way into his intimate circle.

'Other men, for aims opposed to yours, are working on him as you have omitted to do. If you don't react, he will soon let himself be dragged towards a policy you will not be able to accept.

'I believe you may still suceed, however. You must have

personal relations with the Marshal, friendly and trusting; you should go to his private residence every day, so that he learns the news from you and that in all circumstances his opinion may be influenced by yours. You must also place yourself near him in cabinet meetings, so that you can pass on remarks he has failed to understand, etc. All this is perhaps abnormal, but that's how things are. One must have a personal influence on the Marshal at all times. The fate of your policy depends on this.'

But what was the Marshal's own policy? French people every-where, in the occupied and unoccupied zones, in the forbidden eastern and northern zones, in the annexed provinces of Alsace and Lorraine, in the prisoner-of-war camps, those inside France and those outside it in temporary exile, whispered a comforting slogan: 'The Marshal is not saying all he thinks, and he doesn't believe all he says.'

15

Growing Pains for the Free French

De Gaulle's mother, who was dangerously ill, had been evacuated to Brittany. When she learnt of her son's departure for England, she was stirred deeply but showed little surprise. The watchers round her bedside noticed that her spasms stopped when she listened to her son talking on the radio from London. On 26th June the hour of the curfew brought her the well-known voice:

'Monsieur le Maréchal, here is a French soldier speaking to you from across the channel. Yesterday I heard your voice, which I know well, and with some emotion I listened to what you told the French people in order to justify what you have done.'

For a traditionalist family there was something inherently shocking about rebelling against a Marshal of France; yet she saw her son's decision at once as in conformity with the purest patriotism. She had never forgotten her despair as a child in 1870 on seeing her parents in tears at the news that Bazaine had surrendered to the Germans at Metz with 140,000 men.[1] She did not accept defeat. A close friend wrote of her at this time:

'With the rather dour manner of a woman from the Nord, she had a very ardent spirit and a passionate faith. Whole-hearted in her convictions, she sustained them with a fervour which some-times almost carried her away. She rejected all compromises and would go through martyrdom to defend the truth. In some respects she was a thirteenth-century character. Transposed to our times, her idealism took the form of a defence against all assaults on the Church and the Country. Catholic, monarchist, patriot, she loved France with all her being.'

Early in July she told a friend: 'You mustn't believe all they tell you. My son is a good Frenchman.' On the 13th she heard his words for the last time:

'Although this *Quatorze Juillet* is a day of mourning for our country, it should also be a day of underlying hope. Yes, victory

[1] De Gaulle's *Memoirs*, Vol. 1.

will be won. And it will be won, I guarantee, with the aid of France's arms.'

Three days later Henri de Gaulle's widow died. Her last thoughts went to the son who had just proclaimed on her behalf: 'I have picked up the broken sword.' As a boy Charles had gone with his parents to visit a war memorial to men who had died in the 1870 War (which included members of the family). He had deeply absorbed the noble epitaph carved in the stone: 'The sword of France, broken in their valiant hands, will be forged anew by their descendants.'[1]

She died too soon to learn of her son's condemnation to death, pronounced by Vichy's military tribunal at Clermont-Ferrand. When this was mentioned to Pétain in private, he said: 'A mere routine measure – and one which won't be carried out. It's essential to stop dissident movements, discipline demands it.' As for Laval, who saw himself as a new Talleyrand, he remarked: 'Condemning de Gaulle to death is the greatest service you could do him.'

In London the Free French Intelligence learnt that it was 'a pure formality', although some people at Vichy and Paris were firmly resolved to carry out the sentence should the opportunity come. De Gaulle himself wrote in the margin of a note to the future chief of intelligence, Colonel Passy: 'I consider this action by the men of Vichy to be null and void. They and I will have a settling after victory.'

Pétain had called de Gaulle's decision a gamble, but for de Gaulle himself it was an act of faith: faith that the war would be won, with a realization that it might be won without France. He made, in fact, a remarkably accurate forecast of events to come:

'The Germans will sooner or later be drawn into invading the part of France which for the time being is still allegedly "free". This will be a vital necessity for their defence, because the war will become world-wide, and North Africa is bound to turn into a strategic centre so important that both sides will do everything to gain control of it.'[2]

In another speech, however, he claimed that the armistice would surrender intact 'our fleet, planes, tanks, arms, for the enemy to use them against our own allies'. But on this point he

[1] Georges Cattaui, *Charles de Gaulle.*
[2] Colonel Passy, *Souvenirs.*

was wrong: Vichy was never to surrender the fleet. Indeed on 25th June the Marshal had proclaimed in his quavering voice: 'At least honour is safe. Nobody will make use of our planes and our fleet.'

Admiral Muselier, first Commander of the Free French air and sea forces, commented at a later date: 'We sincerely believed that one of the clauses in the armistice envisaged surrendering the fleet to the Germans, because the terms of the agreement which had been communicated to us indicated that naval units were to be disarmed in their port of commissioning, and almost all had been commissioned in the northern ports, occupied by the Germans.' But in practice, thanks to an oral amendment obtained by General Huntziger, head of the French delegation to the Wiesbaden armistice commission, the disarming process took place in the ports of the south. There was nothing absurd, though, in suspecting secret clauses to the armistice, since without any agreement the frontier posts were already set up again on the 1914 boundaries.

This belief by the Free French may have been one of the causes of the incident at Oran in Algeria, when the British gave an ultimatum to the French warships, and on the ultimatum's rejection sank or damaged several ships. After the war Admiral Menzies, Chief of the British Intelligence Service, stated: 'We had false information which said the French fleet was to be ceded to the Germans. Don't forget, also, that the French in London had helped to create a particular state of mind, by declaring that the fleet was going to fall into German hands.'

At the time de Gaulle was furious. He asked Admiral Muselier to warn the Admiralty: 'Unless you cease firing at once, all French volunteers will leave for Pondichéry' (India) 'or Saint-Pierre and Miquelon' (islands in the Atlantic). And to Colonel Passy he raged, in accents more like those of Admiral Darlan: 'These crazy English, these criminals! They are shedding French blood. They still find means of rubbing in our capitulation. They can't resist their desire to humiliate France's naval power.' Yet he recognized in the last resort that the British, planning for war to the bitter end, were right to take steps against Germany gaining control of the French fleet.

There were many sacrifices he had to accept for the fulfilment of his mission, the mission of 'assuming the mantle of France at the worst moment of her history'. He had to rebuild France, but first had to build up his own reputation. 'Churchill will launch me like a new brand of soap,' he once observed – the cynical realist taking over from the romantic patriot. He also realized very quickly that in face of the Salazar-type régime established by Pétain, his support and authority would come from the people, from 'the France of the métro'; nor did he think the Marshal had any hope of developing his 'national revolution' under the heel of the occupier – that was pure illusion.

The appeal of 18th June had originally been to members of the forces; but 'more and more civilians responded, and we were still the only people acting in an organized manner; so we found wider responsibilities coming to us'.

This is amplified in a subsequent letter of his to President Roosevelt: 'We have been told that we should have nothing to do with politics. If that means it is not our business to take part in the party struggles of the past or to dictate one day the country's institutions, we have no need at all of such recommendations, for it is indeed our principle to abstain from such pretensions. But we do not shrink from the word *politics*, if it means rallying for the war not only a few troops but the French nation, or if it means upholding the interests of France with our allies, while defending them against the enemy.'

De Gaulle meant also to be the boss. His second day in London Vice-Admiral Muselier (three stars) accepted orders from de Gaulle (two stars), who had admittedly been recognized by the British cabinet forty-eight hours before as head of the Free French. Muselier has later stated: 'I did not want to take advantage of my superiority of rank vis-à-vis an acting brigadier-general; it would have weakened the war effort of the newly born Free France.'

One of the most brilliant trainees at the Naval College, Muselier was an extremely brave and resolute sailor with wide experience on the high seas, the obvious man to command the Free French sea and air forces, which were much larger than the land ones. It was he who found the Free French their symbol, the Croix de Lorraine (in memory of his father who came from that province), originally a sign for painting on ships and planes; although de Gaulle in his *Memoirs* mistakenly attributed its invention to Admiral d'Argenlieu.

De Gaulle was equally authoritarian with his Intelligence chief, Colonel Passy. The latter was worried about the state of morale among the Free French, who had for weeks or months been without news of their families, and suggested that de Gaulle might address a few words of encouragement to them. 'Directly I had finished speaking,' Passy recalls, 'the General got up, his face set and hard, and said to me: "I don't need any lessons from a whippersnapper like you".'

In de Gaulle's eyes the war was indivisible. A reserve officer, a member of the nobility, was expressing his scruples on the eve of the Dakar expedition: he was afraid Frenchmen might fire on other Frenchmen. 'What did you come to London for,' de Gaulle demanded scornfully 'if you weren't ready for civil war?' In his cold reasoning there was no real distinction between civil war and any other sort – there was simply war, a conflict where sentiment was out of place. There were the good and the bad, with nothing in between. In war the country knew nothing of pardon and pity. Had a sovereign ever hesitated to open fire when a province was to be reconquered? Did human blood count, when France's blood was flowing?

In agreement with Churchill, de Gaulle hoped to establish himself at Dakar. There were two reasons in favour of the plan. First, as the leader of Free France, he hated living in a foreign country; he did not want to be an *émigré* who on the day of victory must return on the British and Anglo-American bandwagon.

But of course it was also part of the grand strategy. To get a footing at Dakar, capital of the black African empire, would mean that France was coming back into the war, and was bringing her British ally bases of vital importance in the battle of the Atlantic. If Dakar fell, the rest of the empire might very well follow suit sooner or later. Starting from French West Africa and French Equatorial Africa, a joint operation could be mounted for Morocco, Algeria and Tunisia.

The Vichy Government, however, learning of the project, sent three cruisers from Toulon, which were unaccountably allowed to get through the Straits of Gibraltar, and eventually arrived at Dakar. On 23rd September Free French forces were sent to land at Dakar, with the following order from Admiral Muselier: 'I forbid you to fire on Frenchmen. I would rather have you martyrs than murderers.' But the batteries of the port, remaining faithful to Vichy, opened fire on the Free French emissaries as their boat was withdrawing. They also fired on de Gaulle's warships and on British ships standing by to come to his aid. Despite a warning three French submarines attacked the British ships, and as a result two were sunk. But Free French forces were unable to make a landing, and when it became obvious that Dakar would not fall without a major operation of war, the British decided on political grounds to discontinue hostilities.

De Gaulle was in despair, even confessing to one of his companions: 'I went through a terrible time. I thought of blowing out my brains.' Meanwhile at Vichy Pétain was saying: 'After a blow like that, de Gaulle will be damned lucky if he keeps any credit with the British.' (Before giving the order for resistance, the Marshal had heard with interest a suggestion from Charles Trochu: 'Here's a magnificent chance for a change of policy: give Dakar up to General de Gaulle.' He even asked Trochu for a written report, but did not follow the suggestion up.)

The world could not help registering the loyalty shown to the Marshal at Dakar, and de Gaulle's lack of success. In the bitterness and humiliation of defeat, compelled to remain on foreign soil, de Gaulle, although outwardly polite, became more irritable, touchy and arrogant than ever, and soon acquired a reputation among the British as an impossible person to deal with. General Spears's wife, the novelist Mary Borden, who mounted a hospital unit for the Free French forces, wrote of him: 'I believe pride is the basis of his character. I think he felt the dishonour of France as few men can feel anything, and that he had literally taken on himself the national dishonour, as Christ according to the Christian faith took on himself the sins of the world.'

There were other resemblances to the Christian faith, based on de Gaulle's own hard-and-fast alternatives of good and bad. For instance, an emissary of Major Loustaunau-Lacau came from Vichy, via Casablanca, Tangier, Gibraltar. He and Major Bonhomme were at this time convinced that Pétain and de Gaulle would sooner or later be reconciled, in view of their past relations. The gist of the letter was 'Bravo, keep it up. Here we are doing what we can with the Marshal. We are building up our resistance. We are trying to take advantage of the situation as best we can.' De Gaulle gave the emissary a letter, which on the subject of the Marshal said: 'Philippe has the rope round his neck which he put there himself.' But he told the emissary: 'He who is not with me is against me. You must join those who obey *me*.'

The Marshal too could quote the scriptures in a somewhat exorbitant way: 'De Gaulle proclaims the illegitimacy of my government. *There* is his original sin.' But de Gaulle asserted: 'It is I who embody legitimacy, it is I who have brought away with me the treasure of French sovereignty.'

Clearly legitimate power is a concept with fluid boundaries: it can authorize generous revolutions against powers established in strict legality. For de Gaulle it wiped out the act of rebellion and justified the resistance of 18th June. The Vichy régime was illegitimate because it was only there at the enemy's discretion. 'There cannot be a legitimate government which has ceased to be independent. Genuine legitimacy is a rejection of the occupier's yoke.' And again: 'There is no longer a truly French Government in existence. . . . The establishment at Vichy, which claims to bear that name, is unconstitutional.'[1]

To which the Marshal retorted: 'Legitimacy, constitutionality, *c'est moi*. The process of my attaining power was legal and I gained the assent of the overwhelming majority of French people. Quote me a régime which enjoys a more striking legitimacy.'

Basically, Pétain could very well accept that de Gaulle carried on the fight against the enemy, but he should 'put himself at the head of a Legion, like Garibaldi. He should limit himself to fighting the Boches. But there you are – always his terrific pride.' Garibaldi – de Gaulle: on such terms Pétain was quite disposed to cry '*Vive de Gaulle*'. But that '*le petit* Gaulle' should claim to have risen to supreme power, should identify himself with France – never!

And de Gaulle himself said 'Never!' to British suggestions that French volunteers should be enrolled in His Majesty's forces, with an epaulette saying 'France'. France, reduced to a piece of cloth on a battledress: what a humiliating, heartbreaking idea!

[1] Manifesto delivered by de Gaulle from Brazzaville, Oct. 1940.

16

A Banner and a Cross

'I am not your successor,' the Marshal told Albert Lebrun, the last President of the Third Republic, 'since a new régime is beginning. Monsieur le Président, the painful moment has come. You have served the country well, but the Assembly's vote creates a new situation.'

At the official audience when Lebrun took his leave, he was sent packing in a few minutes. 'It was very brief,' Pétain told Paul Baudouin, the Foreign Minister. Lebrun in fact became one of his *bêtes noires* ('He was responsible for the disaster, I showed him the door'), along with the radical and socialist schoolteachers 'who flouted patriotism', with Herriot and Blum, with the Third Republic in general, with the parties in particular ('These gentlemen are incapable of bringing off anything but defeats'), and with members of parliament ('They infuriate me with their chatter').

On the form of the new State the Marshal did not have very firm ideas. To General Serrigny he appeared 'very much attracted to American institutions.' To Marcel Peyrouton, Minister of the Interior, he said: 'Let us apply presidential government to France. The head of State and the head of the government must be one and the same person. A supreme court. The legislature must not leave its strict preserves: voting on the budget and the main laws, examining major problems after the government has declared its position.'

Discussion on such points, however, remained somewhat academic, since his régime was always a personal and authoritarian one. Even before Lebrun's departure, Pétain had addressed the country as Prime Minister without submitting his speeches to the head of State. Yet he maintained that he had no dictatorial ambitions. 'Do you see me as Caesar at my age?' he asked, and told a delegation of senators: 'I don't want to be a dictator or a Caesar.'

Laval, who had done much to bring him to power, began to change his tune. Warned by an ambassador that the Marshal detested him, Laval answered: 'Don't I know it! The old man has acquired a taste for power and is clinging to it. If I had known that, I would have called upon Marshal Franchet d'Esperey instead.' (Considering his views, the latter would certainly have refused.)

General Weygand, Minister of National Defence, was furious at the government accepting breaches of the armistice agreements. 'Don't forget we have been beaten,' Laval told him. 'I know that better than anyone, alas,' Weygand retorted. 'But there are different ways of accepting defeat. *You* wallow in defeat like a dog rolling in muck.' 'Oh, Weygand!' Pétain protested at the unparliamentary language.

With very rare exceptions major questions of general policy were not debated in the cabinet. On many occasions members of the government learnt of important decisions from the papers. The Marshal presided over cabinet meetings with a distrust of long arguments: 'The cabinet is not for debates. Everyone has to put his case in turn.'[1]

Monsieur Peyrouton was hesitant about accepting the post of Minister of the Interior. Looking at him with those cold and steely blue eyes, the Marshal said: 'We are at war. That's enough, you have only to obey. If I were told tomorrow to wash the dishes, I would wash the dishes. Go and sit in your place.'

On the Marshal's cabinet methods, Peyrouton has recorded: 'He never let the subject be changed. We did not speak on matters other than those of our department, unless he specially asked our opinion. But he never asked me mine, for instance, on foreign policy.'

His ministers were like staff officers. After a cabinet meeting he would sometimes summon one of them, hand him a law produced by one of his personal advisers and simply tell him: 'Here, sign this draft; it must be sent to the *Gazette*.'[2]

His preference was for privy council meetings, in his office at eleven in the morning, with the principal ministers present, Foreign Minister, Chancellor, Defence, etc. 'During all the time I was a minister,' says Admiral Auphan, 'I never heard the Marshal make a statement in the cabinet on general policy. But we did consider the world situation in the privy council. I pre-

[1] Vice-Admiral Fernet, *Aux côtés du Maréchal Pétain*.
[2] Robert Aron, *Histoire de Vichy*.

sented the reports of our naval attachés, and was always repeating to him: "the game is not over. Taking into account the
production in United States dockyards, the decisive stage will
come in 1943. At that time we must be ready to reverse our
policies."

'. . . Obviously, the Marshal did not always grasp very clearly
the world view of the conflict; he was living a lot in the past, no
doubt. He saw the United States coming into the war, but as in
1917, without appreciating America's industrial potential. I must
not exaggerate, though. For most of the time I felt I was talking
to someone who listened to me, not to a failing old man. He
followed me well enough in my statements of the situation,
though sometimes one had methodically to recapitulate the
same arguments.'

On the other hand, Charles Pomaret, the Minister of Labour,
was 'not absolutely sure on reflection that Pétain had fully
grasped the distinction between armistice and surrender.' At one
point in June 1940 indeed, Pétain accepted the principle that
while *he* stayed in France, part of the government should leave
for North Africa, armed with delegated powers; arrangements
for their going were made, but cancelled. At the cabinet meeting
on 15th June his attitude was certainly ambiguous: Pomaret had
the impression at first that he was going to ask for an armistice
'on the military level, army to army, which would not necessarily
mean its acceptance by the whole government'.

What were the Marshal's real feelings? Deep down he had
only one wish, Germany's defeat. In private he spoke of the
Boches, and confided to General Boucherie: 'The swine aren't
going to win the war, all the same.' He sometimes repeated 'We
got them before, we'll get them again.' He called Hitler a
'savage', a 'dangerous mediocrity'. His only real interest left was
France itself; for the rest he showed increasing indifference to
world events, the hazards of war and human suffering. The first
measures against the Jews were taken, and when General
Mordacq, once a principal private secretary to Clemenceau,
came to see him – 'Monsieur le Maréchal, you are dishonouring
our uniform' – Pétain told him to go to hell. Political refugees,
and also ninety ex-Legionnaires of German origin, were handed
over to the Germans. Foreigners who had enlisted as volunteers
during the battle of France were interned in labour camps.

131

Pétain had met Hitler and actually shaken hands with him; but for Pétain this meant little enough. He told a friend afterwards: 'If the people who think we might surrender the fleet knew how determined I am to scuttle it, they would be reassured.' Indeed in a 'policy of hypotheses', as against de Gaulle's 'policy of certainty', the Marshal's only fixed principles remained three firm negatives: not to become involved in war with Britain, not to sign a peace with the Germans, and not to abandon the Empire. 'I shall do nothing irreparable between Britain and us,' he said. 'And I shall keep the friendship of the United States.'

The determination to avoid starting hostilities in Africa against the British was one of his reasons for arresting Laval; Laval, of course, was soon afterwards released, thanks to the arrival at Vichy of Hitler's emissary, Otto Abetz, accompanied by two armoured cars. Abetz brought an invitation, from Hitler to the Marshal, to go to Paris on 15th December to receive the ashes of the Duke of Reichstadt, buried in Vienna. Pétain declined the invitation.

Paul Baudouin was impressed by the Marshal's powers of dissimulation: 'He did not consider himself at all obliged to explain his policies.' Weygand said sadly: 'I've never met a more secretive man than Marshal Pétain. He reveals nothing, even to me, of his intentions and thoughts. It is impossible to know what he is really thinking.' As for Laval, 'I can never forget that on 13th December, a few hours before having me arrested, he shook hands with me affectionately. He had never been so friendly to me as on that day.' The Marshal himself observed cynically: 'You can't trust anyone with a secret, except unfaithful husbands. They are used to lies.'

Released by the Germans on the Marshal's request, General Laure soon admitted: 'Pétain is our banner, but also our cross.' General Campet, a principal private secretary, remarked: 'Questions of sentiment did not enter into it for the Marshal. Only questions of reason counted.'

Dr Ménétrel, head of his private secretariat, even listened at doors, to stop anyone coming in who might get the Marshal in a moment of weakness to sign some dishonourable order or telegram. (Some months later microphones were secretly installed in his office and in the visitors' waiting-room.) Paul Baudouin used to keep himself informed on the audiences given, 'so as to go up to the Marshal afterwards, comfort him, hammer in the nail of an idea, and if necessary dispute the opinion of the person he had just seen. He tended to think the same as the man who last spoke to him.'

He was still a mixture of remarkable lucidity and periodical brief blackouts, losses of memory, failure of understanding. But even after these a few hours of rest and a good night would restore the balance and leave him mentally and physically alert. More seriously, there was a connection broken between his intellect and his will, the cancer which had eaten away 'the man of character'; and the leader of the great days, who had cultivated a subtle pride above accepting easy compliments, was now quite ready to listen to exorbitant flattery in public. The incense of power went to his head. He reminded Laval: 'I possess more powers than Louis XIV.'

The leader who had declared: 'I hate the lies which have done us so much harm' did not always observe a scrupulous respect for the truth. 'The quality he lacked most,' wrote Herriot, 'was frankness. He was capable of going back on a promise, of concealing qualifications and ulterior motives under an appearance of agreement. . . . Pétain always deceived you with his incredible cunning.'

Churchill regarded Pétain with a mixture of pity and exasperation. There were many rumours about underground contacts between the British Prime Minister and the Vichy Government. One of the skilful diplomats who maintained these contacts was Pierre Dupuy, *chargé-d'affaires* at the Canadian Embassy, who negotiated in particular through Jacques Chevalier, Under-Secretary and shortly after, Minister of Education. 'On loan', as it were, from the Ottawa government, Dupuy served directly under Churchill's orders. His diplomatic bag carried an invisible label 'intelligence service', and he gave extremely valuable help to the intelligence officers of the French Army, the counter-espionage men, and some unknown heroes disguised as T.R. (*Travaux ruraux*). 'Mr Dupuy,' said Churchill, 'is my little window on Vichy.'

Directly he arrived at Vichy, Dupuy went to see the Marshal. It was a bad day. Pétain was half asleep and unable to follow the conversation. Suddenly a name brought him out of his doze – de Gaulle.

'Ah, de Gaulle,' he exclaimed, 'I know him well. I had him on my staff and am the godfather of his son. He's not easy, you'll have trouble with him – see if you don't. You are unlucky. It would have been better if you'd had a general like Mittelhauser at the head of the French who refuse to give up the struggle. . . . I understand very well that some Frenchmen are carrying on the fight, that young men want to continue the war. If I were forty years younger, I shouldn't be here.' He reverted to pessimism. 'But when the French Army couldn't hold on, what do you expect the British to do?'

Dupuy: 'It's only a phase in the war.'

Pétain: 'The Gaullist radio accuses me of being a traitor who has sold himself to Germany. It's disgusting. I am thinking of nothing but the interests of France. I could live so peacefully in the Midi. I am defending France as I defended her at Verdun.'

Dupuy: 'In wartime, language quickly becomes exaggerated. . . . With all the respect that I owe you, Monsieur le Maréchal, I am not sure that History may not prove very harsh towards you, both over the present period and also when you were at the top of the French military hierarchy, between the two wars.'

Pétain: 'I couldn't do anything . . . the governments . . .'

Dupuy: 'Then you should have gone, not stayed.'

All of a sudden the old soldier seemed crushed. 'I shall be shot,' he told Dupuy.

On better days he believed that defeat would regenerate France, that the country would find a new strength, as it had found after the 1870 War. 'That's no way for a *man* to talk,' de Gaulle commented on the other side of the Channel. 'I would quote Foch at him: "They'll never get me to admit that defeat more than victory will help restore our fortunes."'

De Gaulle remembered, too, the advice once given by Captain Bonhomme to those who visited the Marshal: 'If you want to drop a brick, talk of Foch to Marshal Pétain.' So from Radio Brazzaville the General proclaimed: 'Marshal Foch! A French soldier comes respectfully to make his report to you. We have decided, Monsieur le Maréchal, immortal leader that you are, that we shall follow your example, that it is you and no other we shall obey.'

17

Darlan chez Hitler –
and the Consequences in Syria

One of the most complex characters in Pétain's cabinet was Admiral Darlan, formerly a 'good republican' with left-wing sympathies, almost the only French military leader who had actively supported the anti-Franco forces in the Spanish Civil War. At Bordeaux, in June 1940, the chief engineer of the navy, Jules Moch (a future Prime Minister of the Fourth Republic), told Darlan: 'The Germans will demand that the French fleet should be surrendered to them.' Darlan replied: 'I shall never surrender it to them. . . . I shall finish my career on an act of splendid indiscipline. We shall leave together for England . . .'

His 'act of splendid indiscipline' was not carried out until November 1942, after the Allied landings in North Africa, and in the meantime, instead of going to England, he became Minister for the Navy in the Pétain Government, then also Vice-Premier, Foreign Minister, and Minister of the Interior. From the end of 1940, for some fifteen months, he eclipsed Pierre Laval as the real power in France, keeping in close touch with the German leaders, and expressing gratitude to Hitler for not 'obliterating France from the map of the world'. Enjoyment of personal power was no doubt a dominant motive in his actions, but they were also part of Machiavellian plans, which he called 'realist', to assure a new future for France.

On 11th May 1941, he was received at Berchtesgaden by Hitler. It was a day of national celebrations in honour of Joan of Arc, and according to an official telegram from Otto Abetz, 'Darlan did not hesitate to stress the date and the French national saint's struggle against England.' Jacques Benoist-Méchin, the Secretary of State who accompanied him, has given a long and striking account of the reception, which illustrates Darlan's attitude very clearly:

'On our arrival at Munich we were driven to Salzburg in one of Hitler's private cars. . . . At Salzburg, we were lodged in a hotel which used to be part of the Bishop's Palace, and were given rooms with huge beds. . . . We only stayed there about two hours, obviously a disappointment to Admiral Darlan, who was looking forward to sleeping in a former Bishop of Salzburg's bed.

'The Admiral was very tense, and tried to mask his impatience by sudden whims. . . . He said: "I am going to issue an order so that it can be issued from Salzburg. Besides, it will be the first time the French Navy has won a success in Austria!" After reflection, he decided on a decree changing the regulation place for naval officers to wear their *Légion d'honneur* . . .

'He was in full uniform as Admiral of the Fleet, with a sword. He showed it to me. On the pommel there was a dauphin's head with laurels on it, and alluding to his title as Marshal Pétain's successor . . . he said to me: "You see, already!" (The sword had been given him on passing out of the Naval College.)

'It had been agreed between Darlan and me that at Berchtesgaden we should be received together by Hitler, so that my fairly fluent knowledge of German would enable me to start a direct conversation. "In this way," the Admiral said, "I shall have plenty of time for reflection, and I shall even be able to repudiate you if necessary." These plans, as it turned out, could not at first be put into practice . . . for the Admiral and I were separated.

'I was shown into a small room where I was locked in: I was told that these were the customs of the house; that the room led out into a passage which was right by Hitler's *salon*, and only separated from it by a heavy tapestry; and that Hitler could not tolerate the slightest noise of coming and going, while he was in conference. My room opened on to a semicircular balcony with a splendid view over the Bavarian Alps as far as Salzburg.

'Ambassador Abetz had informed us of Rudolf Hess's flight to Britain the previous night. Thinking it over afterwards, I felt convinced that Hess, who was born in Alexandria, spoke English fluently, and did not hide his pro-British sentiments, knew of Hitler's imminent attack on Russia, and wanted to avoid this campaign starting before a compromise peace had been reached between Britain and Germany.

'I had been told that if the interview between Hitler and Darlan proceeded without incident, the Chancellor would invite us to take tea; otherwise we should be driven straight back to Munich. I had to wait from 3 p.m. to 5 p.m., in growing impatience. I knew Darlan had only a limited competence in the field of foreign affairs, that he was impulsive, nervy, in fact anything but a diplomat, and he would be facing Hitler and Ribbentrop alone. At five o'clock, to my great relief, I was ceremoniously invited to come and take tea in the great *salon*, an immense room with an enormous fireplace, in which huge logs were burning. There was a heavy porphyry table in the centre, sofas and chairs, and opposite the fireplace a vast bay window, through which you could see the scenery I had admired.

'By an ingenious device, this window could be lifted at will, so that you felt you were on a terrace. The walls were a cream colour, with bright oak panelling; as ornament, a splendid tapestry coming from Schönbrunn Palace, representing a victory of Prince Eugene, and a Titian, a gift from Mussolini. No papers anywhere. Hitler had a horror of papers. When he wanted to discuss a question, he called for the competent person and his file, shot questions at him, but retained nothing in writing himself.

'I had proof of this. In my presence, he questioned an aviation official, asking him a mass of details on the circumstances of Hess's flight, the exact amount of petrol he had taken, the type of plane, the authorizations he must have had to use this plane, the breaches of service regulations he might have committed, etc. Understandably, Hitler seemed very uneasy, and preoccupied with this Hess business. I realized later he was afraid Hess would inform the British Government of the plans for attacking Russia – as he may well have done.

'This was the first time I had seen Hitler in private, and I studied him closely. His eyes and whole face were extraordinarily mobile. You could follow the slightest emotions on his face, as on a cinema screen, expressed with great variety and intensity. I compared him mentally to a dynamo.

'He was dressed very simply as was his custom, whereas Ribbentrop was in full uniform as the Reich's Foreign Minister, wearing a big green dolman with golden embroideries on the sleeve which showed the German eagle holding the terrestial globe in its claws. There were also the interpreter Schmidt and Otto Abetz.

'I was introduced to Hitler. Then Admiral Darlan, anxious to

137

pay a compliment, said he had been impressed by the march of the German Army into the Balkans, and this campaign seemed to have gone like clockwork. Hitler answered that in his opinion there were many things wrong with the German Army. His face darkened. The Admiral, trying to back down, said: "At least that was my impression as a spectator." The interpreter Schmidt made a mistranslation, using the word *Sachverständiger*, which means expert, instead of *Zuschauer*, which means spectator. Hitler's face grew even darker, and I realized that having been irritated by generals' opinions, he would find it highly presumptuous for Darlan to talk as an "expert" rather than a "spectator". I was wondering whether to correct this mistake when luckily servants came in to announce that tea was served.

'Darlan sat on a couch beside Hitler. I took my place on another chair, and then Hitler launched into a violent diatribe against England, which went on continuously for two hours, without taking any further notice of our presence or making the slightest allusion to France, just as if we didn't exist. The interpreter Schmidt briefly summed up Hitler's ideas from time to time, to enable Hitler to take a breath, and then he would start over again, repeating that he would annihilate England, that England was an obstacle to the peace of Europe, etc. He must have been completely preoccupied by the problems arising from Hess's flight.

'All the important conversations had taken place before my arrival. At the end of the interview, however, I took advantage of a respite to point out that the Wiesbaden Armistice Commission had already exacted a very heavy toll from France in many fields, and that in my opinion these economic concessions should be balanced by substantial political concessions to our country.

'Hitler answered: "I will think about it. My services have not yet provided a complete account of the situation." I told him there was nothing surprising about this, seeing that many of the German local authorities had made requisitions or purchases unknown to the Wiesbaden Commission, while the Commission had just added to the already heavy charges with which France was loaded. The interview ended on these exchanges, and afterwards we went straight back to Munich. Ribbentrop received the Admiral in his mansion near Munich, and the reception was again between him and Ribbentrop alone.'

On the journey home, Darlan told Benoist-Méchin about his private interview with Hitler: 'I asked what the Chancellor meant by the policy of collaboration, and if this collaboration was going to continue to function one way only. I told him that, considering all the concessions we had made, I would like to have some compensations: in other words, give and take. I asked him, following my acceptance of the transit through Syria of a certain number of aeroplanes for Iraq, for the maintenance of French sovereignty in Syria and the Lebanon, and that no effect should be given to Italian claims on that region. Hitler promised that to me. I asked him if all this could be confirmed in a written communiqué, with the agreement to be drafted after our return to Paris.

'I also asked for a guarantee of the integrity of our empire in Africa. He gave me this guarantee. He added that he would claim only the German colonies which had had to be ceded by the Treaty of Versailles. I pointed out to him that an ally of his had designs on our colonial empire. Hitler answered: "As far as the French colonial sphere is concerned, I cannot give a written agreement at present, because of Italian claims. I cannot oppose Italy at this juncture, but count on time to settle things. The war is going to be carried eastwards, and in the eastern basin of the Mediterranean I shall find compensations for Italy, to stop her turning her eyes westwards."

'I again broached the question of Syria, and Hitler replied: "I am not thinking of Syria, because in my opinion Italy must not be left in an exposed situation. Syria is a world crossroads, a territory difficult to hold. Italy is not strong enough to be sure of holding it. As to Tunisia, I think you will emerge with merely frontier rectifications in the south of the country."'

'Admiral Darlan seemed delighted by the way things had gone,' Benoist-Méchin concludes. '"The system of give-and-take," he told me, "puts me on a level nearer equality than we were before. I am going to present more and more substantial counter-claims. Your job will be to try to broaden the basis on which negotiations are conducted."

He was very optimistic. I was less so, I must admit, fore-seeing that we should still have very considerable difficulties to overcome.'

The consequences of Darlan's interview certainly aggravated the situation in Syria. De Gaulle intended that at all costs Syria and the Lebanon, mandated territories where the authority of the Vichy Government held sway, should come into the strategic resources of the Allies. 'I was under no illusions, alas, about the possibility of successfully liberating France without French blood being ever spilt by other Frenchmen.' He was horrified by the conference at Berchtesgaden, exclaiming: 'Darlan has grovelled!'

The stakes were high. The anti-British revolt fomented in Iraq by Axis agents seemed likely to destroy the keystone of the British position in that part of the Mediterranean, spreading south to Mosul and Suez. The Free French forces were standing by in Palestine, and de Gaulle gave this exposé of the situation: 'You see the German pincer movement – Suez and Ethiopia must be held. Otherwise the Germans will break out into the Mediterranean, overrun Tunisia, march on the Persian Gulf, reach the ports of India. From Damascus, Rayak and Beirut their planes will be able to bomb the Canal without any trouble. The offensives based on Syria will be combined with Rommel's.

'Darlan at Berchtesgaden means German planes in the Syrian sky. The Admiral will be quite unable to resist all Hitler's demands. France will be betrayed in the Levant, as she was in June 1940: a soldier does not obey traitors. If the Germans get a footing in Syria with the complicity of Vichy, everything will collapse. Battle will have to be resumed from South Africa, which means two extra years of operations. . . . From national interest and duty we are compelled to stop the Germans getting control of Syria, or even infiltrating into it. . . . The battle in the Mediterranean is on. . . . I do not force anyone to fight against Frenchmen in such conditions. A cruel and painful choice is imposed on us. I leave it to your consciences to decide.

'In Dentz's Army, are our fellow-Frenchmen going to surrender to the enemy the land that France has entrusted to them? Will they lose their honour without firing a single round against the Germans throughout the war? Let us cry out to them: "*Aux armes!*" Let us fire on the Boches!'

The British were hesitant about using the French forces in this campaign, and only yielded to de Gaulle's insistence. For the Free French themselves, 'a cruel and painful choice' was indeed involved, and Admiral Muselier for one opposed de Gaulle here:

'The authorization which Darlan gave the Germans in May 1941, to use Syria's airfields at the time of the complications in Iraq, made this operation in Syria indispensable. I consider that while supporting the British, we should have avoided taking part in it ourselves, for a clash between Frenchmen was bound to have a disastrous effect on French opinion; and I was absolutely decided never to take part in an action which could lead us to shed French blood. Not only was my conscience against it, but I was sure that disunity and civil war might grow out of such conflicts, which ought to be avoided at all costs. General Leclerc agreed with me, but de Gaulle put pressure on General Catroux, and in the end the operation was decided on. . . . I am still convinced that the struggle would have been much less difficult for the British, had the Free French not taken part in it.'

De Gaulle took a different view: it was important, on the contrary, not to let the British become mixed up in French internal questions, or get a footing in territory where the Tricolour waved: 'It's a French affair.' He found it inconceivable that the sacred principle of national sovereignty should be disregarded. Besides, here was a unique chance to offer an important contribution to the Allies' common effort.

The fighting in Syria was fierce. There were no signs of defection in the troops commanded by General Dentz, the Syrian High Commissioner. De Gaulle cabled to Churchill:[1] 'Resistance is pretty tough. It is mostly due to sense of honour, professional tradition, and habits of discipline in officers and troops who carry out a mission once it has been given them.'

General Dentz himself was very much a man to carry out missions given him. He came from Alsace, and his patriotism was beyond suspicion; his parents, in fact, had left the province after the 1870–71 War in order to remain French. A brave soldier, he was temperamentally allergic to politics, but readily accepted the argument in Darlan's telegrams, the gist of which was: 'The Germans have given out that the fate of the whole empire depends on your attitude in Syria. By defending yourselves, you will remove the pretext for their occupation of the bases and ports in North Africa.' As to Pétain, he did not feel

[1] Quoted by Admiral Muselier in *De Gaulle contre le Gaullisme.*

141

called on to explain general policy to his generals: they must simply do what they were told. He sent Dentz the following telegram:

'Admiral Darlan telegraphed you yesterday on the subject of the Franco-German negotiations. I wish to express my personal emphasis on the importance of these negotiations and on my resolve to carry out without reserve the policy emerging from them.

'The allusion made to Syria is to confirm your plan of defending with all your resources the territory placed under your authority, to ensure, as at Dakar, the freedom of its skies, to show our desire, in conditions which I know are politically and materially delicate, to collaborate in the new order.'

The same day General Weygand, then governor-general of Algiers and Vichy's delegate-general in French North Africa, had received a telegram substantially the same as the first half of that sent to Dentz. Pétain, however, had told General Bergeret, Secretary of State for Air, who was anxious about the secret agreements with the Germans that Darlan might have made: 'Don't worry. The extra clauses will not be applied.' In the cabinet, contrary to his usual practice, Pétain asked all his ministers for their opinion. The clauses in question were clearly 'against honour and dignity'. There is no testimony from Darlan's own mouth (he was assassinated at Algiers in December 1942), to say whether he intended to apply them or was just trying to outwit Hitler.

Meanwhile Dentz considered how the Marshal expected him to carry out this policy 'without reserve'. 'A fine mess they've got us into,' he confided to Admiral Gouton. 'Yesterday the British accused us of having surrendered it [Syria] to the Germans; tomorrow the Germans will accuse us of having surrendered it to the British. Such is the situation of a man ordered to hold the Levant without having ever been told his government's real intentions.'

For a moment Dentz thought of putting an end to the agonizing struggle: he asked the British for a truce. Then he relapsed into the reflex of unconditional discipline and withdrew the request. A soldier, even though a general, was neither his own master nor his own government. It was not his business to decide whether he liked or disliked the orders which had been given him. A fine mess indeed, which meant that the Free

French were shouting insults at him on their radio: 'General Dentz is a liar, General Dentz is a German.'

On the 'loyalist side', in the officers' mess at Damascus and Beirut, the Free French were called 'vile mercenaries', and de Gaulle a megalomaniac usurper – wasn't his real name Cohen? – a traitor, whose action on the 18th June was dictated by personal ambition. A Free French intelligence officer got hold of the following service note from a company commander (dated 31st May):

'Sub-sector Merdj Ayoum – western sub-area. I state the attitude to be taken in case of Gaullist action:
  (1) fire without warning on any group of individuals, whatever their uniform, who seek a parley;
  (2) capture alive any individual bearing a flag of truce, and take him to the headquarters of the sub-sector.'

At London, in the inner circle of the Free French, terrible conflicts of conscience arose, and some vigorous opposition was shown. Some said of de Gaulle: 'His personal aim is to get himself recognized as the embodiment of France, exactly like Marshal Pétain, and this fact will soon make him see Pétain as the main enemy.'[1]

De Gaulle was certainly fighting on two fronts with equal vigour. He greeted an air marshal, who had come from Africa to join the Free French, by shouting 'France has to be at war on Germany's side to prove the guilt of the men of Vichy'. The air marshal was shocked and amazed. 'All at once the veil dropped, and I realized that at Carlton Gardens they were fighting Vichy much more than they were fighting the Germans.'

No doubt he had misunderstood de Gaulle's thesis, which could be presented in simple terms. The General saw only two possible alternatives: the policy of Free France, or the possibility of complete collaboration with Germany, as advocated by Marcel Déat. (De Gaulle had seen something of Déat before the war, and recognized the logic of this extreme attitude.) In one sense, Pétain's policy seemed to him more dangerous than Déat's: it maintained an illusion, it sowed division, it took the rank and file of good Frenchmen out of the battle. There should be only two camps, without a no-man's-land in between, leaving no room for doubt.

[1] Admiral Muselier, op. cit.

143

As it was, the element of personality intervened, making a choice of two loyalties. De Gaulle and Pétain were almost like two heroes locked in personal combat, and in consequence something of what we should today call 'the personality cult' was inevitably brought in. At Deraa, near the frontier separating Syria from Transjordan (as it then was), Colonel Monclar of the Foreign Legion told de Gaulle: 'I'm sorry, but I'm not marching. I enrolled with the Free French on the understanding that we should not be engaged against France.' '*La France, c'est moi*,' de Gaulle answered witheringly. (Fifteen years later General Monclar told the author: 'Having studied the files on Syria, I am sorry I did not follow my Free French comrades in 1941'.)

In fact the Churchill–de Gaulle agreement of the 7th August had specified: 'This force will never be allowed to bear arms against France.' The clause had been imposed on the British by de Gaulle, but as he explained in his *Memoirs*, Vichy was not France. It did not mean that the Free French must never fight other Frenchmen; 'one was obliged, alas, to anticipate the contrary, Vichy being what it was'. Unknown to almost all the Free French, the agreement was completed, with explicit statements on these points, in an exchange of secret letters between Churchill and de Gaulle.

As regards Syria, de Gaulle probably thought that with the war extending to the Middle East, Dentz's Army would come over to the Franco-British forces. But for the Levant Army, France was still Pétain, not de Gaulle. At the armistice signed at Acre in mid-July, out of 20,000 men only a few dozen officers and 2,000 soldiers joined de Gaulle, almost all Légionnaires and African troops. Nearly a year after Dakar, the French Army turned its back on de Gaulle for the second time.

Almost 1,100 men from Dentz's Army and 800 Free French were killed in the fighting. They were all buried together in the Damascus cemetery, with the same epitaph on their tombs: '*Mort pour la France.*'

18

Negotiating from Weakness –
in London and at Vichy

'A man may have friendships,' de Gaulle observed, 'a nation never ... don't forget that our allies are also our adversaries.' He was weighed down with bitterness at the vital need for large-scale British help, and gratitude too was permissible for a private individual, not a 'public man', who represented a nation. He indignantly rejected all doubts concerning the capacities or potentialities of France: 'We should get nowhere if I began speaking sceptically through false modesty.'

To quote again from *Journey down a Blind Alley*, by Lady Spears, 'To come to the British as a suppliant, with the disgrace of his nation burned on his forehead and in his heart, was intolerable. But he could look to no one else; his own people failed him; the French officials reviled or snubbed him; the troops turned their back on him; the response to his appeal was pitiable. The weaker his position, the more arrogant he became.'

Although France's debt to the British and Americans increased, de Gaulle acknowledged its extent less and less. In a cable sent from Brazzaville to the Free French at London he said: 'We must spread the idea that the present war is only an episode in the world war started in 1914. France's contribution to the common cause of liberty is to be measured from 1914. It is the same with her sacrifices and consequently with the reparations of all kinds to which she will be entitled.'

The Americans were even worse than the British. They offered not Curtiss planes but medical aid. In August 1941 de Gaulle cabled from Aleppo to René Pleven, who was on a mission to Washington: 'You have no doubt explained that we are not asking the United States for any charity, but simply the means of fighting. I gather that at present the State Department is offering drugs, but not arms. We refuse drugs without arms.'

Moreover, President Roosevelt recognized only the Marshal's France, and kept an ambassador at Vichy, Admiral Leahy, his friend and confidant, to whom he wrote at the beginning of his mission: 'Marshal Pétain occupies a unique position both in the French people's hearts, and in the government. By virtue of the existing constitution, his word is law, and nothing can be accomplished if he opposes it, unless it is done without his knowledge. In his decrees, he uses the "royal we", and I deduce from this that he intends to govern.'

Weak, isolated, sometimes ridiculed, unable to show tangible evidence that the tide had turned, de Gaulle made desperate efforts to bring France back into the war on the Allied side, and thereby modify fundamentally the relation of the forces within the alliance. First of all he pleaded with General Weygand by letter to resume the fight at the head of French Africa. Weygand's ultimate aim was revenge on the Germans, but he believed that any premature action would end by making it easier for the Germans and Italians to seize North Africa. Anyhow, he talked of de Gaulle as a traitor who deserved to be shot.

Undeterred by this refusal, de Gaulle sent a messenger with a personal letter to Admiral de Laborde, commander of the fleet at Toulon, inviting him to establish secret contact in case the Germans should violate the armistice and the fleet were obliged to put out to sea; in this eventuality, allied air protection for the ships would be assured.

The messenger reached the Admiral's villa one evening, and had himself announced as a Monsieur Lucas, an accountant. When he was alone with the Admiral, he disclosed his real identity: 'Admiral, let me introduce myself – Captain Fourcaud from General de Gaulle's personal staff. Here is the object of my visit.'

The Admiral listened impassively till Fourcaud had finished. Then his face turned scarlet. 'And Dakar, Monsieur?' he demanded.

Captain Fourcaud: 'I am only too pleased to talk to you about Dakar, Admiral. It is very simple. There was a terrible Jew and Freemason called Thierry d'Argenlieu. There was another terrible Jew and Freemason called Bécourt-Foch. They approached on a small motor-boat, armed with a white flag. They did not even have a revolver on them. They were fired on . . . .'

Admiral de Laborde: 'Monsieur, if you had been on board

146

my ship, I would have had you arrested on the spot. You are here in my home. I content myself with throwing you out like a tramp.'

There were dangerous enemies even among his allies. Pétain claimed to have 'saved Charles de Gaulle's life', and told a privileged member of his staff: 'A messenger from London came specially to pass on to me, through one of my ministers, the remark made by one of the most prominent people in England: "De Gaulle is a nuisance to us. He thinks he's St Joan. Well, we're going to burn him, and we shan't need a stake as we did in 1431. We'll only have to let the Vichy Government know the day and time of his coming flight to the Middle East, to give them the flight schedule. . . ." I told the messenger: "I have not received your communication. I refuse to do anything dishonourable. The British must cope with de Gaulle themselves."'[1]

Meanwhile, the Marshal at eighty-five seemed to look forward serenely to the future. He had acquired some acres of land, and cultivated his small domain. He also succeeded in ending a long-standing anomaly over his marriage: in 1920 he had only been able to go through a civil ceremony with his wife, since she had had a divorce; but now, with some hesitation, the Vatican agreed, for reasons of state, to the annulment of his wife's first marriage – and the wedding was celebrated discreetly, by proxy, in the Palace of the Archbishop of Paris. This helped to maintain good relations between the Marshal and the Church.

The Vichy régime functioned more or less adequately, and in some fields the country was administered very well. Many members of the government were men of goodwill, guided by concern for public service and the country's interests. There were two or three others, who were considered, no doubt justifiably, to be directly in the pay of Abetz, the German Ambassador.

[1] *Translator's Note:* This mysterious episode is attested by members of Pétain's cabinet and staff, notably the late Jacques Chevalier, who discussed it in detail with the author and wrote notes on it which he proposed to have published posthumously; Pétain, in his cell after the war, confirmed the facts of the story. For diplomatic reasons, the author has suppressed the name of the prominent person involved. There is no testimony available on the British side, the story as it stands seems barely credible, and I can only think the suggestion was part of some subtle secret-service trap for Vichy.

De Gaulle followed the whole Vichy experiment with interest, and wrote: 'In the financial and economic sphere its technocrats undoubtedly showed skill despite all setbacks; and the social doctrines of the "national revolution" – corporative organization, work charter, family privileges – contained ideas which were not without attraction. But the fact that this enterprise was mixed up with the capitulation could only turn the masses towards another mystique.'

Consulted in this period of 1941, together with the other members of the Council of Free France, Colonel (later General) Leclerc, included among his suggestions: 'Suppress all the political parties. Promise to retain certain useful measures of Marshal Pétain's, in particular those which reinforce the central authority and favour the family.'[1]

De Gaulle, himself like his 'typical Frenchman', part royalist, part Jacobin, dreamed of a republic purged and muscular, in a system without political parties. After victory was won, the mission of Gaullism, if God willed it, was to bring France not a national revolution but a national renewal of political structures. He could already see the rise of a great Workers' Party, which might form the centre-piece of the Fourth Republic.

However, morale in unoccupied France was gradually going down. In July, Vichy's Intelligence gave the following picture: 'The population's state of mind in the past three months is marked by a general weakening of confidence and veneration towards the Chief of State, whose popularity had remained intact until the end of winter, and by development of the already existing hostility towards his immediate collaborators. The policy of collaboration is less and less understood. Its latest manifestations (Berchtesgaden conversations, the Syrian business, breaking off diplomatic relations with the U.S.S.R.) are interpreted by the population as a whole as showing base servility.'

Then, in the autumn of 1941, something happened which almost changed the entire story. Following the death of the German field-commander of Nantes, killed by unknown assailants, near the cathedral, twenty-seven political internees were shot at the camp of Châteaubriant, sixteen hostages at Nantes, and five at Paris. At Vichy someone had perhaps whis-

[1] De Gaulle's *Memoirs*.

pered to the Germans: 'Take a few wretched Communists, they won't be missed.'

But when Pétain, the man of marble, heard of the shootings, he burst into tears. His permanent secretary noted: 'I saw this old man, called morose, cynical, and cruel, cry like a child.' The United States Ambassador wrote: 'The sincerity of the grief felt by the Marshal over these mass executions is beyond doubt.'

In front of his colleagues the Marshal exclaimed: 'We cannot remain here any longer. We are dishonoured. The bloodbath must be stopped. Tomorrow morning, it is decided, I shall go and make myself a prisoner. I shall be a hostage. Prepare the car. Communists or not, the men shot were first of all Frenchmen, and the bullets which killed them were enemy bullets . . .'

Even after the armistice, Pétain had always slept the sound sleep of the military leader who must remain fresh and alert for the next day's action. But that night he did not close his eyes. It was planned that Charles Trochu, Mayor of Paris, Roger de Saivre, the Marshal's principal private secretary, and the *député* Vallin, would accompany Pétain over the border into occupied France. All were ready for the sacrifice.

They had counted without the collaborating ministers, several of whom began a methodical undermining of the Marshal's resolve. 'You can't do it. . . . You are France . . . these outrages are committed by Jews or foreigners. . . . Even de Gaulle condemns them.' And soon Pétain's heroic decision was abandoned, vanished without trace. De Gaulle commented: 'I have long ceased to cherish any illusions. The Marshal will go from concessions to surrenders. He died in 1925.'

One day in November 1941 de Gaulle, for whom self-control was a matter of principle, came to see Maurice Schumann, radio spokesman for the Free French. The General was pale with fury, on hearing of a telegram which Pétain had sent – apparently one of the cases where the Marshal's signature was extorted during a 'blackout' period. The telegram was to the colonel commanding a Legion of French volunteers with the German Army on the eastern front. It said: 'You are upholding a part of our military honour.' Of course Vichy apologists murmured: '*Une part* – observe that *une* can mean *one part*;

149

implying that there is another part elsewhere. You see what I mean . . .'

No doubt everyone, including those in the Resistance, interpreted in his own way the Marshal's words and thoughts, both explicit and implicit. A few weeks before, he had spoken of 'French unity'. In an underground pamphlet General Cochet wrote: 'The Marshal made a speech yesterday. He called for the country's unity to be maintained, and added: "the pride of France is not only the integrity of her territory, but also the cohesion of her Empire." One could not say with more subtlety, and yet with more precision, given the prudence made necessary by the circumstances, that Germany's victory is the thing we must fear above all.'

At that date, Hitler's *bête noire* in French uniform was not de Gaulle, but 'Weygandt', as the Führer furiously pronounced the name; already at Berchtesgaden he had attacked Darlan on the subject of the delegate-general in North Africa. On the 12th November Otto Abetz laid siege to Pétain once more: relaxation in Franco-German relations still depended on the departure of the Germanophobe General Weygand, whose presence constituted an obstacle on the road to a united Europe.

Shocked and indignant, Pétain resisted fiercely, but weakened bit by bit, and Weygand was summoned to Vichy; he arrived on the 16th November. Major Bonhomme, still the Marshal's aide, saw that the irreparable would soon happen. During these days his 'chief' seemed in full form physically and mentally, with no blank spells or lapses of memory; but Bonhomme was not deceived. It was the collapse of character, not intelligence, that he feared. 'The driving belt has snapped,' he said. He and Loustaunau-Lacau (the other aide) even considered with a wing-commander a plan for leaving by plane for London, putting the Marshal on the plane at the last minute. 'We will make de Gaulle a gift of poison,' they said. The most fantastic projects were conceived in the hothouse atmosphere of Vichy; but the Germans evidently treated seriously the possibility of such action; for at a later date, they sent a detachment under Otto Skorzeny specially to stop the Marshal leaving suddenly or even being kidnapped.

At the time of the 'Weygand crisis', however, Bonhomme was

more concerned to strengthen Pétain's resolve, if it could possibly be done; and he knew a way it might be. He arranged an urgent secret interview with a man called François Valentin, and gave him advice on how to treat the Marshal. A moderate *député* for Nancy (Lorraine) and youngest member of the 'Popular Front Parliament', Valentin had enlisted as a volunteer in 1939, became a captain in the Light Infantry, then liaison officer to General de Lattre's 14th Infantry Division. After the armistice Vichy had created a fighting Legion, with the original aim of using it for 'camouflaged mobilization' if the occasion arose; Valentin was Director-General of this Legion.

'Monsieur,' Bonhomme began, 'I have not the honour of knowing you well. I have asked you to come here because in these decisive hours I owe you the whole truth. I admire you and have confidence in you.

'Here it is. The Marshal is to receive three people who will insist on his not yielding to the Germans and their henchmen over General Weygand. The three are Monsieur Caziot, General Bergeret, and you. The Marshal will not even listen to the other two, a minister and a secretary of state. You are the only one who can exercise any influence.

'Unfortunately you do not know old Pétain. The circumstances have forced us to maintain a legend. For years and years I have served the Marshal, and whatever happens, you may be assured, I shall serve him till the last; I shall never desert him. But today he has become a monster of egoism. It is his age. That business about "giving himself to France" doesn't cut much ice any more. If you tell him in order to stop Weygand going: "Think of the soldiers of 1914–18, the men of Verdun, the veterans, etc.", he just won't hear you.

'I know him. You must bang on the table, shout and yell: "Monsieur le Maréchal, they will hang you! They'll spit in your face. They'll burn your fine house at Villeneuve-Loubet." Then he will begin to listen. I beg and beseech you, for France and for the Marshal himself, don't retreat. Say all that to the Marshal, without hesitation. Whatever it costs, plunge in. Don't be frightened. Don't be afraid of speaking frankly. Look at Laval, *he* understood. He called Pétain an old crackpot to his face!'

Half standing, resting his powerful hands on his desk, Bonhomme panted for breath, his face white with emotion.

Valentin felt as if he had received a blow from which he would never recover.

On the 18th November ten people met in Pétain's private office. The Marshal stood behind the Empire table. To the left was Darlan, in civilian clothes, as was General Bergeret. To the right were five heads of Vichy's 'Legion', including Valentin. Darlan went straight to the point:

'Every time I have made contact with the highest German authorities, the question of Weygand has been raised with me. The Führer himself brought it up at Berchtesgaden. General Weygand made some private remarks which came to the ears of the Germans. This is the sort of irresponsible talk which poisoned the atmosphere. I draw your attention to the fact that General Weygand has not been superseded. He keeps the prerogatives of an active general, but the position of delegate-general in Africa is abolished. In consequence General Weygand has been recalled to France.'

Still standing, Pétain supported himself on the back of his chair with his left hand. His right hand was used to stroke the back of his neck with a paper-knife. His eyelids flickered, a sign that he was highly excited. His voice rose, but almost as if he were communing with himself in a Shakespearean soliloquy:

'For a long time now the Germans have been asking us to retire Weygand. I have always refused. Today I am obliged to resign myself to it. I have insisted on obtaining an interview with a high German personality, in order to find out what Germany wants.

'Much is said about collaboration. I don't know what it is. I accepted the principle of it at Montoire, on condition that the applications were clearly stated; they never have been. Every time I tried to get them clear, I was faced with someone who had no real authority. So I asked to see an important leader, with whom I could discuss matters to some purpose.

'Monsieur Hitler informed me that my request would be satisfied on one condition, that I recalled General Weygand from Africa. I summoned General Weygand and explained the situation to him. He put his post at my disposal. I immediately let the Germans know that I had fulfilled their condition.' For a moment the Marshal paused, to take up a paper from his desk. 'Here is the telegram I have just received. It is the notification of a meeting with Goering.'

François Valentin took a step forward, clenched his fists, and began to plead the greatest cause of his life: 'Monsieur le Maréchal, we soldiers regret that for the first time we must disobey you. You are surrounded by conspirators who enmesh your person in a net that grows tighter and tighter, from which it will soon be impossible for you to escape. You will find yourself alone, robbed of the means to defend France's last hopes. From the depths of our hearts we implore you: do not sacrifice General Weygand. It won't do any good. The Germans won't show you any gratitude. Besides, Hitler has other worries. He is heavily engaged in Russia . . .'

Hammering his points home with passionate eloquence, in an atmosphere of terrific tension, the head of the Legion launched into the final charge with extraordinary violence:

'Look out, Monsieur le Maréchal, look out for your own skin! We beseech you. Otherwise the French will one day spit on your uniform.'

The old soldier wavered, looked round for someone to rescue him, and said nothing whatever in reply. The attack had inflicted a deep wound, but it failed in its effect: there was no reprieve for Weygand. The meeting had lasted nearly an hour, and all those present left in a state of exhaustion. Valentin said afterwards: 'It was worse than I had imagined. He is completely lucid, but age has destroyed his will-power. And so we Frenchmen with sincerity and enthusiasm go into battle, remembering his past services, behind the empty façade of a glorious soldier.'

Valentin went straight to the Hôtel du Parc, where Weygand had reserved a room. He told Weygand what had happened, and said: 'In these conditions, mon Général, I shall leave at the same time as you. And I shall not be alone. All my friends and colleagues are resigning.'

'No,' cried Weygand, 'don't do it. You have still failed to understand anything about the Marshal. Pétain has no will-power left. Stay, and stop his mistakes. If you all leave, you don't know what he may do.'

In any case Weygand himself had no idea what was going on, and complained once more of Pétain's secretiveness: 'He summons people to see him, consults them, listens to them, but never tells them yea or nay. It's quite impossible to find out what he's thinking. He proved he had great confidence in me by trusting North Africa to me without asking the slightest question about what I meant to do there. Yet never once did he discuss with me any questions of general policy, even at the worst moment of Darlan's agreement with the Germans.'

Weygand left Vichy with Colonel Gasser, his Chief of Staff, and flew to Marugnano, near Milan, where he was met by his loyal colleague, the diplomat Pierre de Leusse. 'There you are,' he told de Leusse, 'Pétain has thrown me out. He has surrendered to the *Diktat* of Hitler, and some bastards who lick Abetz's boots.'

De Leusse and Gasser tried to seize the opportunity. 'France does not know that you've been removed by order of the Germans. The official communiqué has not yet been made public. Your plane is here. It's a magnificent chance. Let's take off at once. Tell the Boches and Vichy to go to Hell. You can send Pétain at elegram saying *"J'y suis, j'y resté"*. No one will come to try and dislodge you.'

Weygand shook his head, and said sadly: 'I can't do it, my friends. I shall never make Frenchmen fire on other Frenchmen. I haven't the right to, and I shall never take that responsibility.'

So he was divested of all military powers, although remaining nominally delegate-general in Africa, one small concession Pétain had gained. But he had no influence, he remained in France, and after the Allied landings in North Africa in November 1942 he was arrested by the Germans; he was interned until freed in 1945.

His removal in 1941 had caused a considerable stir in the Allied camp. Admiral Leahy, before writing to Roosevelt, asked to see the Marshal and noted: 'The Marshal repeated twice: "I am a prisoner." The aged dictator was no more than a pale reflection of the man who had once been the great leader of a great people. . . . Although one may very well consider with full sympathy the difficulties the Marshal has to face this winter, it seems necessary to abandon all hope of trying to give some backbone to a jellyfish.'

As for François Valentin, he too abandoned that hope some months later, in May 1942. He resigned his post, and joined the underground army. A recorded message from him was smuggled out of France, and broadcast from London, introduced by Maurice Schumann with the words: '*Légionnaires! François Valentin vous parle.*'

Valentin's message concluded: 'It was our mistake to think you could restore a country before liberating it. You don't rebuild a house while it is still burning.'

19

Which Is the Real France?

'I find him more the Emperor than ever,' General Spears cabled to Winston Churchill early in 1942, on the subject of de Gaulle. There was a joke going the rounds that when asked what was the greatest cross he had to bear, Churchill answered 'The cross of Lorraine'. It was also known that he sometimes in private referred to de Gaulle as Frankenstein, after the robot monster who gets out of control (really the monster's creator). 'No, General de Gaulle,' Churchill told him angrily, 'you are not France, however much you claim to be. I do not recognize you as France.'

And in the presence of René Pleven, leader of the 'French National Committee' in London, Churchill asked: 'Where is France? I agree, of course, that General de Gaulle and those who follow him are an important and respectable part of the French people. But outside them, another authority could no doubt be found, which also has its authority.' To which Pleven retorted: 'Well, whether you like it or not, the map of France is now called de Gaulle.'

Towards the Allies, de Gaulle made intransigence into a system. 'I was charged with the interests and destiny of France. In the extremities to which she had been reduced, no compromises were possible. What would have happened to France if Joan of Arc, Danton or Clemenceau had been willing to compromise?'

There were even rumours that de Gaulle claimed to hear voices, almost believed himself the reincarnation of St Joan. It is true that he was convinced of his mission, which had started in June 1940, and had written to the Pope concerning it, of 'circumstances which were perhaps providential'. But it was natural for national leaders to identify themselves with their country's great leaders of the past; Roosevelt on occasions compared himself to Washington and Lincoln. In any case de Gaulle was well aware of the importance of 'image'. As he had written himself in *Le Fil de lépée*, 'Every page of the *Commentaries* shows us how carefully Caesar measured his public actions . . . and

Napoleon always appeared in conditions to strike people's imaginations.' So, to foster his own myth, de Gaulle may well have been ready to adopt heroic pretensions as part of deliberate policy, which could sometimes lead to self-caricature. But his 'madness' certainly inspired tremendous loyalty and enthusiasm among the Free French, and there was one point where he followed St Joan without any histrionic exaggeration: his impassioned faith in the spirit of France.

There was an occasion when Colonel Solborg, of the U.S. Army's intelligence, acting on personal instructions from Roosevelt, submitted to de Gaulle a proposal which (as Solborg realized) the General was unlikely to welcome: 'General, the United States Government declares itself ready to fit out immediately, with the most modern equipment, a French division, or else a Franco-Anglo-American division, which would be put at your disposal, on condition that you commanded it in the field.' There was a terrifying silence, after which de Gaulle roared: 'Then who is going to command France?'

Christian Pineau, who had escaped from unoccupied France on a Resistance mission, conferred with de Gaulle every day for a month; and de Gaulle hardly ever talked about the Germans; he was obsessed, apparently, by his quarrels with the British and Americans. The fact was that even before Pearl Harbor, he had declared to one of his staff: 'Of course the war will go on for years, but in a sense the Germans are already beaten. Unfortunately, we are going to make such mistakes on the western side that when the present conflict is over, there will be all the factors necessary for a war against Russia.' (At the same period he ordered: 'No more official contact with Vichy. It is finished: there is no longer any hope of a volte-face. Vichy is too far gone on the road to collaboration!')

At any rate, assuming the war would eventually be won, and that France could only play a tiny part in the victory, de Gaulle gave the political problem a priority over the military one: what counted most was that France should be on an equal footing in the framing of the peace treaty. The Allies were sometimes clumsy, no doubt, and sometimes not disinterested, in their dealings with himself, and matters concerning France; but invariably to attribute everything they did or said to the basest motives only, amounted almost to paranoia. It came from being completely self-centred, or France-centred – in de Gaulle's case practically the same thing.

The socialist *député* Felix Gouin, after a last discussion with the imprisoned Léon Blum, was at Gibraltar on his way to England, when he met de Gaulle, who was visiting Cairo and Beirut. 'We often have the impression in France,' Gouin told him, 'that there are serious disagreements between you and Churchill. The Vichy Press is always making great play with it, and being triumphant about it. How much truth is there in all that?'

'The General's face darkened. A slight shadow came over his brow, and he answered gravely: "Yes, our British friends are not always easy to deal with. You know them, but I think I know them better than most of our people do. The fight to the death they are at present carrying on against the Reich aggravates in them that fierce will to power which is the dominant feature of their race. It is that, no doubt, which makes them forget and infringe the interests of others, and think only of their own." The General paused for a moment; his hands were trembling slightly, his eyes gleamed, and then he brought out words I can still hear today: "You see, my duty is simple. Till victory, I am accountable for what makes France a great people and a great country. So I shall yield nothing of the elements which make up that greatness. The weaker I am," he rapped out, his voice suddenly hardening, "the more intransigent I shall be in defending our rights and getting them respected."'

Arriving in London, Gouin had the impression of finding 'a sort of reduced copy of the Pétain Government. The slogan *Liberté, Égalité, Fraternité* was suppressed in all the official documents. It was a principle of the National Committee that representatives of political parties should never find a place in it as such.'

Churchill's fierce assertion to de Gaulle, 'No, General de Gaulle, you are not France . . .' was delivered at the height of an Anglo-French crisis: the British were trying to establish in Madagascar an administration under their direct control. In May 1942 British forces made landings, to forestall a possible landing by the Japanese. Suspicion of Vichy intentions prompted the British to extend their administration over the whole island, which they succeeded in doing by the end of September. When de Gaulle heard of the original landings, through a Press agency, at 3 a.m., he cried: 'An intolerable attack on French rights.' That evening he is said to have murmured 'After the war I shall reach a reconciliation with Germany on the continent.' Oh, *perfide Albion!*

Churchill did in fact explain to de Gaulle: 'I don't want Madagascar! We have no ulterior motives. Rightly or wrongly, we thought we should meet less resistance from the Vichy troops if we went in alone.' But relations were so bad at this time that the Free French intelligence believed the British authorities had plans for removing de Gaulle and assigning him to a residence in the Isle of Man! The United States was playing a predominant part in every sphere of the war, and in consequence de Gaulle accused Churchill of being merely Roosevelt's lieutenant: he was sometimes near to calling Churchill a traitor to his country's interests. Bitterness and resentment seemed to be his main emotions, making him hard, ruthless and unfair. Could anything touch this man's heart?

De Gaulle has described in his *Memoirs* the occasion when Sir Alan Brooke, chief of the Imperial General Staff, brought him news of the glorious resistance by General Koenig and the Free French forces at Bir Hakim, near Tobruk. 'I thanked the messenger, dismissed him, and closed the door. I was alone. Oh, how my heart beat with emotion, how I sobbed with pride, and wept for joy!' At last the real France had shown herself again.

Colonel Solborg (of the unsuccessful Roosevelt mission to de Gaulle) had talked to the General about Vichy: 'I have carried out several fact-finding journeys in Africa. I have received impressive co-operation, for instance, from Governor-General Boisson at Dakar, General Noguès in Morocco, and many other major or minor officials and officers. You can find good Frenchmen on the Vichy side, who have a particular idea of their duty.' De Gaulle broke in to say: 'There are no good Frenchmen who have not followed me.'

In the autumn of 1942 Colonel Solborg received another mission from the White House, to try to obtain an audience with Pétain. General Donovan had appointed Solborg chief of special operations, and from Lisbon he held the threads of all the U.S. intelligence networks operating in Europe and Africa. It was a few weeks before the Allied landings in North Africa:

he was to ask Pétain in great secrecy whether he would be ready for a sudden 'flit' to Algiers.

Solborg arrived at the Hôtel du Parc. He saw the Marshal alone, and found it impossible to get into a real discussion. That day Pétain was living in the past, evoking the Great War, General Pershing, and the 'boys' of the U.S. Expeditionary Force. (Admittedly, his 'blank spots' were sometimes put on, as were fits of deafness.) When he returned to the present, it was to talk of dinner. He took a menu out of his pocket, read it with satisfaction, and said: 'Ah, we have a good meal today.' Solborg returned to Lisbon bitterly disappointed, and reported to Roosevelt that nothing much could be hoped for.

The end of that audience was typical. When Clemenceau's son came to ask the Marshal not to let Paul Reynaud and Georges Mandel fall into the hands of the Germans (they had been imprisoned by special order in the fort of Portalet), Pétain answered: 'I can't do anything. The Germans call the tune. No ill-will on my part; believe me. I can't do anything. . . . Do stay and lunch with us, I've got some good lobsters from Corsica today.'

Despite the general poverty and severe rationing in unoccupied France, there was always a 'good table' morning and evening at the Hôtel du Parc. Nothing very remarkable about that: in the 1914–18 War, it was a principle with Pétain, and also with Joffre, that the worse things were going, the more the chief's morale must be maintained with good meals. But now, as sometimes happens with the very old, Pétain was like a small child, hating to miss his food. Others besides Solborg felt that when the Marshal had to make a fateful choice, he might well be unconsciously influenced by petty details of meals and domestic comfort. (The latter consideration, incidentally, included feminine company besides his wife's; for he was still not too old to have a roving eye. His long-suffering wife accepted the fact with very good grace.)

Public opinion on the whole did not notice anything wrong, for a good reason. Jérôme Carcopino, then Minister of Education, has described two appearances of Pétain's with only a short interval between them. The first was an audience given to delegations of students, in the gardens of the Sévigné Pavilion. 'Straight as a ramrod, in a well-cut jacket, simple and smiling,

160

the wonderful old man, as if he had drawn a renewal of vitality from these young people's acclamations, decided, against the usual custom, that the introductions should be made separately. In vain did his aide object that they would be there for three hours, and it would be extremely tiring. The Marshal stuck to his guns, and the procession of 250 students began. Their names were called one by one, and for each of them he tirelessly improvised some witty remark or picturesque reminiscence.'

Forty-eight hours later, Carcopino paid the Marshal a visit. 'He received me at 5 p.m. in the Hôtel du Parc. He was unrecognizable. Seeing him so depressed, his features sunken, his face deathly pale, a man who looked as if he had aged several years in two days, in a state of physical and mental collapse, I found it hard to believe that this was the same man I had seen two evenings before, erect in stance, walking with springy steps, his eyes alive and his words incisive, who had inspired with his verve and spirit the 250 young people he had talked to.'

There was a rumour that he took drugs, but Ménétrel, secretary and physician, only gave him oxygen, and treated his kidneys with an old-fashioned apparatus inherited from Ménétrel's own father, who had himself been the Marshal's doctor.

At moments when Pétain was completely lucid, and realized his own state, he was horrified. 'Pity me,' he said to Carcopino, 'now that I am only a man adrift. . . . I have never offered you a photograph of myself. I hasten to repair that omission. But I would hate to offer *you* that picture of the Pétain of 1942. It is the picture of the 1919 Pétain I would like you to keep as a souvenir of me.' He chose a shot of himself riding on his white horse in the Champs-Élysées, in the victory parade on the 14th July.

Sometimes he would declare: 'I am dishonoured, I must go.' Or 'I am the rampart of France. I have made a gift of everything, even my honour.' He questioned Monsignor Chappoulie, representing France's cardinals and archbishops, on the subjects of sacrifice and of St Joan, with implicit reference to his own case. Often he confided: 'I am suffering martyrdom.'

On de Gaulle, Pétain spoke sometimes with an almost paternal sympathy, sometimes with extreme severity and no understanding at all for the struggle he was carrying on. As an example of the former attitude, he told Charles Trochu: 'I am

161

with General de Gaulle at heart. He is a good Frenchman. He has a lot of trouble with the British! He's defending the interests of France there. If I had had the chance to do it, I might well have gone with him.' Learning that Captain Billotte, the son of a dead general whom he had known well, had just arrived in London, having escaped from Germany via Russia, the Marshal told one of the captain's uncles: 'Please send your nephew the following message: Uncle Philip is delighted to know you are in London. If he were your age, he would be there too. Congratulate him. This has given de Gaulle an excellent officer.' On one occasion he declared firmly: 'General de Gaulle will not be deprived of French nationality.'

Yet at another time he could inform the Americans: 'There is one point on which I shall not compromise: it is the subject of the activities of the traitor de Gaulle.' Colonel Solborg heard him say: 'De Gaulle should be shot.' Mr Matthews, the American *chargé-d'affaires*, telegraphed to his government: 'The Marshal has reached the conclusion that ... those who are not ready to place confidence in him can only be the enemies of France.' And earlier, to Ambassador Leahy, whom President Roosevelt called 'my watch-dog at Vichy', Pétain gave the impression of 'cherishing a private hatred for de Gaulle' – 'a creature who bites the hand that fed him.' Again from Leahy: 'The Marshal yesterday spoke to me in detail of the Gaullist movement, in which he sees his government threatened by a group of traitors.' There seemed no longer any question of trying to bring about a reconciliation: beyond the international conflict and the struggle for France's interests, in the whirlwind of events, with whole continents aflame, there was still a bitter duel carried on, a duel to the death, between former master and former disciple.

At bottom the Marshal continually hoped for Germany's defeat. Sometimes he foresaw this: 'Hitler has met his match, he won't survive.' More often he thought that the Nazis would fail to impose their hegemony, but that the Allies would also fail to destroy them. His pessimism always returned, and seeing no possibility of victory for either side, he could only hope for a compromise peace. 'The belligerents will remain facing each other, and no one will win. Then I shall have a chance to say something at the conference table.' He failed to realize that the relation of world forces had been shattered, and – as always, a champion of the defensive – he was so impressed by the 'Atlantic Wall' that he thought the Allies would come to grief against the continental system built by Hitler. 'They will never succeed in landing.'

Pétain's Minister of Health was a certain Dr Grasset, who held radical opinions but was little involved in the major questions of politics; he devoted himself exclusively to public health. Dr Grasset has written as follows in his unpublished *Memoirs*:

'The Marshal certainly had surprising physical vigour, and was extraordinarily well preserved. He had no loss of faculties, had a spring in his step, read easily without glasses. He had a fine face, a distinguished carriage, above all radiated authority and even a sort of majesty. This undoubted personal magnetism, which was rather formidable, came more from his presence and the glory of his name than from his conversation. Beyond doubt he had extensive knowledge and could form sound opinions on a variety of subjects; but he only really dominated a discussion when it was on matters concerned with the training of military leaders.

'From contacts with him over more than two years, I remember two characteristics in particular. First, he detested contradiction. In cabinet meetings, when he had let his own feelings be known and nominally questioned one of his ministers on the same subject, you soon felt he was offended if the minister, although putting it with the greatest deference, expressed an opinion which did not strictly agree with his own.

'I think this was due to the traditions of military discipline. In the army, an officer never has anyone contradicting him. Whatever his rank, he gives an order which must be carried out without discussion or protest. When you get to the top ranks, you end up unable to conceive that an order once given *can* be contested or even that a question may have several solutions, which it is best to discuss in depth. They say the Marshal could be influenced behind the scenes, i.e. when his intimates made suggestions, but he was clearly upset in the cabinet when his ideas were not immediately accepted.

'The other characteristic I remember particularly was his apparent lack of emotion. It may be said that this is an extremely valuable quality for a general directly facing the enemy;

and perhaps it is. When I returned from Lorient after the raid which destroyed the town, I reported to the Marshal on the terrible damage and suffering I had seen, including the maimed little children, to whom I had promised to send toys from him. He approved my intentions, but obviously registered the suffering and physical damage as a military leader would see it, without letting any emotion come through.

'This lack of emotion may well have been one factor in his remarkable physical preservation. . . . Emotional shocks, impressionability, all the gamut of psychological states up to anxiety neuroses, wear out the organism, destroy its resistance and hasten its decline. The Marshal was lucky to be preserved from such deep or violent reactions; he thus maintained an enviable equilibrium and showed a very rare serenity. Being impassive defended him against the onslaughts of old age.'

Robert Schumann, who was a colleague of Pétain's in the short-lived Reynaud Government of spring 1940 (as Under-Secretary of State for refugees), has recounted his arrival at Vichy the following year: 'Arrested by the Gestapo, interned for several months, I succeeded in escaping. I wanted to warn the Marshal about the terrible situation of the annexed provinces [Alsace and Lorraine]. Alas, he cut me short. "All that," he flung at me, "would poison Franco-German relations. These affairs would complicate France's food supplies and general situation."' Schumann departed, horrified.

Yet this was the man who in the last century had chosen the career of a soldier with the noble ambition of liberating the lost provinces, and who in 1918 asked Poincaré to be allowed to receive his marshal's baton in newly recovered Metz. On the other side of the picture Robert Aron, in his *Histoire de Vichy*, writes, 'Receiving the Mayor of Metz, who told him that the people of Alsace and Lorraine felt they were being abandoned by the government, Pétain could not restrain his tears.' General André Laffargue, a special minister to deal with all questions of the two provinces, intervened bravely and often successfully with Pétain on their behalf, until an ultimatum from the Germans forced the Marshal to dismiss him. But the men who always remained of particular concern to the Marshal were the officers and men in the P.O.W. camps. Perhaps with memories of the first-war *poilus*, he kept them constantly in mind.

With regard to the Jews, the two sides of Pétain's character were often in conflict. He started with anti-Semitic tendencies, and at a cabinet meeting in 1940 insisted that the Ministries of Justice and Education should contain no Jews. And he half condoned the deportations in August 1942; according to a private diary of General Bridoux, Secretary of State for War in the Vichy Government (27th, 28th August), 'four thousand stateless Jews were driven back into the occupied zone, and seven thousand collected in camps were about to leave. The Marshal had an interview with the Papal Nuncio about it, telling him of "the favourable attitude to the Jews held by some French priests, who knew nothing about our situation". A prominent member of his cabinet rushed into Pétain's office in great distress: 'Monsieur le Maréchal, I was at the indoor cycle track yesterday where the Jews are being rounded up. It was terrible, terrible; the women and children, the babies torn from their mothers' arms. And French police helping the disgrace.'

The Marshal seemed equally moved. He banged on the arm of his chair: 'How can this ever be redeemed? We can never redeem it, never.' But a minute later the Minister heard him add: 'It's true these Jews have not always had a good influence on the country.'

In the first few months of the Vichy Government Pétain had subsidized resistance networks. But from 1941 the Gestapo infiltrated into unoccupied France, its agents received identity cards from the French police, and also facilities for tracing secret radio sets with special wireless-tracking vehicles. Some of the army's intelligence services collaborated, while others continued to help the Resistance. The latter even succeeded in placing a microphone in the Gestapo chief's hotel room, so that they could listen in to direct German communications between Paris and Vichy; it functioned with great success for two months. But Gaullists or alleged Communists in 'Unoccupied France' were hunted down, tortured and killed, with French help, by 280 Nazi police; and there were tens of thousands of people in prisons or 'administrative camps' for 'ideological' offences.

The Marshal showed no special leniency towards those who had spied for the Germans (or Italians). Between July 1940 and

November 1942 (when the French Army was dissolved) eighty-two convicted spies were condemned to death, although the sentence was commuted in the cases of fifty-three of these. They had been convicted by court-martial, and could appeal to the head of State; but Pétain always followed the opinion of the Appeals Tribunal or found that it agreed with his own. Many appeals were rejected.

Despite everything, the French still acclaimed the great soldier, and he began making ceremonial journeys round the country every Sunday, to be sustained by their applause. 'Come with me,' he said to Admiral Auphan, Secretary of State for the Navy, 'and see France's welcome.' Returning from one such journey, he confided in the car: 'In the work I have to do, the people's acclamations are quite essential to me.' When he passed by, women could be heard saying: 'How handsome he is!' and some even rushed up to cut buttons off his greatcoat as a souvenir. Veterans of the 1914–18 War marched to their places singing patriotic songs : '*Tremblez, ennemis de la France.*' The atmosphere was highly charged with emotion, and tears flowed.[1]

Pétain loved the delirious crowds, the children waving little flags, 'eager hands stretching forward through frantic ovations, the avenues bright with bunting'. 'My young friends,' he would say, 'later on you will be able to tell your children: I saw Marshal Pétain.' 'You see,' he declared, 'this is the people. We understand each other well.' Those who watched the official journeys observed that 'when he feels the enthusiasm is high enough, he sweeps aside all protection and dives into the crowds to "go round the track", as he puts it'.

There was one innovation in these ceremonial journeys: he would always attend High Mass in a cathedral or church. One day a Cardinal said in his sermon: 'Pétain is France and France today is Pétain. To restore our wounded country, the whole of France is behind you, Monsieur le Maréchal.' No wonder that Pétain could claim: 'I have all the priests with me.'

In most of the dioceses the *Semaine Religieuse* published the sermons which had been preached: 'The duty of closing ranks round legitimate leaders. . . . Let us close our ranks round the leader and father who today embodies France. . . . Respect

[1] Robert Vaucher (special envoy from Switzerland), *Quand le Maréchal prend son bâton de pèlerin.*

authority legitimately established in the country. . . . Since 10th July 1940 Marshal Pétain has been the legal holder of power. . . . The Marshal could have wrapped himself in his glory and looked down on events from above. Instead, he was ready to take on himself the country's humiliations and sufferings. . . . French citizens are not only the friends but the subjects of Marshal Pétain.'

De Gaulle, receiving the *Lettres pastorales* in London, was infuriated and bitterly wounded by these words from the Episcopate. '. . . The government of Marshal Pétain is France's legitimate government. . . . The Gospel teaches us that a kingdom divided against itself shall perish. . . . The Apostle told the Romans: "There is no power but of God; and the powers that be are ordained of God. Therefore he that resisteth the power, withstandeth the ordinance of God." When he wrote that, the head of State was called Nero. What would St Paul say today when our head of State is an old man full of glory and years, honours and merits, animated by the purest and most upright intentions?'

Monsignor Guerry, Archbishop of Cambrai, secretary of the Assembly of Cardinals and Archbishops of France, gives the following account of church doctrine on 'the powers that be', in his book *L'Église catholique en France sous l'Occupation*:

'When the French State was defending the country's life, interests and rights, when it resisted the demands of the occupying power, when it formulated a programme of moral truths and worked for the restoration of natural communities, the Church respected its authority and practised loyalty towards it.

'When, however, the French State, under pressure from the invader, yielded or was obliged to compromise, when it reached the point of sacrificing the country's fundamental rights and of compromising France's future (as in the problem of forced labour in Germany), when it attacked the moral law or violated the rights of human personality, then the Church organized resistance and asserted its independence. In both cases it was serving the country's good.'

In fact the last visit to Vichy of a French Cardinal was in October 1942: Cardinal Gerlier, the only Cardinal in unoccupied France, intervened on several occasions in favour of church schools, better prison administration, trade union rights, and to obtain reprieves for Communists condemned to death. There were many other prelates and clergy to emphasize that reverse side of the doctrine: they made solemn protests against the persecution of the Jews, the operations of Darlan's Fascist militia, the institution of court-martials for civilians; they refused to let religious ceremonies for the victims of air-raids be turned into demonstrations against the Allies; they refused to fall in with the 'anti-Bolshevik crusade'; they repeatedly refused to receive Laval at the Assembly of Cardinals and Archbishops; they offered asylum in monasteries to countless hunted patriots; they spoke in defence of international law.

The Church therefore was not so solidly behind Pétain after all; but were the people? De Gaulle saw the photographs and films of the Marshal's journeys. Colonel Pierre de Chevigné said to him: 'Mon Général, in a few years all these Pétainists will be Gaullists, because then you will be representing good order against Communism.' 'Get out,' de Gaulle told him angrily.

In de Gaulle's eyes the repercussions on the domestic front were regrettable, but not too serious; he knew what crowds were worth. Certainly he took a great interest in Pétain's attitudes before the public. During the projection of a film, one of the first men to join him said: 'Look at those crowds, mon Général. Look at that old workman with the military medal. Pétain passes, he opens his coat and shows on his tunic his own military medal. I admit to you that I myself, here at your side, am moved to tears.'

'That only proves,' said de Gaulle, 'how idiotic one can become when one gets sentimental. Listen – the Marshal is the greatest actor of our time. These ceremonial journeys remind me of a strange incident. When I was battalion commander at Trèves, I remember the Marshal inviting me personally to attend the celebration of the anniversary of Verdun. We had breakfast together. The Marshal sat on at table for some time, so I ventured to ask when we were due to reach the cathedral.

'"Leave it to me," he answered, and looked at his watch. At the exact minute chosen by him, we got into the car, and arrived at the cathedral. But the Marshal, instead of going through the main door opening on to the nave, entered by a side door giving access to the chancel. The clergy, the generals, the prefect, the authorities, the *députés* in their tricolor sashes, the flag-bearers of the veterans, the whole crowd – found themselves obliged to go back on their steps. There's been a mistake, it was thought; but no, it was a piece of stagecraft. The Marshal wanted to make *his* entry, not the one expected. I repeat, he's the greatest actor of our time, a real artist.

'One of his great virtues has also been patience. Today he knows how to exploit glory after obscurity, as he once exploited obscurity after glory.'

20

Divisions in North Africa

November 8th, 1942: '*Franklin arrive! Franklin arrive*'! Every hour the B.B.C. broadcast the code phrase which announced the Allied landing in North Africa. De Gaulle heard the news in the early hours from his Chief of Staff, Colonel Billotte, who had himself been informed at 4.30 by General Ismay, the British Chief of Staff. 'The Americans made us keep it secret from you,' the latter told Billotte, 'because the intervention of the Free French would complicate everything. I understand your bitterness. Overcome it.'

De Gaulle's reaction was a mixture of surging hope and indignation. At first anger was uppermost: 'Well, I hope the Vichy people throw them into the sea. They can't break into France like burglars.' And soon afterwards the Gaullist weekly in London, *La Marseillaise*, said: 'France has suffered an immense wrong. The occupation by our American allies of a land which cost us so much blood, affects the country more seriously in a historical perspective than the occupation of French *départements* by the Germans because it damages her honour.'

However, by 11 a.m. hope had triumphed in the General's mind. He had great difficulty in drafting his speech; indeed this was perhaps the one and only time with any of his writings when he had someone else prepare a synopsis for him. At 11 a.m. he addressed the French people: 'Here is the great moment! Here is the hour for good sense and courage! Everywhere the enemy is reeling and giving ground. If we rally now through you, from one end of the Mediterranean to the other, it means that France will have played her part in winning the war'. And for the benefit of the North African Army, he added: 'Rise and aid our Allies. Join them without qualification. Fighting France makes this appeal to you. Don't worry about names or forms. Only one thing counts, saving France.'

Military successes, however, were balanced by complete political confusion, heightened by the presence of Darlan in Algiers. 'You see the Vichy by-product,' de Gaulle observed to

170

Schumann: 'From Berchtesgaden to Algiers.' In fact the Admiral had begun revising his position from the beginning of 1942: in February and March he sent his son Alain, a reserve officer in the signals intelligence of the Marines, on several secret missions to Algiers, where he contacted the U.S. consular authorities, and met Robert Murphy, President Roosevelt's special envoy in Algiers; at this time the Admiral expected the Allied landings to take place in the spring of 1943. After the landings he told the officers of Morocco in an order of the day: 'Don't forget that Machiavellism is an old rule of international politics.'

Under an arrangement with General Eisenhower, Darlan assumed responsibility for the civil administration in North Africa, as a temporary measure.

In a secret session of the House of Commons Churchill had this to say of Darlan and the whole situation:

'I hold no brief for Admiral Darlan. Like myself, he is the object of the animosities of Herr Hitler and Monsieur Laval. Otherwise I have nothing in common with him. But it is necessary for the House to realize that the Government and to a large extent the people of the United States do not feel the same way about Darlan as we do. He has not betrayed them. He has not broken any treaty with them. He has not vilified them. He has not maltreated any of their citizens. They do not think much of him, but they do not hate him and despise him as we do over here. Many of them think more of the lives of their own soldiers than they do about the past records of French political figures. Moreover, the Americans have cultivated up to the last moment relations with Vichy which were of a fairly intimate character and which in my opinion have conduced to our general advantage. At any rate, the position of the Americans at Vichy gave us a window on that courtyard which otherwise would not have existed . . .

'Admiral Leahy has been Ambassador to Vichy until quite recently. He lived on terms of close intimacy with Marshal Pétain. He has at all times used his influence to prevent Vichy France becoming the ally of Germany or declaring war upon us when we have had to fire on Vichy troops at Oran or Dakar, in Syria or in Madagascar. On all these occasions I have believed . . . that France would not declare war; but a factor in forming that opinion was the immense American influence upon all

171

Frenchmen, which influence of course increased enormously after the United States entered the war. Admiral Leahy is a close friend of President Roosevelt, and was recently appointed his personal Chief of Staff. The attitude of the United States executive and State departments towards Vichy and all its works must be viewed against this background . . .

'I now turn to examine a peculiar form of French mentality, or rather of the mentality of a large proportion of Frenchmen in the terrible defeat and ruin which has overtaken their country. I am not at all defending, still less eulogizing, this French mentality. But it would be very foolish not to try to understand what is passing in other people's minds, and what are the secret springs of action to which they respond. The Almighty in His infinite wisdom did not see fit to create Frenchmen in the image of Englishmen. In a State like France, which has experienced so many convulsions – Monarchy, Convention, Directory, Consulate, Empire, Monarchy, Empire and finally Republic – there has grown up a principle founded on the *droit administratif* which undoubtedly governs the action of many French officers and officials in times of revolution and change. It is a highly legalistic habit of mind, and it arises from a subconscious sense of national self-preservation against the dangers of sheer anarchy. For instance, any officer who obeys the command of his lawful superior or of one whom he believes to be his lawful superior is absolutely immune from subsequent punishment. Much therefore turns in the minds of French officers upon whether there is a direct, unbroken chain of lawful command, and this is held by many Frenchmen to be more important than moral, national or international considerations. From this point of view, many Frenchmen who admire General de Gaulle and envy him in his role nevertheless regard him as a man who has rebelled against the authority of the French State, which in their prostration they conceive to be vested in the person of the antique defeatist who to them is the illustrious and venerable Marshal Pétain, the hero of Verdun and the sole hope of France.

'Now all this may seem very absurd to our minds. But there is one point about it which is important to us. It is in accordance with orders and authority transmitted or declared to be transmitted by Marshal Pétain that the French troops in North West Africa have pointed and fired their rifles against the Germans and Italians instead of continuing to point and fire their rifles against the British and Americans . . .

'All this is done in the sacred name of the Marshal, and when the Marshal bleats over the telephone orders to the contrary and deprives Darlan of his nationality, the Admiral rests comfortably upon the fact or fiction – it does not much matter which – that the Marshal is acting under the duress of the invading Hun, and that he, Darlan, is still carrying out his truest wishes. In fact, if Admiral Darlan had to shoot Marshal Pétain, he would no doubt do it in Marshal Pétain's name . . .'

This analysis is confirmed by Eisenhower in his post-war book, *Crusade in Europe*: 'It is possible to understand why de Gaulle was disliked within the ranks of the French Army. At the time of France's surrender in 1940, the officers who remained in the army had accepted the position and orders of their government and had given up the fight. From their viewpoint, if the course chosen by de Gaulle was correct, then every French officer who obeyed the orders of his government was a poltroon. If de Gaulle was a loyal Frenchman they had to regard themselves as cowards. Naturally the officers did not choose to think of themselves in this light: rather they considered themselves as loyal Frenchmen carrying out the orders of constituted civilian authority, and it followed that they officially and personally regarded de Gaulle as a deserter.'

One of the officers who took this view of de Gaulle was General Henri Giraud, military governor of Metz in 1939, given command of an army in Holland on the outbreak of war, and taken prisoner by the Germans and kept under vigilant surveillance at Koenigstein. But Giraud, as he had done in the First World War, escaped from German captivity. He reached unoccupied France in April 1942. With great difficulty he managed to get out of France by boarding a British submarine (almost getting drowned in the process), and joined Eisenhower's forces. On the day of the Allied landing in North Africa, he broadcast an announcement that he had assumed the command of the French forces there; and after Darlan's assassination, on Christmas Eve, he was unanimously chosen by the French Council to be High Commissioner in North Africa, as well as Commander-in-Chief.

Although there had once been no love lost between de Gaulle

and Giraud, the former expressed great patriotic enthusiasm on hearing that Giraud had escaped from Germany. 'Giraud is the only man under whose authority I could work,' he declared. Colonel Passy sent a letter to a high-up contact in the Resistance in France: 'General de Gaulle instructs me to request you to make the necessary arrangements for General Giraud, escaped from Germany and presumed to have arrived in Switzerland, to be helped across to England as soon as possible. General de Gaulle is convinced that the Vichy authorities would hand General Giraud over to the Germans should he go through unoccupied France. He asks you to warn General Giraud of this fact, if the General gets in touch with one of your representatives.'

Giraud, who had in fact gone to unoccupied France, gave Pétain a pledge not to join de Gaulle, but refused any promise not to take up arms against the Germans. He was an ardent patriot and a man of indomitable courage. From the fortress in Germany he had written his children a letter forbidding them to resign themselves to defeat, 'and admit that France can rank after Italy, Spain and Finland'. His daughter died in a concentration camp, after he had refused an exchange of hostages from which his family would have benefited. (Several members of de Gaulle's family were in Nazi camps at the time – among them his brother Pierre, his sister and brother-in-law, and his niece – and like Giraud he sadly refused to accept such a privileged exchange.)

Giraud was the complete soldier, feeling somehow inhibited in mufti; in uniform he was calm and self-assured. He believed in the legitimacy of his own position and in his priority over Gaulle, because militarily he had the higher rank and politically he had been invested with power by a college of high officials. From the lack of harmony between him and de Gaulle, easily understandable on both sides, much trouble was to spring in the next months.

As for Marshal Pétain, he was now by-passed in the main events of war and policy. On the 11th November the Germans responded to the North African landings by overrunning 'Unoccupied France'. Everyone expected the Marshal to make for North Africa and resume the struggle on the Allies' side. But he resisted all solicitations. Weygand implored him: 'It's the

174

beginning of deliverance . . .' The Marshal replied: 'I shall not leave. I am responsible for the fate of the French people, for the workers in Germany, the prisoners, the refugees from Alsace and Lorraine, the Jews threatened with general massacre. I shall not leave, even if I were to lose all my glory. I have made the gift of my person to France. If I go, Déat, Doriot and Darnand will declare war on our former Allies.'

The American diplomats who saw Pétain before they left Vichy never questioned his sincerity in this stubborn resolve to stay in France. However, the Swiss Minister, Mr Walter Stücki, wrote to his government: 'If he had given his resignation at the decisive moment of 11th November, or better still had left France, he would have spared his country the terrible suffering of a fratricidal struggle. It is true that by staying at Vichy, Pétain served France materially, since the Germans, instead of being able to impose their power, were obliged to negotiate on questions of requisitioning property and recruiting labour; but this advantage did not compensate for the devastating psychological damage which his decision caused in France and in the minds of the best of her sons.' The seeds of the 1945 purges, setting Frenchmen against Frenchmen, were already sown.

Dr Ménétrel used to recommend visitors to Pétain to 'get hold of him when he is fresh'. When the decisive choice had to be made, Pétain started a cabinet meeting lucid, but tired quickly and lost the thread of the discussion. Some members of the cabinet left his office declaring in horror: 'The Marshal isn't there any more.'

In full uniform, carrying his Marshal's baton, von Rundstedt notified Pétain of the invasion of the 'Southern Zone'. Pétain read out a solemn protest, then said: 'Monsieur le Maréchal, I ask you to give an undertaking on the fate of escaped French prisoners of war.' The fate of prisoners still preoccupied him as much as ever.

The Germans guarded against any impulses to leave which Pétain might still have had, by a little judicious blackmail: reprisals, deportation, etc. He gave way: 'If I go, the French will suffer the fate of the Poles. A commander never abandons his troops. It's the first principle they teach at Saint-Cyr. My troops are the French people.'

'You think too much of the French people and not enough

175

of France,' General Serrigny told him. 'The war will be finished in a few weeks or months.'

A key argument was presented to him: 'Algeria is France.' 'That's true,' he said, and decided to leave, then changed his mind again. His advisers returned to the charge: 'You did not hesitate to order fire at Dakar, in Syria and elsewhere. Defending the principle of French sovereignty is only justified if the principle is respected in every context. It's the hour of decision.'

The hour of decision passed. The last attempt was made by Wing-Commander de Gorostarzu, who broke into Pétain's bedroom and kept up his pressure on the old man for twenty minutes: 'Monsieur le Maréchal, there is no longer a free zone. You no longer have a reason to be here. I have a very fast American plane at my disposal.' (This was a Glen-Martin, disarmed, based at Vichy. The Vichy Army retained eight Glen-Martins.) 'It will only take a few hours. This evening you will be in Algiers. The German pursuit has not yet started.'

Pétain said: 'I have promised the French people to stay with them. . . . The Americans have occupied one side of the Mediterranean. The Germans will occupy the other side. It's all in the game.'

He had a bad headache that day, and after a few minutes told Gorostarzu in a sharp, cutting tone, which signified that discussion was at an end: 'Flying and high altitudes are absolutely forbidden at my age.' In vain did Gorostarzu plead that they would be flying by night, and at a maximum of five or six thousand feet. Although as a young man Pétain had obtained a flying certificate, he did not like planes. When he was ambassador to Spain, he had refused to go to Paris in a twin-engined plane sent by the Air Ministry – with Gorostarzu as pilot. The refusal was repeated now.

In London de Gaulle commented: 'From June 1940 at Bordeaux, to Vichy in 1942, this has been one of the secrets of the war: everything would have been different if the old Marshal had liked flying. But he will never, never fly.'

The Allied landings in North West Africa coincided with Montgomery's advance in Libya, which drove Rommel's Africa Corps back into Tunisia. By May 1943 the German armies in

Tunisia surrendered, giving the whole North African coast to the Allies. But the French in North Africa were still confused and divided; and it was not till June 1943, through the efforts of General Catroux, that an agreement was reached for a French Committee of National Liberation to be set up, directing the French share in the campaign of reconquest; Giraud and de Gaulle were co-presidents of the committee.

De Gaulle had been cooling his heels for some months after the landings before he was allowed to set foot once more on 'French soil'. *'Bonjour,* Gaulle,' Giraud addressed him, with the patronizing air of pre-war days. *'Bonjour, mon Général,'* de Gaulle answered respectfully, biding his time; but he had already decided that Giraud was too much a supporter of the old order and if left with sole authority would maintain in France a régime like Pétain's. Bolshevism would become inevitable with 'a new Vichy under American control'. The people would be bound to rush into the communist fold. 'The Americans will win the military war but the political winner will be Stalin.'

Giraud, on the other hand, feared that de Gaulle would establish a 'totalitarian system' after the war and carry out a 'disturbing' foreign policy. Some fervent republicans from the Free French side, such as André Labarthe and Admiral Muselier, went over to Giraud; and others were heard saying: 'Let's opt for Giraud. At least we can get rid of him when we want to. We shall have de Gaulle for years and years.'

The United States was backing Giraud heavily. At the White House there was still talk of the 'so-called Free French', and Roosevelt's sympathies went to Giraud, whose military stature seemed likely to make possible a revival of the French Army, and who did not meddle in politics. Mr Rives-Childs, appointed American Ambassador at Tangier in 1941, has analysed this basic attitude fraught with consequences both immediate and for the future:

'What were the reasons that impelled us to establish a policy of opposition towards de Gaulle to which we clung with the greatest persistence until forced to retreat before the march of events? Sentimental considerations and a refusal to face the truth? These two factors certainly played their part. It has been suggested that Roosevelt's policy at this period towards France, and the persons of Pétain and de Gaulle, was influenced by the

Catholic Church in America, which was very well disposed towards Pétain owing to the concessions he had made to the French Church in 1940. The fact that a large number of Roosevelt's closest advisers, as far as French affairs were concerned, belonged to the Catholic faith, is certainly significant. This is not to attribute to them anything but patriotic sentiments in embracing the cause of Pétain, Darlan and Giraud; but it explains their conservative inclinations, drawing them naturally towards Vichy. Whatever the reasons, there is no doubt that Roosevelt and Cordell Hull felt an almost pathological aversion towards de Gaulle.

'I realized these feelings after a conversation I had with the Secretary of State [Hull]. His face went scarlet, and he launched into a violent diatribe on the first mention of de Gaulle's name. At the same period, I met Admiral Fénard in Washington, absolutely desperate at being unable to get access to the White House in order to hand over a personal message from de Gaulle for Roosevelt. The day of my return by plane to Tangier, a few weeks before the invasion of France by Allied forces, I had a conversation with one of my old friends, working as a special assistant to Mr Hull. During the discussion my friend assured me that according to the State Department's information de Gaulle would not be supported by even half the French people when our troops landed. I was staggered. *"Au revoir,"* I said, "I must catch my plane. I can say only one thing on leaving: God help our government if it bases its policy towards France on such erroneous calculations."'

Robert Murphy, President Roosevelt's envoy, suffered the repercussions of these misjudgements, for which indeed he was held personally responsible by de Gaulle. Murphy had been in French North Africa for thirteen years, first as senior state official, then as consul-general. On the 14th July 1943 de Gaulle presided over a military parade, followed by a big popular demonstration. Formerly welcomed with pathetically little applause, he now received continuous ovations. On his left were Harold Macmillan, the British Minister of State, and Robert Murphy. A young man of the Resistance behind them heard the following dialogue:

Murphy: 'What a reassuring sight! How French I have felt for the last thirteen years!'

De Gaulle: 'Really, monsieur? *I* have felt French for two thousand years.'

Certainly de Gaulle was far from accommodating even to his fellow Frenchmen. Officers arrived from France to resume the fight, including one of the hopes of the French Army, Colonel Ély, who had been seriously wounded in 1940. Since then he had risked his life in Underground operations. 'Why didn't you join us sooner?' de Gaulle asked him.

'You see, mon Général, there were a great many of us who thought that the Marshal and you, considering you used to be on his staff, were fighting the same battle, he in France and you outside.'

De Gaulle rose angrily. 'Whatever made you think that? There's not a single word in any of my speeches that could have given you the right to think it.'

'Mon Général, we obviously did not suppose that you would say explicitly in your speeches that there was an understanding between Pétain and yourself. There were the Germans to think of!'

'The Marshal and I no longer have anything in common. The Marshal died in 1925. The pity is that he is still the only person not to realize it. I knew him well, it's true; but now he has become a man with a heart of stone.'

At one stage things looked very black for de Gaulle. Giraud claimed to have fears of a sudden *coup* directed against himself, and on this pretext established a sort of state of siege within a radius of fifty miles round Algiers, with tanks patrolling. De Gaulle, facing possible arrest, told one of his officers: 'It wouldn't be funny, eh, if the people opposite were as determined as the Gaullists. The British are at the back of it, but mark my words, Churchill and Roosevelt will climb down. They'll have to, because I'm in the right.'

The British and American commands had reason to be disturbed. They saw whole French units roaming about, with hundreds of French soldiers from the African Army trying to join the Free French, and vice versa; recruiting sergeants were at work for both sides. Eventually Colonel Paillole, with the help of General Koenig and René Capitant, managed to stop the wave of desertions and restore order.

There was, of course, one further complication: the war, and the private wars, were being fought here in an Arab country. One day de Gaulle was in a car with General Juin inspecting a parade. The review of the troops had been splendid. Several regiments of North African light infantry and cavalry had filed through the streets, watched by large numbers of Arabs, many of them shoe-shine boys and ragged unemployed. De Gaulle seemed in such ill humour that Juin asked him what had caused his displeasure.

'Nothing,' was the answer. 'Everything was perfect. But I look at these Arabs, these urchins in rags, and tell myself it's impossible, impossible, ever to turn them into Frenchmen.'

Perhaps it was always impossible; for a conflict generally encourages revolutionary ideas. Attempts to speed up assimilation of the North Africans raised only a faint echo amongst those concerned. The secret summaries produced by Military Security forces reported that at Algiers, Constantine and Setif the walls had been covered with the slogan: 'French citizens, no – Algerian citizens, yes.' The summaries added: 'An Underground paper *L'Action Algérienne* has been circulated. It condemns the policy whereby Moslems are to be progressively integrated into the French nation. It comes out for the definite establishment of an Algerian State governed by an Algerian Parliament. An underground nationalist agitation exists, the exact extent of which cannot be precisely determined. . . . Ferhat Abbas is still leading the Algerian nationalist movement.'

De Gaulle reflected on these symptoms, which confirmed in him a deep conviction: all over the world, through all civilizations and religions, invasions and occupations, nationalism, a feeling as natural as mother love, innate and indestructible, had a grip on men's hearts throughout their lives. Prophetically enough, he declared to one of his staff: 'France's presence in Algeria is a mistake. We have been able neither to assimilate this people nor to allow their own development. It won't last. One day we shall have to go.'

21

The End of Vichy, and the Liberation

All through 1943 resistance was growing within France; the Vichy Government was severely criticized even by its own men. A high official in the Foreign Office reported: 'The government has shown itself incapable of assuring one of its essential prerogatives: the protection of its nationals. Many Frenchmen, including seventy-four officers and N.C.O.s, have been arrested by the Gestapo for having simply carried out the functions entrusted to them; and the government failed even to protest. It is governing against public opinion, about 80 per cent of which is hostile to it. Diplomatic representatives abroad are abandoning it one by one. Only those in countries under the Axis heel are still attached to it, often against their will.'

This report was quoted by Colonel Paillole, who went on to give details of German oppression, including large-scale pillaging of French agriculture and industry, and the requisitioning of French labour. Laval was now effectively head of the government, actively collaborating with the Germans, and in agreement with Hitler had fixed that from May to August 1943 France must furnish 600,000 workers, two-thirds of them to go to Germany.

Nevertheless, the tide had clearly turned against Germany, and Pétain, with little or no power left to him, looked forward to the Americans arriving as they had done in 1917. This led him to a complete reversal of policy, in which he planned for a re-established republic with normal institutions restored. He would still be the legitimate power in France; there was no question of making it up with de Gaulle. On the contrary, he was preoccupied with keeping de Gaulle out of power after the war, and used all diplomatic channels open to him in order to influence Washington in that direction.

He even had a draft constitution drawn up, the text of which was to be conveyed to President Roosevelt. In August 1943 this was hidden in a loaf of bread and sent out to Lisbon, where it was received by Wing-Commander Gorostarzu, already in

Lisbon and in touch with Colonel Solborg, the U.S. Intelligence Chief. Gorostarzu had strict orders not to give anything away to de Gaulle's official representative there, who happened to be a former colleague of Pétain's at the Madrid Embassy.

Roosevelt duly received the text, and sent a reply which Gorostarzu could not deliver till March 1944: 'The Allied armies will shortly be landing. Let the Marshal abandon his position to a *Gauleiter* and retire to the château of Chambord or Chenonceaux. We shall then be able to liberate an imprisoned legitimate government. Let him abstain from all public activity, following the example of the président de la Chambre, Édouard Herriot.'

'That's what the Americans expect of you without delay, Monsieur le Maréchal,' Gorostarzu told him at a secret meeting in the Marshal's summer residence near Vichy. 'Pétain did not give me a definite reply at once,' Gorostarzu records, 'but he showed me quite openly that having promised the French people never to desert them, he preferred to remain at his post as head of State.' After the interview Gorostarzu, hearing that Laval had issued a warrant for his arrest, succeeded in escaping over the Pyrenees to Spain, where he at once informed Colonel Solborg through the American intelligence in Madrid that he had carried out his mission, but did not know what would come of it. In fact, as he suspected, nothing came of it.

At a lively meeting in the White House, Roosevelt had told the Free French representative, André Philip: 'France as France does not at present exist. After our invasion, when elections have taken place, we shall know who is France. For the moment there is no France, so de Gaulle cannot speak in her name. I am not an idealist like Wilson. I am a realist. Darlan gave me North Africa; *vive Darlan!* If Laval gives me Paris, *vive Laval!* If the Marshal gives me France, *vive le Maréchal!*'

Roosevelt talked of de Gaulle as 'an apprentice dictator'; these two exceptional personalities were separated by a wall of incomprehension. Indomitable defender of the cause of liberty, proud of his country and America as a world power, Roosevelt sometimes showed autocratic tendencies, though these were limited by the control of Congress. He cultivated his likes and dislikes, and steered a winding course between firm resolves and wily tactical manoeuvres. James Warburg, one of his closest colleagues in 1933, wrote: 'He believed what he wanted to

HENRI DE GAULLE

'His outstanding intellectual ability was matched by a most unusual moral excellence, and all his behaviour was marked by a rare courtesy; personal grief goes with deep regret to see the disappearance of a representative of the old true France.' (Extract from obituary notice under photograph 'in remembrance')

MADAME HENRI DE GAULLE

'She suffered intensely at the defeat of June 1940. From patriotism and sense of honour alike, she could not admit that this defeat was final. The refusal to compromise was a duty for her as for all Resisters. Her last days were filled with anguish, but also with hope and pride.' (Extract from obituary notice under photograph 'in remembrance')

The five de Gaulle children, Charles in the centre

The four de Gaulle brothers in 1919 (*left to right:* Charles, Xavier, Pierre, Jacques)

De Gaulle's 'intake' at the Staff College. De Gaulle, with white gloves, is sixth from left in second row

Nels, Dinant

Commemorative ceremony at Dinant, Belgium, September 1927. Marshal Pétain and his aide-de-camp, Charles de Gaulle (Mayor in top-hat behind)

Major de Gaulle with his battalion at Trèves

Major de Gaulle and the generals of the Trèves garrison with an illusionist, at the traditional *fête des chasseurs*—the anniversary of a famous battle in Algeria in 1845

Metz, December 1918. Poincaré presents marshal's baton to Pétain. *Behind him, left to right:* Joffre, Foch, Haig, Pershing, Gilling, Haller. Second row: Weygand and Buat

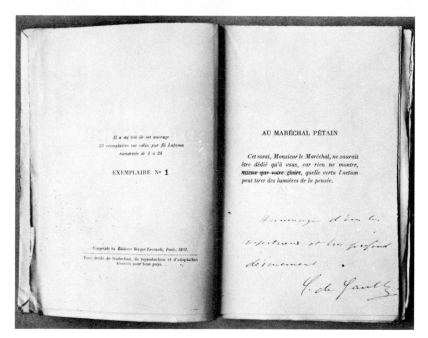

Copy No. 1 of de Gaulle's *Le Fil de l'épée,* given to Pétain, who deleted the word *'mieux que votre gloire'* (see p. 73)

Clemenceau in 1924

General Weygand

The title-page of de Gaulle's
lecture which became Chapter
I of *Le Fil de l'épée*

Commandant DE GAULLE

L'ACTION DE GUERRE

ET LE CHEF

CONFÉRENCE
faite à l'École supérieure de guerre, le 7 avril 1927,
sous la présidence de M. le Maréchal Pétain

IMPRIMERIE BERGER-LEVRAULT
NANCY-PARIS-STRASBOURG
1928

A
Monsieur
LE MARÉCHAL PÉTAIN

QUI A VOULU QUE CE LIVRE FÛT ÉCRIT,

QUI DIRIGEA DE SES CONSEILS
LA RÉDACTION DES CINQ PREMIERS CHAPITRES,

ET GRÂCE A QUI
LES DEUX DERNIERS SONT L'HISTOIRE
DE NOTRE VICTOIRE.

Disputed dedication to Marshal Pétain in de Gaulle's
book *La France et son armée*
(see p. 99)

20 Nov. 42

Monsieur le Maréchal,

Au moment où vous me livrez à l'ennemi, je vous réponds :

Vive la France !

Paul Reynaud's message to Pétain of 20 November, 1942 (see p. 160)

Marshal Pétain's physical vigour at eighty-five

The Marshal on his daily walk with Dr. Ménétrel at Vichy. It would have been easy to assassinate him

Marshal Pétain with cheering crowds at Nancy, end of May 1944. At the end of September de Gaulle came here to be greeted by equal crowds. Looking at photographs of the Marshal's visit, he observed: 'You could make out the same faces'

VICHY, le 11 Août 1944.

Je donne pouvoir à *l'Amiral Auphan*
pour me représenter auprès du haut commandement
anglo-saxon en France et, éventuellement, prendre
contact de ma part avec le Général de GAULLE ou
ses représentants qualifiés, à l'effet de trouver
au problème politique français, au moment de la
libération du territoire, une solution de nature à
empêcher la guerre civile et à réconcilier tous
les Français de bonne foi.

Si les circonstances le permettent,
l'Amiral Auphan m'en référera avant toute décision
d'ordre gouvernemental.

Si c'est impossible, je lui fais confian-
ce pour agir au mieux des intérêts de la Patrie,
pourvu que le principe de légitimité que j'incarne
soit sauvegardé.

Si je ne suis plus libre, *Auphan*
fera ouvrir le pli qui a été remis par moi-même en
1943 au vice-Président du Conseil d'Etat et au
Procureur général près la Cour de Cassation.

Ph. Pétain

'So long as the principle of legitimate government vested in me is safeguarded.' Pétain, in August 1944 (see pp. 186-7)

**MINISTÈRE
DE L'INTÉRIEUR**

DIRECTION GÉNÉRALE
SÛRETÉ NATIONALE

N° 268

Objet : **Notification**
d'une ordonnance de
prise de corps

Affaire :
PÉTAIN Philippe
Maréchal de France

PROCÈS-VERBAL

L'an mil neuf cent quarante cinq

le vingt six Avril

Devant Nous, François CHAVALOR

Commissaire de Police à Direction de la Sûreté Nationale

en résidence à PARIS *Officier de*

Police judiciaire, auxiliaire de Monsieur le Procureur de la République,

en mission à la frontière franco-suisse à Verrières-
sous-Joigne, se présente M.le Maréchal PÉTAIN, domici-
lié à Paris(7ème) Square de la Tour Maubourg N°8, qui
fait l'objet d'une ordonnance de prise de corps, en
date du 23 Avril 1945, délivrée par la Commission d'instruction près la Haute Cour de justice, du Chef d'at-
tentat contre la sûreté intérieure de l'Etat et du
chef d'intelligences avec l'ennemi et qui nous a été
remise ce jour pour exécution.
Interpellé sur son identité M.le Maréchal PÉTAIN
déclare:
"Je me nomme PÉTAIN Henri, Philippe, Benoni, Omer,
je suis né le 24 Avril 1856 à Cauchy-à-la-Tour(Pas d
Calais),de Omer et de Clotilde LEGRAND,Maréchal de
France,domicilié à Paris(7ème) Square de la Tour Mau
bourg N°8.
Je reconnais que l'ordonnance de prise de corps
dont vous me donnez connaissance et dont vous me re-
mettez copie s'applique bien à moi.
Lecture faite persiste et signe.
LE COMMISSAIRE DE POLICE JUDICIAIRE

'Above all, underline my Christian name Philippe,' Pétain asked on his
return to France, perhaps reminding everyone of his connection with de
Gaulle's son Philippe (see p. 208)

Le Jugement du Général de Gaulle
s'est imposé:

1° par une nécessité de discipline
militaire;

2° Comme valeur d'exemple
afin d'arrêter un mouvement
d'exode d'officiers français vers
l'étranger

3° Il est évident que ce jugement
par contumace, ne peut être que
de principe. Il n'a jamais été,
dans ma pensée, de lui donner
une suite.

4° Je suis prêt, au contraire, à
m'associer aux actes qui faciliteront
le retour de l'ordre en France et
l'union des cœurs entre tous les
Français.

Ph. Pétain

A note by Pétain on the sentence of death passed on de Gaulle by a Vichy tribunal (see pp. 123 and 210) believe, and remembered only what he wanted to remember.' A great American and a great servant of freedom, he was no missionary, but perhaps, in the name of the American empire, considered himself the world's leading democrat. Full of generous motives, he meant to restore France, but was hostile to the French colonial system, and did not think France could keep Indo-China, Morocco or other territories. After the liberation of France, he expected the country to be administered by A.M.G.O.T. (Allied Military Government of Occupied Territory).

In all his correspondence with Churchill he used the terms 'occupied' and 'occupation', which understandably roused de Gaulle's disgust and indignation. Occupation by friends who had saved France was almost as bad as the brutal régime of the German *Kommandatur*, because it was an offence against the dignity of France. Moreover, de Gaulle was afraid that if such an occupation were allowed to come into being, it would inevitably lead to a Russian party being formed in opposition to the Anglo-American party. The secret letter he wrote at the end of May 1944 to *Quartus* (Monsieur Parodi), the delegate-general of the Underground Provisional Government, for transmission to *Tristan* (P-H. Teitgen), is extremely revealing:

'My dear Quartus,

'The bearer will hand you something to which I attach great importance.' [Urgent nominations to be made.]

'In the phase about to open, the essential thing is to avoid having action directed by any foreign source. Everything must be centred on the government. No other authority counts. It will be your business to pick out what genuinely comes from the government amidst the hurly-burly organized by London, Washington and Moscow. The opening of operations is near. But developments will not go fast. So the Resistance meanwhile must carry out its battle in depth.

'All my thoughts and confidence are with you,

C. de Gaulle.'

The crucial moment was certainly approaching. Throughout the country the demands of the Resistance increased, and firing-squads got ready. But strangely enough, there were no attempts on the Marshal's life. Every day he went for a walk in the spa city's park, accompanied by Dr Ménétrel. They would sit down on an iron seat, and sometimes Pétain would say, tracing circles in the gravel: 'De Gaulle will have me shot. You don't know him. He's full of spite.' When he resumed his stroll, walking as strongly as ever, there were just two inspectors walking a few yards in front, two others behind, and one on each side of him. To fire at the Vichy Chief of State, to liquidate in spectacular manner the symbol of a policy, would have been the easiest of all operations considered by the special teams of the Resistance.

The Resistance's 'national military delegate', *Polygon* (Maurice Bourgès-Manoury), received a radio message from Algiers, dated the 14th April 1944, confirming agreement to the *Caravelle* mission, for 'execution of Darnand, Henriot or Doriot according to choice'. *Caravelle* (Franzini) wondered which of these, if any, to choose; it would surely be simpler to achieve the political sensation of executing Vichy's Chief of State. The plan was studied, and seemed very tempting compared with the other possibilities; but the decision to go ahead with it needed approval from de Gaulle himself. *Polygon* sent a message asking for the 'green light' and received the following cable in reply: 'No action of this kind. Stick to your own job, and carry out previous instructions.'

At the Hôtel du Parc, the Marshal was now saying: 'I am a prisoner, and I can't escape. At Verdun I had officers, men, munitions. Now I am alone, I have nothing left. Oh, the French people will find out afterwards what I have spared them.'

Eleven days after the cable from London was sent to *Polygon*, Pétain arrived in Paris for an official visit. The French authorities feared serious incidents, but none occurred, except that at several places the barriers gave way before the crowd's enthusiasm. Parisians came out in large numbers and gave him terrific ovations, singing the *Marseillaise*, which had been banned for four years. The Swiss Press spoke of a 'grandiose patriotic demonstration'. The Parisians, no doubt, were acclaiming not Pétain himself but the army, the French uniform, the last of the victorious marshals of the First World War – a symbol to rouse mass emotion in a population long denied any open expression. Pierre Taittinger, then Mayor of Paris, recalls the scene:

'On reaching the Hôtel Bichat, I shall always remember a fat woman dressed entirely in white at the entrance, who might have been waitress, nurse or concierge. . . . When we announced that the Marshal was just coming, she burst out scornfully: "We don't need *that* old monkey."

'Preceded by a few motor-cyclists, the Marshal's car arrived, its tricolour flag tied round with white bows and tassels: there was a burst of enthusiasm. . . . Marshal Pétain shook a few hands, then reached the slut of a few minutes before, who was now transfigured, almost in ecstasy. She began yelling "*Vive Pétain*" in delirious enthusiasm which helped to excite the crowd still further.'

Sinus (General Revers), chief of the Army Resistance Organization, sent a report to London: '200,000 people at least . . . genuine enthusiasm.' On 4th June, two days before D-Day, a film of this official visit was shown to de Gaulle in London, who was very disillusioned. Colonel Billotte analysed the facts, trying to reassure him: 'The Parisians found this their only way of protesting against the Germans: to gather round a Marshal of France in uniform, symbol of France victorious. It's not an act of collaboration, it's an act of resistance.' But de Gaulle, thinking of the near future, repeated his frequent comment: 'The Marshal is an old fox. At the last moment he'll try some trick or other. But he won't catch *me*.'

Pétain himself wanted to get the film sent to General Eisenhower, as evidence of his 'legitimacy'. On 3rd June he told one of his staff: 'Now I've got a tricky bit of diplomacy to do. It's lucky I have friends in the United States. As for the *Wehrmacht*, they still *look* disciplined but that's all that's left. The Germans are incapable of resisting.' In Paris, from the balcony of the Hôtel de Ville, he had spoken in such strong anti-German terms that the speech was censored and altered for use in the Press and on the radio.

After this, however, he broadcast a pro-German speech. When General Serrigny asked him why he had done this, he said: 'I was forced to. The Germans have been putting pressure on me for weeks, and in the end I had to give in. But anyhow what am I criticized for?'

'Above all, for saying that the Germans would protect France.'

'But that's what I think.'

185

'Perhaps, though even when you say so directly to me, I don't really believe it. In any case the French people would never ask to be "protected" in this fashion.'

After the failure of the attempt to kill Hitler on 20th July, Pétain said: 'I think I'll send my congratulations. It's only elementary politeness, from one head of State to another.'

'No!' protested Dr Ménétrel indignantly. 'The French people will never understand that. To them it would mean something far more serious.'

Pétain wavered, and gave up the idea – until Laval pressed him: 'A few formal words.' The pressure lasted for twenty-four hours, then the Marshal signed. The telegram was in his office, ready to go. He had a German general, von Neubronn, with him. Gabriel Jeantet, one of his personal staff, entered, and seeing the telegram said: 'Monsieur le Maréchal, you are dishonouring yourself.' 'What should I do?' Pétain asked helplessly. 'This,' said Jeantet, picking up the telegram and tearing it in pieces. The Marshal looked at him, but said nothing. Then he squashed a fly buzzing about on the wall-map, and exclaimed: 'Look, a Boche! I'm killing him.' Von Neubronn went very red. 'We're too apt to make generalizations,' Pétain remarked blandly.[1]

A few days later, von Neubronn had the doors of the Marshal's rooms smashed open, and the windows broken. The Marshal himself was taken off to Belfort soon afterwards, at the end of August, a prisoner at last in name as well as fact. The *Luftwaffe* were ready to go into action, and the Marshal declared: 'I haven't the right to let Vichy be bombed so that I can go down in history with greater glory.'

During these last convulsions he had finally followed the advice of those who wanted him to join up with de Gaulle. One of the most prominent of these was Admiral Auphan, former Secretary of State for the Navy, who in November 1942 had urged Pétain to order the fleet at Toulon out to sea, following the Allied landings in North Africa. He saw Pétain vacillate and then decide against this, but obtained a belated resistance to the Germans in the scuttling of the fleet at the end of the month. He had kept in touch with men in the Resistance, and

[1] Whatever the Marshal's final decision, although the telegram was never sent, congratulations on his behalf were conveyed orally to Hitler's personal representative.

so was able to start on a mission from Pétain, offering to hand over power to de Gaulle, 'so long as the principle of legitimate government vested in me is safeguarded.'

Auphan first made contact with two ardent young Resistance men in Paris, *Tristan* (Pierre-Henri Teitgen) and *Jacquier* (Michel Debré). *Bip* (Georges Bidault) reported to Algiers, which had authorized the meeting. Further meetings were only to be sanctioned if the Marshal first condemned action against the Maquis, disowned Laval's Militia, etc. Owing to the difficulties of getting these conditions fulfilled, combined with the fact that *Tristan* was arrested, negotiations remained abortive. But Auphan at last succeeded in transmitting Pétain's message to de Gaulle through General Lacaille and then General Juin.[1]

Pétain had told Auphan: 'I am ready to leave the scene so long as the legitimacy of my position is not questioned. Revolution must be avoided. Tell de Gaulle that I never intended to shoot him. Here is his military dossier. . . . The gesture must be tried for the sake of France. . . . But you won't get anywhere. He is too proud.'

During the discussions, the Marshal sometimes seemed to have lost touch with reality. In the presence of one of his private secretaries he made some bizarre remarks: 'One might give de Gaulle a secondary post to start with. Not the Postmaster General, of course. But he might take the War Office. To make him head of the government straight away would be rather rash! He'll have to prove himself first. You need preparation for everything. We'll soon see if he's capable of becoming Prime Minister.'

On other occasions he would say: 'You must tell de Gaulle I don't intend to stay in power long. Just a few months, together with him, to consolidate the unity which our agreement will bring about. Basically we have the same ideas. As soon as possible I shall return to my estate and live in peace.'

At the end of August 1944 a French armoured force under General Leclerc entered Paris, and the German commander surrendered. A day or two later, de Gaulle sat in a big room at the War Office, which he made his headquarters, with the

---

[1] See Appendix 3, Auphan's memorandum to de Gaulle on the need for a legal handing over of power, 25th August 1944 (the day of the liberation of Paris).

message before him: 'The Marshal of France, head of State. . . . I authorize Admiral Auphan to . . . make contact on my behalf with General de Gaulle, in order to find a solution to the French political problem. . . .'

De Gaulle read it in silence. He has described in his *Memoirs* the memories passing through his mind. 'So, in the destruction of Vichy, Philippe Pétain turned to Charles de Gaulle. Here was the end of the terrible series of surrenders when, on the pretext of "saving the property", slavery was accepted. How unbearably distressing that such a policy should be adopted by a glorious military leader in extreme old age. While reading the message transmitted to me on his behalf, I suddenly felt myself confirmed in what I had always known, and full of ineffable sadness. Monsieur le Maréchal! You who once did so great honour to our Arms, you who were once my leader and my example, how low have you been brought?'

In the midst of his triumph, de Gaulle could feel 'ineffaole sadness'; but 'in this case sentiment could not prevail over reasons of State'.

Pétain had offered him a last example – an example to reject: never to stay on 'in affairs' till old age eroded the character and sapped the memory; never to become the 'Pétain of peace' after having been the 'Gaulle of victory'. The Marshal, although haunted by the fear of senility, had failed to keep this strict check on himself. One day he had crossed the line without noticing it. 'May God rest his soul,' de Gaulle murmured, the disciple speaking of his former master, in piety and pity, as of one who was already dead.

The Marshal had not known when to retire, because he had never imposed tests on himself. De Gaulle would subject himself to a severe discipline: the day when he observed that his fantastic memory was deserting him, however slightly, the day when he could no longer deliver a lecture of an hour or an hour and a half without any notes, that day de Gaulle would retire from public life whatever happened and whatever anyone said to him. You couldn't wait for those around you to warn you: entourages never dared to reveal the terrible truth.

And so, things being what they were, the old soldier travelled towards the Reich, protected by the pistols of the German military police. But to the Marshal of 1944 and his approaches de Gaulle could give 'only the answer of silence'. He could not admit a legitimacy he had always denied, the recognition of which would have the effect of retrospectively ratifying the armistice in 1940, and so transforming the appeal of 18th June into an act of indiscipline. He could not accept this principle: he had not disobeyed, since duty and honour commanded him to reject a power which had lost the attributes of national sovereignty. Moreover, in that summer of the liberation, de Gaulle had become convinced that any other attitude would create a revolutionary situation inside France, which he greatly feared.

He was supported in this by some ministers who had arrived in France from Algiers. They admitted that 'in the country districts, among the veterans of the first war, among the clergy, and of course in the middle classes, there are plenty of people who would like to see a de Gaulle–Pétain reconciliation. Can de Gaulle bring this about if he wishes, with all his great prestige? No: it is impossible. It would benefit only the Communist Party. How could one explain that handshake to the Resistance, the deportees, the families of those who have been killed? Pétain has condoned enlistments in the Legion of French Volunteers against Bolshevism, racial looting, the creation of the Militia, court-martials for civilians, operations against the Maquis, etc. You can't absolve him, then condemn those who have committed crimes in his name.'

De Gaulle himself stormed against 'the middle-class armchair heroes, the generals who did not rally to the fight, the bishops who preached too much'. (At the Liberation de Gaulle expressed the wish that about thirty bishops and archbishops who had been definite supporters of Pétain should be replaced.) 'Did they expect that I would save them from the gallows? Oh yes, there were apparently too many Jews and Freemasons round me. The Jews and Freemasons would have been less conspicuous if that lot hadn't kept their feet in their slippers. It's incredible they haven't understood what we stand for.

'Gaullism has been, is and will remain, the school of politics which refuses and will always refuse to let France be a power of the second order. Gaullism is the negation of the *fait accompli*. It is a rejection of pessimism, defeatism, surrender and resignation: that's what Gaullism is. It is a natural reflex, not the faction or coterie it has been described as. It is not a provisional expedient, but an immense faith in France. A great people which ceases to believe in its destiny, which leaves the issue of battle to others, is no longer a country. That is something I shall never accept, for I shall never surrender.'

Meanwhile Pétain was transferred by the Germans from Belfort to Sigmaringen in Germany. There he sent out his pathetic last message to Roosevelt, written on a piece of silk sewn into the lining of a coat worn by a Swiss diplomat. It was too late: he had not retired in time to a château on the Loire, as the President had advised him. But the message arrived in Switzerland, went to Allen Dulles at the Berne Office of Strategic Service. It was eventually transmitted to Roosevelt by Colonel Solborg, who had long been convinced that his government had gone astray in their policies towards France, and that de Gaulle ought to be recognized as head of a provisional government. 'Vichy, London, Pétain, de Gaulle,' commented Solborg. 'Neither the Americans nor the British, nor even the French themselves, can appreciate to the full this great national tragedy and great human drama.'

22

De Gaulle Joins the Big Three

'The supreme battle is engaged. It is, of course, the battle of France.' What joy and pride in the General's voice, as he addressed Frenchmen in the 'last lap'! But he was full of sadness too, not to see more of the sons of France joining in the Liberation; instead, they had left the Allied armies, friends but still foreigners, to play the decisive part.

The landing on D-Day was 'notified' to de Gaulle by Churchill somewhere near Portsmouth – 'and in a railway carriage!' the General exclaimed bitterly. Eisenhower in his proclamation invited the French nation 'to carry out his orders,' promising that 'the French nation themselves will choose their representatives and their government'.

Soon after the liberation of Brittany, de Gaulle went to Rennes, where he visited his mother's grave, and later retrieved some personal papers, including many letters from Marshal Pétain. He received the honours of the American troops, whom General Bradley, with the best intentions, had detached from operations for the occasion. The Tricolour, the Stars and Stripes and the Union Jack waved across the streets, mingling fraternally together. Remote from the cheers of a frenzied crowd acclaiming the 'boys' and the 'Tommies', de Gaulle asked the prefect: 'Tell me what all this is about. We're supposed to be celebrating the liberation of France, aren't we?'

During the reception by the town's authorities Monsignor Roques, Archbishop of Rennes and Primate of Brittany, allowed himself a frankness justified by his irreproachable attitude under the occupation:

'Mon Général, do you know what they are saying about you in some circles?'

'In what circles?'

'In the circles a man of my kind may frequent.'

'And what are they saying?'

'That you are too close to the Communists.'

'Well, they wouldn't say it if more prelates had been with me.'

Yet everywhere in France the people's will was being tested. Very close to the people for all his reserve, de Gaulle immediately made a series of visits: Lyons, Marseilles, Toulon, Toulouse, Bordeaux, Saintes, Orléans, Normandy, Champagne, the Nord, etc. In the suburbs of Paris, Robert Lacoste, Minister of Production, pointed to the crowd: 'You see all these splendid folk, mon Général. *They* didn't come to applaud Pétain.'

De Gaulle: 'You're wrong, my friend. I saw the films of the Marshal's visits. There were at least as many people present, and often the same ones.'

One slight incident marred that day; there was an isolated cry of 'Bravo, Charlot!' That is what Charlie Chaplin is commonly called in France. The General frowned.

The evening after the triumphant visit to Nancy, where Pétain had gone only a few weeks before, de Gaulle was with his family, comparing the photographs of the two welcomes given by the crowd in Stanislas Square. With sardonic humour he observed: 'Look, you'll be able to find the same faces.'

Passing through Lorraine, he was advised by General de Lattre: 'Mon Général, as you go back into France you should take in Domrémy. Joan of Arc. . . .'

De Gaulle: 'You're right. She has deserved it.'

At Montreuil, a tiny little hunchback planted himself at de Gaulle's feet. He drew himself erect, swelling with historic importance, looked up at the General, and addressed him in a slightly reproachful voice: 'We trust you, mon Général, to apply the programme of the National Council of the Resistance.'

De Gaulle: 'And also a programme to restore France, don't you think?'

He did not wish at any price to hold power through the Resistance; as he often repeated, power came to him legitimately from the position he took on the 18th June 1940. What a reversal of roles that the man once 'miserably shipwrecked on Anglo-Saxon shores' should play host to Winston Churchill and Anthony Eden, when they came to Paris for a conference in November 1944. The British Prime Minister and Foreign Minister arrived in the capital on 10th November.

De Gaulle sincerely admired Churchill as a man of tremendous character and indomitable courage. Yes, he was a great man, a very great man. Yet (as the General wrote in his *Memoirs*) it was not so long ago that Churchill 'could not wholeheartedly decide to admit the independence of Free France'; that he had seen Charles de Gaulle as embodying 'an ambitious state which seemed to be trying to recover its power in Europe and overseas. Churchill had naturally felt a breath of Pitt's spirit pass through his own.'

The day after his arrival, Churchill, in R.A.F. uniform, wearing a cap with gold oak leaves, attended a troop review in the Champs-Élysées. They were triumphant hours, marking the resurrection of France and her return to full sovereignty. In response to the cheering crowds, Churchill raised his right hand and gave his famous V sign. . . .'*Vive de Gaulle! Vive Churchill!*' the crowds yelled. Going down from the Étoile towards the statue of Clemenceau, Churchill met a new wave of acclamations; while de Gaulle hissed into the ear of the minister next to him: 'The imbeciles! The cretins! Just look at that: the mob acclaiming that old brigand!'

Such an aside did not mean there could be no personal feelings between the two men; but in foreign policy there was no room for sentiment.

Yet at this point Churchill was more favourably disposed to de Gaulle's hopes and plans than de Gaulle might have expected. He (Churchill) wrote to Roosevelt reporting on the discussions (with a copy of the letter for Stalin), 'I sympathize with the French wish to take over more of the line, to have the best share they can in the fighting or what is left of it – and there may be plenty – and not to go into Germany as a so-called conqueror who has not fought. I remarked that this was a sentimental point which ought nevertheless to receive consideration. The important thing for France was to have an army prepared for the task which it would actually have to discharge, namely their obligation first to maintain an orderly and peaceful country behind the front of our armies, and secondly to assist the holding down of parts of Germany later on.

'On the second point the French pressed very strongly to have a share in the occupation of Germany not merely as sub-participants under British or American command, but as a French command. I expressed my sympathy with this. . . .'

The exchange of views in Paris dealt with problems all over the world: Germany, the Saar, Eastern Europe, Syria and the

Lebanon, the Middle East, the Pacific, and the future peace conference. Since 22nd October 1944 de Gaulle's Government had been recognized by the main powers as the 'provisional government of the French Republic'. 'Well, I hope you're pleased,' said Churchill. 'Here you are, recognized as the legitimate government.'

'Good heavens!' cried de Gaulle. 'Are *you* so pleased, then, when someone calls you by your own name?'

The British delegation left Paris somewhat reassured about France. Churchill: 'This morning the demonstration of French strength was impressive. Before I left England, the people there were a bit scared.'

De Gaulle: 'Of the F.F.I.?' (French Forces of the Interior.)

Churchill: 'Yes. But everything has gone well.'

De Gaulle: 'One is always right to trust France.'

In fact, however, de Gaulle was more anxious than he made out. For months he had been worried by the fear of serious disturbances organized by the Communists and their Resistance Army, the F.T.P. (Franc-Tireurs Partisans). At the end of August the Algiers intelligence had sent *Polygon* the following telegram among others: 'From absolutely reliable source. Quote: after Boches leave F.T.P. ready to take power Lyons; prefect Boutemy made contact with them, holds stations and post office. F.T.P. refuse to recognize military governor and all officers and officials appointed Algiers, claiming their views not republican enough. F.T.P. troops probably already at Lyons, we estimate 1,400 men forming nucleus. List of suspects prepared by them, certain result will be several thousand people shot. F.F.I. abandoning Lyons, await regular troops to retake city. All efforts must be co-ordinated at any price to avoid massacre.'

Was there a danger of the Communist Party taking power? The opinions of the Republic's regional commissioners, even in areas where the central power had difficulty in establishing itself, were unanimous: the Communist Party was only putting out one instruction, to intensify the war effort as much as possible, not creating any disturbances behind the western front. Moreover, Stalin's political designs were not Europe from the Urals to the Atlantic; it was enough for him to get Communism firmly planted in eastern Europe.

It is quite true, however, that the Communist Party proved to have considerable appeal, and (as de Gaulle noted) the events from which France was painfully emerging gave it exceptional chances of triumphing. Admittedly the Americans would not have tolerated any attempt at a rising, and even without Gaullism Italy did not succumb any more than France. The risk, as de Gaulle saw it, was rather that of a future infection, through a 'National Front', which would gradually involve the country in a fatal process – as Czechoslovakia was soon to illustrate. The situation might indeed have gone either way, but de Gaulle had a sort of 'Kerensky complex'.

The patriotic militia formed in the factories and urban districts, amidst the enthusiasm of a national rising, might well provide a war machine if the chance came. This force was armed, whereas the police and the National Guards were equipped in practice only with pistols of very small calibre.

One bargaining point which de Gaulle had, and used, was the return of Maurice Thorez to France. At the outbreak of war the Communist Party leader, following the Russo-German pact, had refused military service and fled to Russia; he was condemned in absence by a military tribunal. At the period of the Algiers Committee the Soviet ministers Vyshinsky and Bogmolov had several times made requests that Thorez should be allowed to return; but de Gaulle always rejected them. Now, however, he signed a decree whereby the Council of Ministers gave Thorez the benefit of an 'act of clemency'. In his *Memoirs* he states: 'Considering the circumstances of 1940, the events which had taken place since, and the needs of the day, I considered that the return of Maurice Thorez to the leadership of the Communist Party might at the time have more advantages than disadvantages.' In other words, as he put it more explicitly to Colonel Groussard, a former commander of the Staff College: 'I brought back Thorez so that I should be able to disarm the patriotic militia.'

And to Colonel Passy, just back from the United States, he observed: 'The Americans are worried about my policy, it seems. In this country, you see, which is at least a quarter Communist, I have no choice. I have two solutions: either to allow the Communists to renew their organization and put at the head of them one of the leaders of their military resistance with a halo of prestige around him; or to bring back Thorez who, because of that business of his leaving his unit, will always carry the slur of desertion.

'My basic aim, made easier by the treaty with the Soviets, is to bring France right back into the war and launch into the battle of production with all our resources. For this the co-operation of the Communists was indispensable to me. There, you see: I'm right. All the Communist leaders are now getting on their soapboxes to tell the French to roll up their sleeves!'

De Gaulle attended in person the awards of the Liberation Cross to Communist underground fighters. He told Jacques Soustelle: 'We must swamp the Communists in democracy.' The key to his policy can be summed up in the chronology of events: dissolution of the patriotic militia and home guard (28th October); decree of act of clemency for Maurice Thorez (6th November); appeal by Thorez 'Fight on, right to Berlin. This is the only task for the moment, the law for all French people' (30th November); General de Gaulle's arrival at Moscow (2nd December); conference of the French Communist Party's central committee (21st January, 1945). The secretary-general pronounced against the maintenance of armed groups whatever they might be; he appealed to the Communist Party's 'national mission' and called for a million men to serve in the forces.

At a later date Jacques Duclos, prominent among the Communist Party leaders, told the author: 'We pronounced for the dissolution [of the militia] in order to avoid incidents. They were incompatible with our policy, which was to carry on with winning the war, to intensify the national effort in the struggle against Nazism.'

Invited to join the government, Thorez showed himself to be a 'real statesman', as de Gaulle often repeated. As a Frenchman who put Communism first, he no doubt needed greater courage in 1939 to desert his regiment than to remain a sapper in the army. But now he proved to be a Frenchman first, a Communist second: here he was at Paris, contributing to national unity. As things turned out, it looked as if the president of France's provisional government, going to Moscow to sign the Franco-Soviet pact, had carried out an exceptional performance of political lion-taming.

He wrote in his *Memoirs*, concerning the patriotic militia: 'You could feel they were ready to apply a pressure which would either coerce the legal power or get control of it.' And later, to a journalist: 'At the Liberation, arms were in the hands of the Communists, and the F.T.P arm-bands served as a passport to respectability. I had to bargain to get the militia disarmed. I bargained indirectly through the return of Maurice Thorez. But I never agreed to give the Communists one of the key posts in the State, such as national defence, the interior, or foreign affairs! Without de Gaulle, the Communists would have seized power in France.'

However, the fear of internal disorders pursued de Gaulle even to Russia. At Baku, putting on his fur-lined coat, he exclaimed: 'This is a perfect trip. But I only hope France won't get into a revolution while I'm away.'

From Armavir, Mosdok and Stalingrad to Moscow, along the Caspian, or through white expanses broken by churchless villages and tractor stations, the railway journey, despite copious meals, seemed endless. Five days! Anxious to make good use of the time in the carriage saloons with their tasselled green curtains and fine Russian leather, Mr Bogmolov, who had long represented the Soviet Union at Vichy, often referred to the time he had spent there. De Gaulle became distinctly irritated: 'Look, Ambassador, what characterized the men of Vichy is the fact that they always wanted to play some card or other: the German or the English or even the Russian card. We are not playing at all. We haven't got an English card or even a Russian one. For us there was and is only France.' His face grew animated, he picked up his smoker's kit and leant over the table: 'You see, Ambassador, we remade France with matchsticks.'

Ilya Ehrenburg, the famous Russian author, had dedicated his book *The Fall of Paris* to de Gaulle. Opening it, de Gaulle exclaimed: 'Ah, if we had had 5,000 miles in which to retreat, it's we today who would be writing *The Fall of Moscow*.'

Stalin – de Gaulle, it was certainly a meeting of two giants. De Gaulle commented on the red Tsar: 'He's a despot, and means to be. He's a man of genius. He has political genius, but also, alas, a genius for evil.'

Stalin certainly had a sense of drama, décor and scene. Even de Gaulle, although he did not show it, was riveted by the man. While Molotov and Bidault were involved in lengthy negotiations on the Lublin Committee and the fate of Poland, Stalin several times interrupted his conversation to make cutting remarks about them, with a wink at de Gaulle: 'Oh, these diplomats! What a race! Bulganin, go and fetch me a machinegun and sweep all that away for me.' Then he advised his guest: 'Thorez is a good Frenchman, don't put him in prison, not straight away anyhow.' At the time of the toasts he turned towards de Gaulle's chief secretary: 'I drink to Monsieur Palewski, Polish patriot.' Protests. Stalin: 'French? But a Pole always remains a Pole.' This rather crude joke was greeted with constrained laughter for several minutes.

Such was the small provincial leader, transformed into a great Russian nationalist, of whom Lenin said: 'He's a Genghis Khan who has read Karl Marx.' A truculent and terrifying dictator, his constant cunning and will to power were at least partly in the interests of Soviet Russia and the proletarian revolution.

Physically, he was disappointing to the imagination: in khaki uniform, wearing the medals of a Hero of the Soviet Union, despite high black boots which shone like mirrors, he still looked a short squat figure – he was only five foot five. He had a thin sallow face, deeply wrinkled eyes, and thick, close-cut, well-combed silvery hair. The voice which could doom thousands to death or torture was not thunderous but if anything rather weak. Yet underneath all this there was an indefinable sense of fierce energy. Emmanuel d'Astier wrote in *Les Grands*, 'many worshipped or hated him: no one could love him. In History he will rouse only pride and terror.'

According to his moods and schemes, tragedian or comedian, friend or enemy of the people, Stalin wore several masks: satrap or patriarch, tyrant or little father, jovial Georgian or cruel demi-god. His humour readily took a sadistic turn, and the tormentor enjoyed using jokes to terrorize any who came in contact with him.

He was delighted to demonstrate his talents to de Gaulle, whose character he had grasped shrewdly enough. 'You are a stiff man,' he remarked, raising his glass of vodka to the Franco-Russian alliance. 'France now has uncompromising leaders who do not yield. It's good, very good. It's what France needs.'

De Gaulle was not deceived by smooth words, nor by the outward appearance of Communism in practice. The Moscow crowd, mute and passive, made him think. 'The silence of the sea,' he commented. 'It's the domination not of a party, but of a man. The régime is not popular. It is against nature. Still, we shall have these people on our hands for a hundred years!'

In his foreign policy de Gaulle continued to show all the intransigence Stalin had attributed to him. Talking of France's partners, he grumbled: 'They are cowards. They're only strong through our weakness. They will feel our unshakeable resolution. They will capitulate. They will lie down!'

'But, mon Général,' a Minister objected, 'if Stalin and Roosevelt and Churchill talked like you, we should be at war every morning. What would happen if each of the Big Four were a de Gaulle?'

'You are right, my friend. But then, you see, there is only one de Gaulle.'

23

'Peace Is Exasperating'

Allies and adversaries, of course, did not always bow to the inflexible will. In these cases de Gaulle had mastered the art, it is true, of retreating while apparently advancing. According to an opinion in common circulation, de Gaulle is a master of cunning. This is only half the truth. A disconcerting Machiavelli, he offers a striking example of fidelity to his ideas and permanence in his objectives, if not in his tactics. He puts in black and white the ends to which he is working: often, indeed, he has made them so 'blindingly' clear that the world seems too dazzled to grasp them at all; it all looks so obvious that no one dare believe his eyes. Contrary to the legend, de Gaulle has been revealed on many occasions as an example of devastating simplicity. Simplicity then becomes cunning – one day he admitted: 'I pretend to be pretending, so that I can better conceal my real plans.'

'There is only one de Gaulle.' But alas, that de Gaulle was not sitting round the conference table at Yalta in February 1945 with Stalin, Roosevelt and Churchill. He could not accept such exclusion! That August he said in a speech: 'How many Frenchmen, buried in their native land for two thousand years, must have turned in their grave when it was known that the fate of vanquished Germany had partly been settled without France having her say?'

The affront had already been avenged, however, in May, when Germany surrendered, and Field-Marshal Keitel saw General de Lattre take his place beside Eisenhower, Montgomery and Zhukov. 'What!' cried Keitel. 'The French too?' This was a moment of triumph for de Gaulle's unconquerable heart. By a miracle France had been pulled out of the abyss to sit at the victor's table with the Great Powers. By a miracle France was erect again, stripping off the mentality of the 1940 defeat. As a Great Power once more, she occupied German territory, planted her colours on the Rhine and on the Danube. Such was the reward for political combat, a reward which could never have been won by a 'Garibaldi Legion'. By his genius, against all appearances and all reasoned hope, de Gaulle had brought his humiliated country, whose prostration he could not bear to see, back into the camp of the victors. For the demons of bitterness and shame he had substituted the familiar spirits of victory. 'I have wiped out the defeat,' he exclaimed on one occasion.

But had the French really 'won the war'? he wrote in his *Memoirs*: 'I dreamt how exalting it would be for them to take part in an adventure as wide as the world. However harsh the realities might be, I could overcome them, since it was possible for me, following Chateaubriand's phrase, "to lead the French by dreams".' De Gaulle had already been wondering whether it was not time for him to depart. Here is part of his address to the officers of the victorious troops on the Atlantic front: 'I wonder how far some people imagine that I am indispensable to the restoration of France. . . . They would like to have me considered a miracle worker or a magician. . . . I am neither the one nor the other, and even if I were, I should refuse to intervene.

'France is sick, she is like a body which is breaking up. If I wanted, I could put her in an orthopaedic corset, and, holding her at arm's length, give her an outward appearance of health. . . . But as soon as I opened my hand and unlaced the corset, she would fall, never to rise again. No, certainly, I shall not do that.

'The cure must be her own work. She must recover health of herself. Inside this heap of decaying matter there must surely, inevitably, be a healthy seed which will generate its own resurrection. But the seed must be born and grow from the French people themselves. . . . Only then will a gardener chosen by the nation bend over it, lavish his care on it, help it to grow and proliferate so that in the end it smothers all the rest.

'It matters little who this gardener is. Whether his name is de Gaulle or not . . . he will be sure of success, for the body of France will have proved by its proper reaction that it was worthy to live and become strong again.

'If France cannot accomplish this act of energy, if she cannot carry out this act of faith on which her resurrection depends . . . so much the worse for France. In that case she will no longer be worthy to survive.'

201

But to change the metaphor once more, de Gaulle was the captain who had weathered all storms. Now the storms were already dying down, how, he asked in his *Memoirs*, 'could the flame of national ambition, rekindled under the ashes by the gale, be kept ablaze when the wind fell?' For the moment peace reigned, a state which said little to de Gaulle. He confided to Georges Bidault, his Foreign Minister: 'One only governs well in time of war'; and another favourite theme was that 'Administration is mean, petty, pernickety. Government is painful, difficult, delicate. War is horrible, to be sure, but as for peace, it's exasperating.'

In practical terms things were not going as he wished in those early months of peace. He deplored 'the old French propensity for divisions and quarrels'. The parties came back to life, and he complained to some leading socialists: 'The parties are again becoming detestable. . . . Your socialists will return to their vomits, anti-militarist or something else. When de Gaulle is no longer there, you will see them all getting worked up, anyhow – the *députés*, the priests, the military . . .'

One evening, in the intimacy of his room at the War Office he confided some of his ideas on French politics.

'Before the war my thoughts on political institutions were what any officer of my training would think: Parliament, crises, instability of power, the parties. I thought, too, that outside this shadow-theatre, France drew her strength from the great national institutions, the army, the intellectual aristocracy.

'Then I left for London. I hoped I would be joined by the heads of the public bodies, the churches and the military staffs. I looked to those who had an official position and were then in London – but saw them gradually return to France.

'Then I saw the poor folk arrive, the privates, the Dunkirk sailors and Breton fishermen, the little people. In the end I was able to build Free France with them – and with some others, it's true, but first of all with the people.

'The people, though, are becoming undisciplined again. They are returning to disorder, mess, the parties. The parties! The misfortune of this country remains, that the right is against the nation and the left is against the State!

'Perhaps one individual can be held responsible for what was done in the bad days as in the good days. I am not very convinced of it, however, since that individual was responsible to France, and France's true wishes.'

For the moment the one individual governed, in the difficult and delicate times of peace. If the main storm had abated, there were plenty of minor ones, including a new quarrel with the British over Syria and the Lebanon. When this came up in the cabinet, he found Bidault strongly opposed to his views. He consulted the rest of the cabinet in turn, but they supported Bidault. Following Lincoln's famous remark when opposed by everyone else in a cabinet discussion –'seven noes, one aye, the ayes have it' – de Gaulle announced: 'I have collected your opinions. They do not agree with mine. The decision is carried unanimously.'

His decision, that is: ministers were to play only a consultant part. De Gaulle boasted: 'When I am annoyed, all they think about is climbing under the table.' Some were less ready to lie down, however, and he told one of these bold spirits severely: 'For you, to negotiate is to capitulate.'

'Mon Général, I am as good a Frenchman as you are.'

'You may be; but the next time you won't be a cabinet minister.'

One of his most devoted supporters, responsible for an essential department, burst into tears in front of several of his colleagues after a personal humiliation from the General, who had added for good measure: 'I chose the most stupid man because I thought he would be the most loyal.'

'You talk to me of the people, of my ministers,' he exclaimed before one high official. 'But there is only de Gaulle.' As for criticisms, 'We can't stop people criticizing us. But then, you know, other people's opinions matter so little.' Of men in general he complained to Pierre-Henri Teitgen: 'In the last resort the best of them is worth no more than the worst.' To Henri Ulver: 'Men have no importance. The only one who counts is the leader commanding them.' In fact he did not at all care for striking personalities and strong characters; he preferred individuals who did what he said and did it readily. One could catch an echo of Clemenceau talking to Maurice Barrès: 'I have always despised men. It's a pity, but that's how it is.'

The Second World War was over, though perhaps a third war was on the horizon. Since Pearl Harbor de Gaulle had foreseen only a calm at the end of the storm, to be followed some time by a new conflagration. Even on that day in December 1941 when he heard over the radio of the Japanese attack, he predicted to Colonel Passy, after a period of meditation: 'Now the war is definitely won! And after it the future has two phases in store for us: the first will be the rescue of Germany by the Allies; as for the second, I fear it may be a great war between the Russians and the Americans – and that war, Passy, the Americans will lose!'

Still, by the end of 1945 the guns were silent for the time being over most of the world. General de Gaulle remained president of the provisional government, but felt very much alone. Sometimes it gave him a harsh pleasure to be alone, and solitude was his constant temptation: 'Solitude is my friend,' he remarked in his *Memoirs*. 'What other friend can satisfy when one has been face to face with History?'

He began to listen to the songs of the sirens, bidding him make his final appearance, then go: not a real final appearance, but one after which he could prepare for return at the moment of danger; the country, deprived of its captain, would soon be threatened by such a moment. The resurgence of the parliamentary system was becoming inevitable, and he had no use for the 'shams' of that democracy. However, the time for dictators in the style of ancient Rome had gone. He dreamed of a régime which would take away the importance of the *députés*, and allow their part in the government to be limited in favour of technicians, technocrats and non-party men. The executive must not come from parliament, nor the head of State from a party. No old-fashioned despotism; but the power must have a head, not the hundred heads of the parties, doomed to weakness and liable to decadence. Colonel Passy collected some of the General's disillusioned observations:

'It's impossible to govern . . . the parties. . . . Between the country's interest and party interest, the parties always choose their own. . . . You see, Passy, I know very well what should be done. Unfortunately, Marshal Pétain has done it before me.'

24

The Last of Philippe Pétain

In April 1945, learning that he was about to be tried in France in his absence, Marshal Pétain wrote to Hitler asking to be released:

'I cannot, without losing my honour, let it be believed, as is insinuated by some tendentious propaganda, that I have sought refuge in a foreign country so as to evade my responsibilities. I can answer for my actions only in France, and I alone can judge the risks which this attitude may entail. I therefore must urgently request Your Excellency to grant me the possibility. You will certainly appreciate the decision I have taken, to defend my honour as leader and protect by my presence all who have followed me. That is my sole aim, and no argument could make me give up this project. At my age, the only thing one still fears is not to have done one's full duty; I wish to do mine.'

Whether or not in response to this appeal, the German authorities released Pétain from the château at Sigmaringen, along with other French internees. But while a full collaborationist like Marcel Déat made for the Italian Tyrol as French forces advanced into the Alps, Pétain showed the same obstinate determination to return to France as he had earlier shown not to leave it.

This was decidedly inconvenient for de Gaulle. At the beginning of 1944 he had declared in Algiers: 'The Marshal will have to face trial like the rest. The best thing that could happen to us would be for him to die before our landings in France.' After the Liberation he told his colleagues: 'If the Marshal returns, it will be politically impossible to avoid trying him, and this will only lead to reviving divisions among the French people and disturbing national unity.' Now when de Lattre asked for instructions should the Marshal present himself at the outposts of the 1st French Army, de Gaulle answered: 'send him to Switzerland.'

On his release Pétain did indeed go first to Switzerland, which was ready to grant him asylum, although having denied it to

Laval. De Gaulle would have liked the Marshal to stay there, and secretly informed the Swiss Government of the decision, without even consulting his chief ministers. De Gaulle's hope was that although France was bound to ask for extradition, the Swiss Government would refuse it; France could then quietly drop the demand, and the implicit agreement need never be brought up. Unfortunately, the Swiss authorities were unable to change Pétain's mind: the Marshal recalled the enthusiastic reception he had been given not so long before in Paris, Nancy and elsewhere; and no doubt realized well enough that his return would embarrass de Gaulle.

When it became clear that nothing would stop Pétain returning to France, de Gaulle summoned some of his chief ministers, and also General Koenig, military governor of Paris. 'So they are restoring him to us,' he sighed, 'He's coming back. What a pathetic business! The Marshal cherished the illusion that he was serving the national interest, outwardly firm and protected by his own cunning. Really he was just a plaything in the hands of intriguers all round him. The guilty men of Vichy must be arrested, but I wish I could have left the Marshal out of it. What a terrible pity! So he's going to give us trouble right to the end. . . . He possessed so many qualities. Why did he do all he did under the occupation? He was a great man, but old age is a wreck – in public affairs you must never let yourself grow old.'

He sent General Koenig to meet the Marshal at the Swiss frontier, near Pontarlier, giving Koenig instructions to this effect: 'I don't want any incidents – see nothing happens to him.'

On the 26th April the eighty-nine-year-old Marshal Pétain, with his wife and entourage, drove off in three cars to Vallorbe, the Swiss town nearest the frontier. One of those accompanying him was a very loyal follower, Admiral Bléhaut, former Secretary of State for the Navy. He said to the Admiral: 'De Gaulle's full of hatred, he's a man whose heart can't be touched. Do you think I'll be shot?' On the way to Vallorbe, indeed, he passed through conflicting moods. Sometimes he was worrying over the trial, not knowing a good man for his defence counsel. At other times he seemed to forget about the trial, but expected to receive military honours at the frontier. 'I was willing to be the country's shield. . . . We'll have to reach an understanding with de Gaulle.'

The Marshal and his party were given a meal at the restaurant in Vallorbe station. While they were there, a French official came to see Madame Pétain, telling her there was no warrant for her arrest and that on reaching French territory she would be asked whether she agreed to be interned with her husband. She answered that she wished to be interned and to stay with her husband as long as possible.

The Swiss police had taken great precautions to see that all went smoothly. Some of their officers went ahead to the actual frontier, and soon after their arrival General Koenig came up to the barrier to meet them. The police report continues thus:

'General Koenig said a few words to us, thanking our country in flattering terms for all we had done under the occupation for French prisoners, deportees and internees. . . . A section of Swiss soldiers, commanded by a lieutenant, presented arms when Marshal Pétain's car arrived at 7.25 p.m., followed by those of General Debeney and Admiral Bléhaut. No one got out of the cars and the formalities were carried out very quickly.

'We took our leave of the Marshal and Madame Pétain, who both seemed very moved. They thanked us again for the welcome which had been given them in Switzerland and assured us they would never forget it. The car went on a few yards and then stopped on the other side of the frontier. The Marshal got out, saluted all round, but no one responded. The guards lining the road did not present arms, and the civilians did not remove their hats. General Koenig was in front of him and brought his hand to his cap. The Marshal held out his hand, but the General did not extend his. He bowed slightly twice and asked the Marshal to get into the car.'

According to another account the Marshal said to Koenig: 'I've heard a lot about you.' To which Koenig refrained from answering: 'I should think so. You condemned me to death.' In fact Koenig had been given this mission by de Gaulle because of his authority over the F.F.I. (French Forces of the Interior); he found it a very distasteful and painful one.

The Swiss police report goes on: 'With police and Republican guards on both sides, the cars proceeded as far as the frontier station. Everyone was asked to get out and go into the customs

shed in turn. The Marshal there signed the legal form acknow-
ledging his arrest. When he was asked to give his titles, he
answered: "I believe I am still a Marshal of France."

'Once the formalities were completed, he resumed his seat
in the car, but the driver was replaced by a policeman. . . . The
whole convoy was then conducted under escort to the station
five miles from the frontier where the special train was waiting.
It was composed of two second-class coaches, one first, and a
special coach reserved for the Marshal. . . . Militia controlled
the doors of each coach. The train reached Pontarlier at 9.57
p.m. A crowd estimated at 1,500 people came to the station.
Demonstrators cried: "To the stake", "to death", "traitor",
etc., even spitting at the coach occupied by the Marshal. A
quarter of an hour later the special train left Pontarlier amidst
yells from the crowd. Three minutes later detonators placed on
the track went off as the train passed. It stopped, and about a
hundred people in the vicinity took advantage of this to shout
abuse.

'The French authorities did not seem too delighted at the
Marshal's arrival in France on the eve of the municipal elections,
and the general opinion was that the Germans' release of the
Marshal was only a skilful trick of theirs to disturb the minds
of the French. On the other hand . . . there are many people
who, although convinced Gaullists, refuse to consider the
Marshal as a traitor to his country and would be scandalized
if he were condemned to death or degradation.'

When he was signing the form required on his arrest, the
Marshal is said to have come out of a deep reverie and stated
in a toneless voice: 'My usual Christian name is Philippe.
I request, no, demand, that this be underlined in the arrest
form.' This demand was made so that it might remind de
Gaulle of Pétain's connection with his son Philippe.

Sometimes Pétain claimed to be godfather, but not always.
The question came up one day during his first internment, in
the Fort of Montrouge. Two nuns were attached to him, chosen
for being very anti-Pétainist during the occupation. They relate
that 'the hall was adorned with a large photograph of General
de Gaulle, which Pétain was bound to pass going to and from
his exercise periods. We very often noticed him smiling at the
photograph and giving it a knowing little nod. One day he told

us: "It is a glory and an honour for me to have been his patron at the Staff College," We asked him: "Are you the godfather of Philippe de Gaulle?" He said he was not.'

'They keep asking me whether you are Philippe de Gaulle's godfather,' his wife complained. 'What am I to answer?'

Pétain: 'Say you've forgotten.'

Madame Pétain: 'What do you take me for? You could at least tell *me* the truth.'

Pétain: 'Don't bother your head over it. I won't say anything more.'

De Gaulle himself, questioned by a friend, denied categorically that Pétain had ever been godfather to his son, though ready to admit that Philippe had been named with Philippe Pétain in mind. At any rate the Marshal was still proud of the connection, and sometimes expressed friendly feelings towards de Gaulle in conversations with the chaplain who visited him. 'They tell me General de Gaulle is losing his popularity,' he said once. 'I can't take any pleasure in that, for if de Gaulle does not succeed what will become of France?'

The old man soon rediscovered the faith of his childhood. He attended Mass on Sundays, missal in hand, and made regular confessions to the chaplain, who also received many confidences outside the confessional. 'I sacrificed my person to France,' he told the chaplain, 'but France failed to appreciate it. I knew they wouldn't when I undertook this assignment.'

Here are some other observations of his noted by the chaplain: 'To die in Paris is the only joy I have asked God to grant. He has granted it to me. Like many others, I have been tempted to run away, because I was not understood. But I always resisted it, simply by thinking that my sacrifice would do some good. . . . May they one day understand, these poor French I love so well, who are preparing their own misfortunes. . . . Now my sacrifice is complete. They will be able to say and do what they like: it matters little to me.'

At other times he would defend his skill in resisting German demands. 'The Germans called me *der alte Fuchs*, the old fox. *Ich* bin *ein alter Fuchs.* . . . Never think it was easy at Vichy. But I didn't expose myself. An infantryman must never stick his head out of a hole too soon.'

He often returned to his relations with de Gaulle: 'I only

asked to pass on to de Gaulle the legitimacy of my position. But all the same I had worked and done something for France's recovery. Why has he refused to take this into account? I know de Gaulle well. He was constantly in trouble throughout his career. I settled all the difficulties. He is the only officer on whose behalf I intervened. You see how he thanks me and where it has led?

'Of my relations with de Gaulle this is all that is left: he called his son Philippe because of our friendship. Why did he not take the hand I held out to him? I had received the power legally. I had not seized it. They came to find me and offer it.

'Look, here is the note I wrote concerning the condemnation to death of Charles de Gaulle. I never wished him any harm.

'I have no hatred for anybody, not even for my enemies.'

His examining magistrate found some lapses of memory, whether real or feigned; but when he was lucid, Pétain showed himself careful, reflective, cunning, devious. He did not care to be pestered on minor points: 'A Marshal of France does not concern himself with local details. See the minister responsible.'

He reverted continually to the monologue on de Gaulle, sometimes with pathetically little sense of present realities. 'An ambitious fellow. Pride will destroy him. Mark my words, pride will destroy him. . . . This young man has done very well. He was a first-rate officer. I thought very highly of him. He dedicated his works to me. He should have come to see me. From the point of view of government he lacks experience. He has a great deal to learn, a great deal. I could have been useful to him. I had a lot of things to teach him. He wants to govern without my advice. It's a mistake. He had a good opening for coming to me – his books, *Le Fil de l'épée*, *La France et son armée*. I would have told him: "There you are, my friend, this is the way to manage France's affairs."'

There was a passage from the former book which suddenly had a remarkable application. 'The prestige [of a leader] depends first on an elemental gift, a natural aptitude, which defies explanation. The fact is that certain men, almost from birth, spread an air of authority, the secret of which you cannot analyse; which can astonish you even while you are feeling its effects.'

So it was in the opening of Pétain's trial, in the Paris Court of Appeal, in mid-August 1945. 'Bring in the accused,' the presiding judge ordered, and the old soldier appeared through a small door: khaki uniform, military medal, silk sash, white gloves. Majestically he brought his hand up to his cap and saluted the whole court. Here he was, charged with treason and collaborating with the enemy, held up to public obloquy; almost all those present were deeply hostile to him. Yet when they saw him come in, they rose to a man, as if obeying some magnetic impulse. One of the barristers told de Gaulle that evening: 'I must admit, mon Général, that the scene was rather striking.' 'Of course,' said de Gaulle. 'I've always said the Marshal was a remarkable old fellow.'

When the charges had been heard, Philippe Pétain stood erect, and without spectacles read in a firm voice the statement which had been prepared for him. It closed on these words: 'A Marshal of France does not ask anyone for mercy. Your judgement will have to face God's judgement and posterity's. They will suffice for my conscience and my memory. I leave it to France.'

Several of the leading pre-war statesmen were present in the court: among them Lebrun, Daladier, Reynaud, Blum, all liberated from Nazi prison camps. In the course of his devastating testimony, Léon Blum turned towards Pétain and remarked: 'I look at that face of stone. I don't understand the Marshal. There is a mystery in him which I cannot penetrate.'

Some of the army's regular officers did not like the way things were going. 'De Gaulle will let Pétain be condemned to death and executed. If he does, it will be nothing less than parricide.' However, there were no disturbances in Pétain's favour, although the trial roused passionate interest throughout France.

De Gaulle's own wishes had already been communicated to the judges. He had privately seen two of the ministers involved, and told them: 'The Marshal will probably be condemned to death. He must be condemned. Do not let us try to understand the man. Reasons of state are all that must count. But there is no question of my sending the Marshal before a firing squad. Things will be made easier for me if the judges condemn Philippe

Pétain to death, but express the wish that the penalty be commuted.'

Nevertheless, the twenty-seven judges took seven hours to reach a decision: it was a very unusual one. There was a majority vote (fourteen to thirteen) in favour of the death penalty, but they expressed a wish that the sentence should not be carried out. An appeal for mercy received seventeen signatures. General de Gaulle, using his prerogative, immediately commuted the sentence to detention for life.

Pétain was taken in de Gaulle's private plane to the fortress of Portalet, chosen because Reynaud, Mandel and Daladier had been sent there by special order from the Marshal. '*They* came out,' said Pétain now, 'and so shall I. They are sending *me* there in my turn. It's natural. The wheel has come full circle.'

The tables had been turned in another way too. 'During the occupation de Gaulle was condemned to death. The sentence was not carried out. It is the same with me. I have been condemned to death and reprieved. Oh, it's a nice trick of de Gaulle's, a nice trick.'

However: 'De Gaulle really ought to have listened to me. If he had, he wouldn't be having trouble today with his extreme left.'

The president of the French bar had made out Pétain was senile. 'I forgive him. He is very old.'

In the plane he had his first statement at the trial circulated. 'Give it back to me please. If you sold it to the Americans, you'd get a lot of dollars for it. It is a historic document. Afterwards France's children will go and consult it in the national archives.'

He began to lose his grip, forgetting the object of the journey. Once he took his stick and tapped the head of the passenger sitting in front of him: 'Don't fall asleep. I am going to escape.' The Medical Officer in the plane was taking photographs, and Pétain said: 'Take one of me.' The M.O. clicked, to find Pétain had been thumbing his nose.

The head of the department of prisons, whose name was Amor ('À mort, like me,' sighed Pétain,) paid him a visit. After Monsieur Amor's departure, the governor of the fortress noted, 'the guard looked through the spy-hole, and saw the old Marshal sitting on his bed, crying. It was reported to me at once: the first time the prisoner has wept. It will not be the last.' And Pétain himself murmured: 'I can understand Paul Reynaud bearing a grudge against me, for having had him sent to a grim place like this.'

General Héring, the Director of the Staff College at the time when de Gaulle gave his three lectures, was still a loyal friend of Pétain's. In October 1945 he had a private audience with de Gaulle, who received him in a very friendly manner. Héring was anxious to get Pétain moved from Portalet on health grounds, but de Gaulle told him: 'Anyway, I don't intend to leave him at Portalet during the winter. Having regard to his age, we shall progressively improve his conditions.

'The Marshal,' he went on, 'is a great man, who so far as I am concerned, died in 1925. He was too old at Vichy. In 1945 he would have done better not to return to France. He wished to be judged, and he *was*. For reasons of state he had to be condemned, I admit that an army *may* have to surrender, but never a State. No other government surrendered. The French Government ought not to have done so but to have fallen back on North Africa, with all the fleet and the army that could have been collected. Weygand is the most guilty. On 8th June I asked him what he was intending to do, and he answered: "We'll go on resisting on the Seine and the Marne, then it will be finished." "It's never finished," I answered, "as long as there are men to fight . . ."'

In November 1945 Pétain *was* moved, from Portalet to the island of Yeu in the Bay of Biscay. He talked freely to the senior priest on the island, who acted as his chaplain. Sometimes he complained of his bad memory: 'I don't remember things. Now, de Gaulle has an amazing memory. With a memory like his, one can try anything and bring anything off.' A pause. 'You need judgement too. Ah well, history will decide.'

As far as history went, he did not take particular pride in the title of Victor of Verdun. 'At Verdun I stopped the enemy. That was what was needed. But it was Nivelle who took the offensive. My action in 1917 was more important, and if I ever saved France, it was then.'

At a later audience de Gaulle told Héring, who was pleading for Pétain's release: 'You know better than anyone, mon Général, I used to admire the Marshal very much. Those who criticize his part in the 1914–18 War are people with no real understanding. He was a great man. But what concerns us at present is the case of the Marshal in 1940. He should have left France that June: we could have played the card of our Empire. Having concluded the armistice, however, he should not have collaborated with the occupying power. Finally, in 1942, it was his duty to go.'

So Philippe Pétain was not released. He remained imprisoned on the island of Yeu, where he died in 1951.

25

De Gaulle Retires

De Gaulle had made his headquarters in the War Office, an old mansion in the rue Saint-Dominique. He worked away in the *salon*, examining state documents, seeing his ministers. But sometimes at the end of the day, he would break off for a minute or two and pace the room. The minister he had summoned would wait, papers in hand, in a state of suspended animation, knowing he no longer existed for de Gaulle. The great man was meditating.

He seemed to be communing with all his predecessors who had built up the State, Philip Augustus, Philip *le Beau*, Louis XI, Henry IV, Richelieu, Louis XIV, the Committee of Public Safety, the Royalists and the Jacobins; Joan of Arc and Clemenceau were at his side. Steeped in French history, Charles de Gaulle travelled through the centuries, drawing examples, guidance and comfort, large lessons and also little tricks if need be, the wiles of government.

Suddenly he would break the eloquent silence to soliloquize out loud, recalling perhaps the heroic days of 1940, the fateful 18th June: 'It is often imagined that all that was prepared, premeditated. I do not think so. I felt myself taken up by a hand stronger than myself. I was gripped by an idea.

'I became the instrument of a will greater than mine. . . . In the first days of the Battle of France, before I was called to the government, I saw only one end for the poor colonel I then was: to die on the battlefield, leading my regiment. . . . Certainly what I did was in a sense "thrust upon me".

'Politics, you know – the real stuff of politics on the grand scale, which changes the course of events, the destiny of peoples, the future of nations – politics is a matter of the Word. In the beginning was the Word. On the 18th June I changed History by an appeal of forty lines.'

The magnificent reverie over, de Gaulle came back to earth: 'Ah well, let us consider the affairs of State.' The dismal files of government departments rose to the surface again. De Gaulle told several ministers at this period: 'I didn't save France to concern myself with the macaroni ration.'

Alas, the business of government demanded attention to such things. It could not all be done at the heroic level of his answer to General de Lattre, who told him, 'France thinks that . . .' 'When I want to know what France thinks,' de Gaulle interrupted, 'I question myself.'

The president of the provisional government continued to tour the country. Liking solitude, he also liked crowds: the two sentiments are not incompatible, but complementary. Left-wing former members of the Resistance began to express suspicion: 'De Gaulle is playing off the population against the people.'

He carried out his purge. Apart from a certain number of summary settling of accounts or executions, the courts pronounced 2,071 death sentences, excluding men condemned in absence. 'I would assert,' de Gaulle wrote in his *Memoirs*, 'that except for about a hundred cases, all those condemned deserved their sentence. Yet I reprieved 1,303 of them. . . . I had to reject 768 appeals where men had been condemned for personal and spontaneous action causing the death of other French people or directly serving the enemy.'

The case he felt most deeply was that of the poet Robert Brasillach. Madame de Gaulle became concerned for her husband's health: 'He doesn't sleep – it's terrible.' De Gaulle kept telling himself: 'Brasillach gambled and lost, so he must pay. He surely knew the choice he was making. An intellectual's treason, the sin against the spirit. . . . Please pray, Yvonne.'

Brasillach was shot. On his last dawn he wrote these lines: 'This morning the chaplain came to bring me communion. I thought with affection of everyone I loved, of everyone I had met in my life. I thought with pain of their pain. But I tried hard to face my fate in a spirit of acceptance.' The firing squad did their duty; and for de Gaulle, Brasillach too had in his way died for France.

In the last months of 1945 de Gaulle carried out some large-scale nationalization on which even the pre-war Popular Front had not ventured. But on the 1st January 1946 he had made up his mind: he would abandon power before power abandoned him, 'manipulated' by the parties. He allowed himself a week's holiday – the first for seven years – at Cap d'Antibes, then returned to Paris by special rail-car on the 14th January. He was met at a suburban station by Jules Moch, the (Socialist) Minister of Works and Transport. In the car taking him into Paris he informed Moch of his decision.

Jules Moch was appalled: 'You *can't* go. You are the Clemenceau who led the country to victory – how could you make this choice? You agreed to continue your mission. You can't go now, like this, deserting France.'

De Gaulle reflected. After a longish silence he remarked: 'Obviously it is hard to imagine Joan of Arc married, bringing up a family, and perhaps even deceived by her husband.' Another silence. 'Don't reveal anything yet to your colleagues in the government.'

Moch: 'I promise you that. But I should be glad if you would let me report our interview to Léon Blum.'

De Gaulle's reference to St Joan echoed a conversation he had in September 1944, on his first visit to liberated Toulouse, with Pierre Bertaux, an official at the prefecture:

Bertaux: 'Mon Général, how do you see the future?'

De Gaulle: 'I wish to re-establish our institutions.'

Bertaux: 'And how will you fit into this framework?'

De Gaulle: 'Me? Get myself elected? Can you see me standing for election in one small district? No?'

Bertaux: 'So in that case?'

De Gaulle (after hesitation): 'One must disappear.' Another pause. 'If Joan of Arc had married and had children, she would no longer be Joan of Arc. There will come a day when France needs a pure image. That image must be left for France. One must disappear.'

De Gaulle summoned the regional commissioners, as responsible for maintaining public order, to give them priority information of his decision. On 19th January at 3 p.m. they assembled in the War Office and took their places on three rows of gilded chairs in the great Hall of Armour with its plumed helmets, halberds and coats of mail.

'Gentlemen,' began de Gaulle, 'we are relapsing into the confusion of past years which did us so much harm. I am obliged to govern with the ministers the parties have given me.

Most of these ministers, alas, are guided more by the instructions received from their party than by the true interests of France. The result is that I am gradually becoming discredited in the country and, more serious, outside it. This is something I cannot tolerate. It makes it impossible for me to carry out my mission. I must draw the logical conclusion.'

The commissioners sat in stunned silence, while the General looked at his long, patent-leather shoes. There was a severe food crisis on, and he shocked his hearers by continuing: 'I have consulted the statistics of the Paris hospitals. No one has died of starvation. They tell me people are dying of hunger in Paris. Well, it's not true. The supply situation is all right.' (On the same day, however, in a letter to the President of the Assembly, he wrote: 'After immense trials France is no longer in a state of crisis. Admittedly, there is still much suffering among our people, and grave problems remain.')

The commissioners talked to him of the state of mind in their regions and of popular aspirations. The General answered them in much the same terms as he had answered General de Lattre: 'When I want to find out what France is thinking, I try to find out what I think myself.' He added: 'I have put the train back on the rails. I have re-established democracy.'

That evening he declared in private: 'When I chose democracy I accepted the rest.' The rest: that is to say the consequences of a power which no longer depended on one man. He had been governed by the head, not the heart, in *choosing* democracy. At the end of July 1944 just before he returned to France, he had announced at Algiers before the consultative assembly: 'On the political level, we have made our choice. We have opted for democracy and the Republic.' It is hard to imagine a 'natural democrat' using such a phrase. But in a democratic republic Charles de Gaulle was a king without a crown; he spoke nostalgically of 'the kind of monarchy which I recently assumed'.

There was one important reason for his going: he believed a third war was imminent, between the Americans and the Russians; he thought it would come as early as 1946. The war would come to Europe, and the French Communists would be faced with a decisive choice. He must hold himself in reserve, with the aura of untarnished prestige, to save the unity of France at that time.

With only a few more hours left as head of the provisional government, in that room in the War Office whose tapestries had returned the echoes of so many confidences, the General received Robert Prigent, Minister for Population, to deal with a quarter of an hour's government business. The audience lasted for an hour and turned into a Gaullian monologue:

'I wasn't made for this system. . . . I am worn out by parliamentary skirmishes. . . . I must go, so as to hold myself ready for the big events which must be expected. If a conflict breaks out with the U.S.S.R., I alone shall be capable of re-creating national unanimity and avoiding civil war. For the immediate future, the train is on the rails. In the spring there will be grass in the meadows and cattle in the cowsheds.

'You see, Prigent, what this country should have is a king. A great man to be brought out from time to time, in the great and difficult moments. That's what it should have. But all that has been broken, and can't be repaired.'

So he left the government on 20th January, not even knowing who his successor would be. The transmission of powers was assured by the cabinet. Félix Gouin, president of the constituent assembly, was elected president of the provisional government, and complained that he couldn't find any of the State records. The clean-sweep policy had been carried out to the letter.

There were rumours of an army *putsch* being prepared; that General Leclerc had left Indo-China (which he hadn't). 'Get on his track at once,' President Gouin ordered the civil and military authorities. 'If I find Leclerc, should I arrest him?' General Juin asked. 'No, wait,' said Gouin. 'Leclerc is the liberator of Paris, the Parisians have a sentimental attachment to him.'

De Gaulle had told the regional commissioners: 'I hope everything will go smoothly. In any case you will immediately return to your regions, and if there is any trouble, you will take the necessary measures by virtue of the powers you possess.'

He thought, indeed, that the French would demonstrate, but the streets were calm, there were no disturbances: he was mortified. 'The French cannot even show their regret that the power is passing from General de Gaulle – from General de Gaulle to what?'

When the oak falls, said the ancient Greeks, everyone turns

219

wood-cutter. A volcano erupting within, the man of the 18th June noted (in his *Memoirs*) 'a sudden outburst of insults and invectives' from most of the papers and the 'centres of political intrigue'.

Joan of Arc, the true bride, had been deceived. France was an inconsolable widow, spending her time remarrying and then divorcing: as Alfred de Musset once wrote, 'France, Caesar's widow.'

26

Lonely Greatness

Charles de Gaulle is a prime example of what the French call a *monstre sacré* – a term first applied to stars of the theatre like Sarah Bernhardt. In its political context it implies a personality so outstanding that there is something strange and marvellous about it, something almost god-like. The sacred monsters of de Gaulle's kind bestride the world, or at least their own country, like a colossus; they are idolized by their own people, and in their day they seem to personify their country. All these things are true of Winston Churchill, of course, yet somehow he does not quite fit into the scheme: he was too human, he did not keep round him an air of mystery and aloofness, as de Gaulle has done. Perhaps the sacred monster is a species found mainly in France, with her special brand of patriotism; for intense patriotic feeling is at the core of his being.

His own life does not count; he is always ready to sacrifice himself on the altar of the State – he has a vocation for martyrdom. His patriotism, admittedly, is so enclosed in a world of his own that he sometimes seems to take over the country too completely, and no one knows if he is serving France or using her. But for him there is no difference, because he *is* France.

The *monstre sacré* cultivates ambition and pride, he is immensely egocentric. Without these motivating forces he could not carry out his mission, he would gradually decline into a nonentity. He has the highest opinion of his own abilities. Often he sees things clearly; when he is mistaken, he has a natural tendency to blame events for being wrong.

Although idolized himself, he does not like to see other idols set up; so he can also be an iconoclast. He excels in trials of force, he governs well amidst disasters. Abel Ferry wrote: 'Clemenceau, like Foch, is a man who revelled in adversity.' He loves drama, believing that drama, presented to passive crowds, is the best way to make them aware of a serious or tragic situation, to bring an affair to its climax. He likes appearing on a vast stage. A natural actor, he adopts special methods to obtain his effects on people's minds. He 'stages' very carefully his public actions and appearances. His head rules his heart, and in-humanity, by his ethic, may be a necessity of State; compassion is merely sentimental, and sentimentality the worst of weak-nesses. Thus Clemenceau regretted the importunities of Édouard Ignace, under-secretary of state in his war cabinet:

'Unfortunately there was Ignace: The best of men ... he was made for peace. If God existed – but God does not exist – God would have welcomed Ignace to His bosom, for his kind-ness. But I was obliged to cast him out of mine, for his weakness. The wretch spent nights over the dossiers of men condemned to death. In the morning he would come to me pale and stutter-ing: "I implore you, examine this case here." I would jump up saying: "To hell with your case, Ignace." But he would pester me: "Monsieur le Président, surely we could grant a re-prieve. . . ." Then I would take his arm, shake him and shout: "Ignace, Ignace, there is a war on, my friend. What should I care if some poor wretch is shot tomorrow? While we are arguing, a thousand innocent people are being killed."'

The *monstre sacré* is ready to lie; but in his world the meaning of the word is shifted. He does not lie, he tricks and deceives so as to govern in the supreme interest of the nation, an interest of which he alone is judge. When this past master of deception achieves his ends, he makes his confession, and reconciles himself with God – or with himself! According to *his* lights, he has acted for the triumph of virtue and the glory of France: again, for him, the same thing.

He has Plato to support him here: 'If there is anyone who should lie, it is the guardians of the City, to deceive enemies or citizens, when the interest of the State demands it. No one else has the right to touch so delicate a thing.' But he is capable of telling petty lies as well as noble ones, like Briand seen by his adversary Abel Ferry: 'He makes an art of lying. He admits something and denies it at the same time, like water mixing with mud. . . . I despise and hate him, for he is ready to make any sort of peace, the most glorious or the meanest, provided he is the one to make it.'

There is falsehood, of course, in the very idolatry he receives:

he becomes almost a religion for his countrymen, and so, in the Marxian phrase, an opium for the people. He devotes all his powers to France the well-beloved. As he grows old, nears death, he makes desperate efforts to clasp the country's heritage in his arms, full of jealous love: to clasp it alone.

Wise men have said: 'Calling on him sometimes proves necessary in the life of a nation. It is better, however, to try to do without him.' For sooner or later he will be found exclaiming like Napoleon: 'Everyone has loved me – and hated me.'

But this is to generalize about men who, for all their features in common, show wide differences in every field. De Gaulle is more than a *monstre sacré*, he is unique in his kind, there is no parallel with him in French history which cannot quickly be exposed as false. Every two or three centuries, perhaps, a people will bring forth a being of these dimensions.

There is a terrible duality inside him, which keeps him racked by ceaseless conflict. The demons within are struggling with the angels, and if the angels relax their vigilance they may lose the battle. This makes for other contradictions. He seems uncompromising, confident of being always right; yet because of his immense intellect he is continually tormented by doubt. He is even irritated to be treated as infallible. For the outside world he struts on the proud mountain of his 'Moidegaulle', the all-seeing, all-knowing, all-foreseeing hero: if he did otherwise, the mob would not forgive him, and the idol would collapse.

Does he forgive himself? Often he has showed rancour, vindictiveness and hatred, 'natural daughters' of patriotic fervour. In other cases, though he would never boast of them, he has unobtrusively been generous, indulgent, even merciful. But mercy, certainly, is not one of his familiar spirits, partly because he is condemned for life to carry the burden of his amazing memory.

Ordinary mortals will readily forgive if they can forget, if the person they think has wronged them is out of sight and out of mind:

'The hatred for an enemy we feel,
When he's away from us, is half unreal.'

223

Life would soon become intolerable if we did not have this faculty of forgetting. An ancient Greek philosopher used to bid man be grateful to memory and oblivion: 'the one makes life's joys last longer, the other bears away life's sorrows.' For his discomfort, and sometimes the discomfort of others, de Gaulle's sorrows and setbacks and disappointments remain with him indefinitely.

Though profoundly Christian, he has a religion which is very much his own, directed towards penitence more often than love, with the hair-shirt coming before the communion. A dark attraction drives him towards the altars of mortification, a true spiritual son of Loyola, in whom his father had seen the great example. His private morality has remained irreproachable, the standards of his family life exemplary. But even in personal relations he sins at times from contempt of others.

The army often considers him an 'unfrocked soldier', but for de Gaulle the army is like a church. After having taken the oath at Saint-Cyr, you do not leave the army, any more than you leave the church once you have been ordained.

He believes with Nietzsche that 'States are cold monsters. You can't bring sentiment into politics.' Trained at the Staff College, he always means to keep the element of surprise – as expressed in *Vers l'armée de métier*: 'Surprise must be organized. Those who make plans and decisions must of course keep secret all statements, orders and reports, and must mask their preparations; but they should also lay on a thick veil of deception.'

His enemies ask whether he is mad. Yes, as Foch was mad in Liddell Hart's analysis: 'He rarely stooped to explain and allowed no deviation from his own views. With the officers he neither sought nor attained popularity, and to the men he was simply a symbol. Even if he was aware that some of his mystified subordinates declared him insane, he did not mind, for to him *morale* connoted his own soul and, knowing that, he was content.'

De Gaulle suffered terribly from the shames and misfortunes of France, and complained: 'Why is everyone against me? I sacrifice myself entirely for the country.' Was he, is he, a Gaullist himself? There is perhaps a riddle here. Charles de Gaulle the citizen cannot but deplore certain actions carried out by General de Gaulle the political leader. Talking of his supporters, he once said: 'I should not be a Gaullist myself were I not obliged to take into account a phenomenon which takes command over me and which I cannot always explain to myself: the phenomenon of de Gaulle.'

But let us go back twenty years, to 20th January 1946, when de Gaulle abandoned power in the Fourth Republic. He thought the people of Paris would come and demonstrate in his favour under the windows of the *Pavillon de Marly*, where he had taken up residence for the time being. The capital did not move. A crowd one day, only a handful the next: such is the law of history.

He foresaw an imminent conflict between the United States and the Soviet Union. Once again he would become the country's saviour when short-term policies collapsed under the pressure of great events. 'I can hear the Cossacks marching on Paris. War is coming.' His would be the stern task of keeping the Communists, torn between two loyalties, within the fold of France. Already he was looking to the vast expanses of Africa, where the French Government might have to set up a new headquarters. 'The Sahara will replace our Massif Central . . .'

He wanted to prepare hearts and souls for the new test, and thought he had been deserted. He complained of parliament, the Press, the army, the people of rank and title, the episcopate. He paid a visit to Monsignor Beaussart, Assistant Archbishop of Paris, and kept repeating: 'France. . . . General de Gaulle. . . . General de Gaulle. . . . France.' The Monsignor listened in horrified amazement, thinking: 'How can a Christian, a Catholic who carries out all his religious duties, harbour such pride?' De Gaulle continued his harangue. Then the tall figure suddenly bent, he was on his knees. '*Mon père*, please be good enough to receive my confession.'

He installed himself in his property at Colombey-les-deux-Églises, eventually restored after the devastations of war – where he was to stay for twelve years, until the country's call at last came. With the forest opposite, not far from the battlefield where the Gauls once drove out the Huns, he had plenty of time now for meditation, bitter though many of his reflections might be. The man of the 18th June wrote: 'Silence fills my house. From the corner room where I spend most hours of the day, I can look westwards for ten miles – there is not a building in sight.'

Solitude, sadness, grandeur: ten miles of France in front of him, but no French people.

Appendix 1

Why I did not continue the war in North Africa in 1940.

My first impulse was to continue the struggle, but I soon realized that this would mean losing North Africa.

I had reliable information that the Germans had prepared a substantial expeditionary force, which was sent direct to Irun, railhead of the Spanish railways. With the help of the Spanish authorities, they had established a complete plan for rapid transport across the Spanish railway stations to organize this. The first train carrying a detachment of the *Wehrmacht* had already arrived at San Sebastian.

In Morocco the Spanish Army had mobilized three army corps, two of them near the frontier of·the French zone. The French forces in Morocco were almost non-existent. They included no more than a division still in process of formation, which did not even have enough arms to arm all its men. Only the division defending South Tunisia was in a condition to fight.

The planes arriving at Casablanca, coming from America, left the same day for the French front. The Anglo-French fleet could not have effectively prevented the transport of the German troops across the strait. The Spanish Army alone could have seized Morocco. North Africa had sent 180,000 men, armed and equipped, to France. It had only one tank company, removed for the French front despite my protests, and taken prisoner the day it arrived there.

The Anglo-French fleet did not have the mastery and control of the Mediterranean. A powerful German Air Force (120 planes), based on South Italy, made it very difficult to get supplies by sea to our army operating in Libya.

After the armistice I organized two divisions in succession, under the guise of workers in the Atlas forests. Above all I increased the numbers of Goums (Algerian troops), who in Italy, by climbing like cats in the very steep areas of the German positions, enabled the Franco-American forces to win the battle.

227

Appendix 2

Dear Sir,

. . . You ask me why, when others were advocating withdrawal overseas, I considered it my first duty to hold the front till the last minute and keep control of the army.

First, I had decided not to abandon the national territory at any price, unless constrained to this by force of arms. In the last resort, when I saw I was being overrun from all sides, I asked for an armistice to be concluded so that the maximum amount of national territory could be kept under authority of the French Government. In other words, I was always pursuing the same end, first by arms, then by negotiation.

I ask you to turn to the third volume of my *Memoirs*, page 293: 'The armistice saved liberties, lives, territories, wealth. It was as advantageous for France's allies as for France. Those who asked for it – that is to say, I myself as responsible commander, and the Marshal above me with a more general responsibility – hoped this would be the case. This, I believe, is what History will recognize, once passions are appeased and the truth can triumph.'

The truth has not yet triumphed. We continue to live in falsehood. But turn to pages 286–87 of the same volume: 'Today my case has been proved by the course of events. . . . Two years after the signing of the armistice, our American allies undertook their first war operation in the old world; thanks to the possibilities given by the armistice and the policy followed in France and North Africa . . . , they found an Africa inviolate, an African Army eager for action and ready for battle despite its poverty in equipment . . .'

M. de Gaulle recognized in 1944 the full importance of Africa, as a starting point for the liberation of Europe.

Reread the opinion expressed by Mr Churchill to General Georges at Marrakesh, also in 1944, and finally consider the verdict on the armistice of Mr W. L. Langer, who could consult the official documents of the United States and who concludes as follows:

'There was an unoccupied France, governed and administered by the French, with an army of 100,000 men, still preserving at least a degree of independence. Considering the fate reserved for Poland, Norway and almost all European countries, this is saying quite a lot. And if we add that North Africa remained unoccupied, which eventually allowed an entry into Europe, the case for the armistice seems established.'

Secondly, Marshal Pétain was a very secretive man, in the sense that when he asked someone's opinion on a particular point, he listened to the answer given him without expressing any opinion himself. He never confided to me his plan for bringing [North] Africa back into the war, but he always approved my conduct, and in view of my reports to him could not have been unaware of my efforts to that end.

Thirdly, the letter which M. de Gaulle sent me in March 1941 through the intermediary of the British Consul General at Tangier, was not signed by him, and concluded without the normal expressions of courtesy. I considered indeed that as neither the United States nor Russia was in the war, and as M. de Gaulle did not possess any military resources, his blustering speeches would only provoke the Germans into sending control commissions to reinforce those of the Italians.

Appendix 3

MEMORANDUM TO GENERAL DE GAULLE FROM ADMIRAL AUPHAN
ON THE NEED FOR A LEGAL TRANSMISSION OF POWER
(*dated 25th August* 1944, *day of German surrender of Paris, sent
with covering letter dated 27th August.*)

Without having sought it, I find myself the main depositary at Paris of the Marshal's legal powers. Before stating the nature of these powers and the advantages that can issue from this fact, it must be explained how the powers came to me, without my having to abandon any of my own views or independence.

As an ordinary naval captain at the painful time of the armistice, I did not dispute a political fact which was quite outside my scope. The navy had to safeguard its forces and help to feed the country. I worked whole-heartedly to these ends, resisting the Germans as far as possible, replying in kind to the often unjustifiable attacks on our shipping by our British allies, and thinking only of the common good. Eventually I rose progressively to the rank of Naval Chief of Staff.

In April 1942 I was in practice the head of our war and merchant navy, and when Laval replaced Admiral Darlan at the head of government, pressure was put on me from all sides to take the title of *ministre de la Marine*. I accepted the post only from duty, after having expressed written qualifications and made certain conditions, in particular on Franco-German relations; on this subject I received formal but only verbal reassurances from Laval.

I gradually gained the confidence of Marshal Pétain. My independent position in the government often helped in avoiding the worst disasters, until November 1942. I shall relate elsewhere the story, so far unknown, of those days of November 1942 at Vichy, when I hoped to get the Marshal to adopt a position leading progressively to the breaking of the armistice and avoiding the terrible split of France into two sections, each regarding the other as 'dissident'. Let me just say that it was thanks to me, in agreement with the Marshal, that Admiral

Darlan, despite the orders of the Laval Government, had a completely clear conscience in negotiating with the Anglo-Saxons, in releasing the officers from their oath, and maintaining French influence in Africa by keeping damage to the minimum.

As I did not succeed in getting the government of the mother country to take a corresponding position, I handed in my resignation on the 15th November 1942, after having advised the Marshal to reject the policy of full Franco-German collaboration towards which he was being inveigled. Accepting this advice, he abandoned his powers to his head of government, but did not manage to preserve the silence and restraint which were called for.

After long months of retirement, I returned now and then to Vichy, on the Marshal's expressed wish. During these short visits I continually advised him to make gestures of conciliation towards those governing North Africa and to carry out public actions which would show that, at least morally, he was against the policies of Laval.

We had hoped to get Laval dismissed, but a letter from Hitler in 1943 stopped all possibilities of this. A few of us then advised the Marshal at least to make the National Assembly his successor in case of his decease, removing the succession from Laval. As publicly adopting this position might bring about German reactions, it was important to have a legal succession secretly assured until the Assembly could be convened. Such is the origin of the secret constitutional act of 27th September 1943. I did not take part in its drafting and did not know till later of the names it mentioned, which included mine.

With this precaution taken, the Marshal tried to promulgate the public constitutional act of 12th November 1943, assigning his powers to the National Assembly (instead of the Laval Government) in case he was prevented from acting. We know the repercussions of this affair, how the Germans banned speeches, the Marshal adopted a position of semi-prisoner, then hesitated, and then was obliged, following a German ultimatum, to resume his functions and re-establish apparently normal relations with Laval.

After a series of very lively reactions even in the Marshal's entourage, and the arrest of many French people, which I was astonished to find did not include me, French politics fell into the same quagmire as before.

I remained one of the few who could speak to the Marshal in an independent and disinterested manner, and could tell him repeatedly how much I disapproved of the declarations or decisions Laval skilfully extorted from him, to which he privately objected, but was weak enough to tolerate or condone, thinking thereby to spare the country suffering.

Having contacts with people in the Resistance and also loyal friends in Africa, being independent and without an official position, I could help bridge the gap between Frenchmen caused by the different policies in France and Algeria. I found the Marshal sympathetic to my overtures, but because of the Germans he was unwilling to commit himself in writing to an agreement between Vichy and Algiers. From one interview to the next Laval's influence destroyed all the ground gained.

I went to Vichy for the last time on 11th August, on my way to Paris; I wished to have the joy of being in Paris when it was liberated. Without hiding from the Marshal that it was very late in the day, I insisted that he should hold out the hand of friendship towards General de Gaulle, thus giving the French people an example of reconciliation.

He listened to me at last. Believing, as I also did, that I should find Anglo-Saxon authorities before I could make contact with the General, he handed me a written authority. He informed me of the approaches made by the Vatican to the same effect. Finally he showed me the military dossier of General de Gaulle with notes in his own hand, which he asked me to take to the General.

On 13th August I informed a leading member of the Resistance of the written authority I held and of my wish to meet General de Gaulle or a qualified representative as soon as possible. I do not know if this demand, which I renewed several times in the following days, ever reached the General.

On 20th August I heard the news that the Marshal had just been forcibly removed from Vichy by the Germans and taken to Belfort. The last paragraph in my written authority came into play: I opened the envelope containing the secret constitutional act, and noted that, among the members of the college entitled to receive provisionally the powers of the head of State, two were prisoners of the Germans, one was away from Paris, and two others sent apologies for being unable to come. So I remained the only one ... to represent the legitimate power, arising from the vote of the National Assembly on 10th July 1940, with the special mission of seeking an agreement with General de Gaulle ... so as to prevent civil war and reconcile all French people of integrity.

How can this ideal, that of the great mass of French people, be attained? As far as one can tell, the Parisian representatives of General de Gaulle consider that he is popular enough to be recognized in France and abroad, without needing to seek any other ratification (which might embarrass him) except through this popularity and the success of the Allied armies. They believe it is impossible for this government to link up with the Marshal's Government. What one National Assembly has done, they say, another can undo. When the 'sovereign' is a prisoner he loses all legal power.

I think, on the contrary, that the French could later reproach their rulers with having abandoned too hastily the solid ground of legitimacy, and that the legitimacy of the Marshal's powers cannot seriously be disputed. But the question goes beyond the precise legal position, and should properly be argued in the context of future policy and the country's recovery.

Four years of German occupation and accumulated devastations, four years of various propaganda, four years of exile for prisoners, refugees, workers – all this leaves Metropolitan France in a terrible state socially, economically and morally. An immense effort of discipline and redressment is called for. It would be utopian to try to direct this effort in a party spirit, without trying to unite all French people and bring together the 'two Frances' which exist at present. One France consists of those who continued the struggle abroad or in Africa, and later the resistance movements, and who in the moment of success can forget the other section of the French people. That other section is the great mass who remained in their own country, supporting the legal power, despite the sufferings of the occupation; they also believe they have done their duty. Both sections have in their hearts the same feelings towards the enemy and the war profiteers.

233

Each of these 'two Frances' has its extremists; under their influence, each is ready to fight the other. If we do not succeed in uniting both sections which are often working towards the same end by different paths, civil war can complete the ruin of our unfortunate country.

Of course there is no question of acquitting those who are guilty of political treason, who have denounced their fellow-countrymen or had dishonourable dealings with the Germans. But one must distinguish between bad Frenchmen, who too often used the Marshal's name against his will, and the generality of honest people who have loyally followed the ideal represented for them by his legendary figure. They will only rally to the government of tomorrow with a quiet conscience, if legality is respected.

To sum up: the liberation of France leaves two possible alternatives until a legally valid Assembly can be convened: either a government is established on the fringe of legality, which rejects the masses who had accepted that legality, accentuates the divisions between French people, and so is likely to lead us to disorder, impotence and anarchy; or we set up a united government which respects legality and rallies behind it all our fellow-countrymen of integrity and all French efforts.

It seems to me quite possible, by reason of the mission and powers which have fallen to my lot, to find a procedure satisfying the dignity of both Marshal Pétain and General de Gaulle; through their reconciliation a united national government may be established as desired by the mass of the French people.

Sources

Sources used throughout are General de Gaulle's *Memoirs*, the private papers of the late General Héring, and a vast amount of material in the author's files, including oral and written testimony, much of it previously unpublished. Where quotations or statements have been attributed in the text or footnotes to a definite source, some of these sources have been omitted from the list below.

Chapter 1:

Marcel Prévost, *Le Scorpion*.
Jacques Chastenet, *Histoire de la troisième République*.

Chapter 2:

Philippe Barrès, *Charles de Gaulle*.
Roger Parment, *Charles de Gaulle et la Normandie*.
Joseph Teilhard de Chardin and R. P. F. Lepoutre, statements to Pierre Bourget, *Ici Paris* (1958).
General Desmazes, *Saint-Cyr*.

Chapter 3:

General Laure, *Pétain*.
Charles de Gaulle, *La France et son armée*.

Chapter 4:

General Laure, op. cit.
Henri Bordeaux, *L'Année ténebreuse*.
Colonel Carré, *Les Grandes heures du général Pétain*.
J. and J. Tharaud, *Album du Maréchal Pétain*.
General de M. . . , letter published in *Le Maréchal* (1962).
General Serrigny, *Trente ans avec Pétain*.
A. Ducasse, J. Meyer, G. Perreux, *Vie et mort des Français*.
Gaston Bonheur, *Charles de Gaulle*.

Chapter 5:
Charles de Gaulle, op. cit.
William Martin, *Les Hommes d'état pendant la guerre.*
Jean Martet, *Le Tigre.*
Basil Liddell-Hart, *Reputations.*
Jean Pottecher, *Lettres d'un fils.*

Chapter 6:
General Laffargue, *Fantassin de Gascogne* and personal testimony to author.
General Chauvin, and personal testimony to author.

Chapter 7:
L. Nachin, *Charles de Gaulle, général de France.*
General Héring, personal testimony to author.

Chapter 8:
L. Nachin, op. cit.
Journal Officiel (debates in the *Chambre des Députés*), March 1929.

Chapter 9:
L. Nachin, op. cit.

Chapter 10:
G. Loustaunau-Lacau, *Mémoires d'un Français rebelle.*
General Laure, op. cit.

Chapter 11:
Paul Reynaud, *Mémoires.*
Henri Noguères, *Munich ou la drôle de paix.*
J. de Pierrefeu, *Plutarque a menti.*
Commandant Bugnet, *En écoutant le Maréchal.*
General Laffargue, op. cit.
G. Loustaunau-Lacau, op. cit.
Monsieur Daniel-Rops, personal testimony to author.

Chapter 12:
Roger Parment, op. cit.
Le Journal, April 1936.
Georges Duhamel, *France-Illustration.*

Chapter 13:

Paul Reynaud, op. cit, *La France sauve l'Europe*, and personal testimony to author.
Lucien Gallimand, *Vive Pétain, vive de Gaulle*.
Albert Lebrun, *Témoignages*.
Maurice Schumann, *La Voix du couvre-feu*.
Les carnets de René Mouchotte.

Chapter 14:

Jean Giraudoux, *Armistice à Bordeaux*.
General Héring, *La Vie exemplaire de Philippe Pétain*.
Yves Bouthillier, *Le Drame du Vichy*.
General Spears, *The Fall of France*.
Camille Chautemps, *Cahiers sécrets de l'armistice*.

Chapter 15:

Georges Cattaui, *Charles de Gaulle*.
Colonel Passy, *Souvenirs*.
Mary Borden (Lady Spears), *Journey down a Blind Alley*.

Chapter 16:

Albert Lebrun, op. cit.
General Serrigny, op. cit.
Vice-Admiral Fernet, *Aux côtés du maréchal Pétain*.
M. Peyrouton, *Du service public à la prison commune*.
Robert Aron, *Histoire de Vichy*.
Édouard Herriot, *Episodes*.

Chapter 17:

Deposition by Jacques Benoist-Méchin before his trial in April 1945.
Admiral Docteur, *La grande énigme de la guerre, Darlan, amiral de la flotte*.
Letter to author from André Blumel on Darlan's personality.
William Langer, *Le Jeu américain à Vichy*.
'Log-book' of André Lavargne, one of Pétain's Secretaries of State.
Admiral Muselier, *De Gaulle contre le Gaullisme*.
General Laffargue, *Le Général Dentz*.
General Catroux, *Dans la bataille de la Méditerranée*.

237

Chapter 18:

Personal testimony to author from Monsieur du Moulin de Labarthète and Georges Riond.

Guy Raïssac, *Un soldat dans la tourmente.*

Chapter 19:

Admiral Muselier, op. cit.

J. Carcopino, *Souvenirs de Sept Ans.*

William Langer, op. cit.

Robert Aron, op. cit.

Paul Baudouin, *Neuf mois au gouvernement.*

Chapter 20:

J. Carcopino, op. cit.

Winston Churchill, *The Second World War.*

General Catroux, op. cit.

Walter Stücki, *Le fin du régime de Vichy.*

Colonel Passy, op. cit.

Chapter 21:

Personal testimony to author from Wing-Commander Gorostarzu and Colonel Solborg.

Pierre Taittinger, *Et Paris ne fut pas détruit.*

General Serrigny, op. cit.

Major Jean Tracou, *Le Maréchal aux liens.*

Chapter 22:

Winston Churchill op. cit.

Chapter 23:

General de Langlade, *En suivant Leclerc.*

Chapter 24:

Georges Duhamel, op. cit.

Gabriel Delattre, *J'étais premier juré au procès Pétain* (*Histoire pour tous*, April 1964).

Petrus Faure, *Un témoin raconte.*

Joseph Simon, *Pétain mon prisonnier.*

Personal testimony to author from Canon Ponthoreau, Pétain's chaplain on island of Yeu.

Chapter 25:

Letter to author from Robert Prigent.
Letter from Monsieur le Gorgeu, one of the regional commissioners, to the *Nouveau République* (April 1964).

Chapter 26:

René Benjamin, *Clemenceau dans la retraite.*
Basil Liddell-Hart, op. cit.
Les Carnets sécrets d'Abel Ferry.

Index

241